IELTS SUCCESS FORMULA ACADEMIC

THE COMPLETE PRACTICAL GUIDE TO A TOP IELTS SCORE

Stephen Slater & Simone Braverman

One Sided Paper
Centre for English Language in the University of South Australia

www.IELTS-Blog.com   www.IELTSonTrack.com

Published by
One Sided Paper
4, Chalk Place,
Torrens Park
South Australia 5062

Centre for English Language in the
University of South Australia
98 North Terrace
Adelaide, South Australia 5001

Information on this title: www.ielts-blog.com, www.ieltsontrack.com

Copyright © Slater, Braverman 2013
First published 2013

Unless otherwise indicated, all materials on these pages are copyrighted by the authors. All rights reserved. No part of this book (including text, images, audio or video content) may be used for any purpose other than non-commercial personal study use. Therefore, unauthorised reproduction, photocopying, recording, modification, storage in a retrieval system or retransmission, in any form or by any means, electronic, mechanical or otherwise, is strictly prohibited without prior written permission from the authors. Users are not permitted to mount this file on any network servers.

A catalogue record for this book is available from the National Library of Australia

ISBN: 978 0 9873854 0 6

Audio: Stephen Slater

Cover design: Simone Braverman, Derek Murphy

ACKNOWLEDGEMENTS

The authors hereby acknowledge the following for their contributions to this book:

Neville Clark at Disk-Edits Pty Ltd. for audio recording and mastering.

Donna Millen for permission to use recorded extracts from IELTS on Track Listening tests.

Derek Murphy for cover design assistance.

Sally Collyns, Tanya Dahlenburg, Dr Ashish Davda, Sarah Divine, Georgina Hafteh Peter Hanna and Keith Smith, for voice recordings.

IELTS-Blog.com members, but particularly Dharmen, Diana, Eveline, Hemanth, Hon, Irina, Juliana, Lili, Nga, Paramjit, Princess, Rae, Raza, Rodney, Shahin, Shyam, Simone, Tina, Venkatesh, Viet for participation in the trialling of the Listening and Reading test material.

Alex Braverman for assistance with proofreading and graphic design.

iStockPhoto for licensing of the image appearing on the front cover (©iStockphoto.com/SimoneBraverman).

Australian Geographic for permission to use the article "To dam or not to dam", originally published online at http://www.australiangeographic.com.au/journal/ on 21 January 2011.

Other texts were freshly written to test parameters drawing on and integrating information from a wide variety of written sources.

While every effort has been made to contact copyright holders it has not been possible to identify all sources of the material used. The authors and publisher would in such instances welcome information from copyright holders to rectify any errors or omissions.

INTRODUCTION

A **big 'HELLO'** to you from your team of authors, Stephen and Simone. We are glad you have chosen IELTS SUCCESS FORMULA for your exam preparation. They say everything happens for a reason, and perhaps **the reason you're reading this book is that you need a high IELTS score and you want to be confident about how to achieve it for yourself or how to help your students to achieve an above-average IELTS score.**

Many books have been written about IELTS preparation. What makes this one different? As you will have noticed, this book is called "IELTS Success Formula". That's exactly what you should expect to find here – **step by step, friendly guidance on how to overcome your difficulties and achieve a high score in the IELTS tes**t. This book wastes no time and immediately shows you the important aspects requiring attention during your exam preparation. The tips, advice and examples here will help you understand the difference between a lower score response and a higher score response, and you will learn efficient ways of dealing with test tasks to give more accurate answers, faster.

HOW TO USE THIS BOOK

This book was designed to suit busy test takers as well as people who can devote several weeks to IELTS preparation. Here are two possible test preparation plans:

PLAN A: CRASH-COURSE PREPARATION (for candidates who are short of time)

STEP 1. Read through the Listening, Reading, Writing and Speaking lessons while making notes. Pay special attention to secrets and tips on impressing your assessor and achieving a higher score.

STEP 2. Do the full practice test included in this book. Instead of sticking strictly to IELTS time limits, spend some additional minutes trying to implement all the useful tips you have learned in this book.

STEP 3. Analyse your performance: write a brief summary on what you were good at, not so good at, and what to improve. Check your answers against the correct ones in the book and try to understand why you were wrong and why the answers in the book are correct. Then go over our tips once more on the skills you need to improve.

STEP 4. With any time left before your exam, locate and work through the relevant Fitness Activities to improve your performance in the skills that you found difficult in the practice test. IELTS Writing Doctor can help you cover the gaps in your use of grammar and vocabulary, and the rated writing samples and the recorded IELTS-style interview give you insights into how **you** can get a higher score in writing and speaking.

PLAN B: COMPREHENSIVE PREPARATION (for candidates who have more time, or for teachers/students working with our book on IELTS preparation courses)

STEP 1. Work systematically through the lesson for each IELTS subtest with its detailed descriptions, extensive Q/A, and secrets of impressing an assessor and raising your score.

As you read through each lesson chapter carefully, note any information, strategies, tips or advice that are new to you. Underline or highlight the ones that apply to you.

STEP 2. After finishing the lesson for every skill (Listening, Reading, Writing, Speaking), work through its fitness activities and then check your answers.
Analyse any incorrect answers, and try to understand why you were wrong, and why the answer in the book is correct. UNDERSTANDING tasks and mistakes is central to improvement.

Note: if you need some help with your use of grammar or ideas for vocabulary, visit our IELTS Writing Doctor and Top Score Vocabulary in the Writing and Speaking chapters. For a deeper understanding of how to improve your score in writing or speaking, check out the rated writing samples and the recorded IELTS-style interview with a detailed analysis of the speaker's performance.

STEP 3. Take the Full practice test.
You should work through the test under strict test conditions and in the correct order (L > R > W > S) observing correct timings for each subtest. Put into practice as many relevant techniques and insights as possible from each of the four skills chapters you have systematically worked through.

When you have completed the full test, you can check your answers. For the Writing and Speaking test you'll need either to self assess by rating your level in comparison with those in our Writing and Speaking Resource sections, or ask a teacher to give you a rating.

STEP 4. Analyse your test performance and re-test later.
A vital, final stage in our SUCCESS FORMULA is to analyse and evaluate your exit test performance carefully in each of the four subtests and to write brief notes on what you were good at, not so good at, and what to improve. **UNDERSTANDING your performance deeply IS MUCH BETTER THAN JUST DOING** one, new test after another.

After a week, **re-take the exit test, and carefully re-analyse your performance.**

You will by then have applied the IELTS SUCCESS FORMULA! Good luck!

CONTENTS

IELTS LISTENING

Lesson	1
Fitness Activities	20

IELTS READING

Lesson	33
Fitness Activities	57

IELTS WRITING

Overview	75
Lesson Task 1	78
Fitness Activities Task 1	99
Lesson Task 2	127
Fitness Activities Task 2	146
Tasks 1 & 2, Rated Samples	174

IELTS WRITING DOCTOR

IELTS Grammar	195
IELTS Vocabulary	232

IELTS SPEAKING

Lesson	261
Fitness Activities	280
Interview, Rated Sample	298
Top Score Vocabulary	307
Questions for Practice	314

IELTS TEST

Full IELTS Practice Test	331
Answers	355
Audio Transcripts	369

IELTS LISTENING

LISTENING LESSON

First Questions Answered

Q. **How long is the Listening test?**
A. The Listening test takes 40 minutes, where the first 30 minutes are used to listen to a recording and answer questions on what you hear, and the last 10 minutes are used to transfer your answers from the question booklet to the Answer sheet.

Q. **Is the Listening test different for Academic and General Training test takers?**
A. No, there is no difference in the format or contents of the Listening test in Academic and General Training tests.

Q. **How is the Listening test organized?**
A. The recording consists of four sections, which progress in speed and difficulty. Sections 1 and 3 are recordings of conversations between two or more people, and Sections 2 and 4 are recordings of monologues.

Q. **How many questions are there?**
A. There are 40 questions in total in the Listening test. In each section there are 10 questions.

Q. **What topics are likely to appear in the Listening test?**
A. Every section will have a different topic.

Section 1 is an everyday conversation between two people, such as a patient and a doctor, a receptionist and a client, and so on.

Section 2 is a lecture, a presentation or a speech by a person on an everyday topic such as services and facilities available in a library.

Section 3 is a conversation that may include more than two people about study-related matters. Often the participants are a student and a lecturer or a group of students, discussing homework or a university project.

Section 4 is a talk or a lecture on an academic subject, such as historical summary or a presentation of a study the speaker has undertaken.

Q. What type of questions am I likely to get?

A. All the questions will be about the information on the recording; however, the way you need to provide your answers (or, as we call it, 'task type') may differ. The typical task types are below (Figure 1.)

Task type	Example
MATCHING — select the appropriate description (verbal or a picture).	Questions 1–3 Who will pay for the following items: A Mary B Peter C Both Mary and Peter Write the correct letter (**A–C**) next to questions **1–3**. 1 food for the trip _____ 2 accommodation _____ 3 excursions _____ *Need practice? Go to Fitness Activity 1 (Page 21)*
MULTIPLE CHOICE QUESTIONS — select the correct answer.	Question 4 Circle the correct letter **A–C**. The reason Mary prefers to stay in this hotel is A because of the magnificent view B because of the facilities C because of the affordable pricing *Need practice? Go to Fitness Activity 2 (Page 22)*

IELTS Listening Lesson

Task type	Example
SENTENCE COMPLETION — complete a sentence according to what you hear.	Question 5 Complete the sentence below. Use **NO MORE THAN THREE WORDS AND/OR A NUMBER** for each answer. Peter has put a _____ on his packing list. *Need practice? Go to Fitness Activity 3 (Page 23)*
SHORT ANSWER QUESTIONS — write an answer in one, two or three words, according to the instructions, on what you hear.	Question 6 Answer the question below. Use **NO MORE THAN THREE WORDS AND/OR A NUMBER** for your answer. Which country are both Mary and Peter reluctant to visit? _____ *Need practice? Go to Fitness Activity 4 (Page 24)*
FORM OR NOTE COMPLETION — enter the appropriate information in blanks.	Questions 7–10 Complete the travel agency form below, using **NO MORE THAN THREE WORDS AND/OR A NUMBER** for each answer. Customer's name **7** _____ Booking includes **8** ___ adults, **9** ___ children Dates of holiday: 21 April to **10** _____ *Need practice? Go to Fitness Activities 5–7 (Pages 25-26)*

IELTS Listening Lesson

Task type	Example
TABLE/FLOW CHART COMPLETION — fill in the blank cells or blocks.	Questions 11–13 Complete the table below. Write **NO MORE THAN THREE WORDS AND/OR A NUMBER** for each answer. Trip Itinerary | Date	Flight no.	Destination
---	---	---
21 April	CX 1345	**11** _____
25 April	**12** _____	Toronto, Canada
13 _____	FL 131	New York, USA	 *Need practice? Go to Fitness Activity 8 (Page 27)*
SUMMARY COMPLETION — fill missing words in the blanks. You may or may not be given a list of words to choose from. If there is no list, choose directly from what you hear on the recording.	Questions 14–16 Complete the summary below. Use **NO MORE THAN THREE WORDS AND/OR A NUMBER** for each answer. Peter and Mary are planning a **14** _____ together. The **15** _____ they have decided to visit include Canada and USA, where they will be **16** _____ by plane. *Need practice? Go to Fitness Activity 9 (Page 28)*

IELTS Success Formula :: Academic

IELTS Listening Lesson

| DIAGRAM, MAP OR PLAN LABELLING—write short descriptions of up to three words for parts of a drawing. | Questions 17–21

Label the diagram below. Write your answers in the boxes **17–21** on the answer sheet.

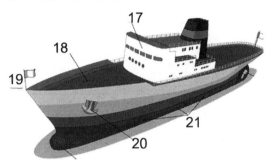

 Need practice? Go to Fitness Activity 10 (Pages 29-30) |

Figure 1.

 Note: in the real Listening test you won't see the task type change after every question—it is common to see a group of about five questions for every task type.

Q. Will I have time to read the questions?

A. Yes, you will have about 15–20 seconds to go over each group of questions before listening.

Q. When do I answer?

A. Once a recording is being played you will need to answer the questions as you listen, because you will hear the recording only once.

Q. Where and how do I write the answers?

A. During the listening test write all the answers in the question booklet. Once the recording has stopped you will have 10 more minutes to transfer your answers to the answer sheet.

Please read the section 'How to Avoid Problems with Your Answers' (Page 14), to make sure none of your answers gets disqualified.

Q. Will I be penalized for writing answers in capital letters?

A. When answering any task with missing words (such as sentence completion, summary completion, note completion, table completion, etc) you can write in uppercase letters (e.g. 'AFTERNOON') or lowercase letters (e.g. 'afternoon'), as you wish. It is probably best to choose a particular way (either uppercase or lowercase) and follow it consistently.

Q. Will I need to re-phrase what I hear in my answers?

A. No, you won't. All the answers are as heard on the recording. You will not need to substitute a word for its synonym or to change its form.

Q. What spelling version should I use, British or American?

A. Both British and American spelling versions are accepted. It is also very important that your spelling is correct, because misspelled answers may be penalized. For example, you can write 'color' (American spelling) or 'colour' (British spelling), but if you write 'calor' the answer will get zero points.

Q. Is grammar important?

A. Yes, grammar is an important part of the Listening test. Any grammatically incorrect answers will not get any points, even if their meaning is correct. If you use a singular form ('apple') where a plural form should be used ('apples'), if you use the wrong tense or verb form ('he go' instead of 'he goes'), such ungrammatical answers will receive zero points.

Q. Is it OK to use shorthand writing in the answers?

A. While it is acceptable to use shorthand writing for your notes in the question booklet, your answers on the answer sheet must be complete. So if you quickly scribbled on your answer sheet something like 'doc. ord.', use the full form 'doctor's orders' when transferring such answers to the answer sheet.

IELTS Listening Lesson

What if I...?   Some Problem Situations

Q. **What if I can't understand what is being said on the recording?**

A. If you have trouble understanding the recording it could happen for several reasons:

Reasons

It is possible that the speaker uses an accent you are not familiar with. For example, people who are used to the American accent may find a British accent hard to understand at first. This shouldn't be a problem as long as you have had some time to train your ears by listening to recordings in different accents that may appear in the IELTS test. The main accents to concentrate on include those from Australia, Britain, Canada, America and New Zealand.

It is also possible that your listening skills are weak, which may make you feel that the words are coming faster than you can recognize and understand them.

Solutions

This doesn't mean you will fail in the exam, because with training and regular work your listening can improve significantly. To develop your listening skill:

- It's a good idea to use recordings that have a transcript (to help you understand every word).

- Listen to a recording daily for 20 minutes, then rewind and listen repeatedly to unclear sentences, to build the speed at which you decode spoken input.

- Try repeating words you hear after listening to help you remember them and the way they are pronounced, and perhaps even to improve your pronunciation.

Q. What if I lose track of the recording?

A. Being focused is very important in the Listening test. The fact that the recording is played only once means that there are no second chances for missed answers. This is why it is crucial that you learn mentally how to block out any disturbance or background noise, while preparing and practicing for the exam.

However, anything can happen, and if you have lost track of the recording there is a way to re-gain control:

• Jump ahead to the two or three questions immediately following the one you missed and you will find the one that the recording is addressing now. This way, you may miss an answer or two but from the question where you have re-established the connection with the recording, no more answers will be lost.

• Try to guess the missed answers instead of leaving their boxes blank on the answer sheet.

Q. What if I am a slow reader and don't have enough time to read the questions before the recording begins playing?

A. There is a solution that may help, especially with Sections 2, 3 and 4.

At the end of each section you get about 30 seconds to review your answers. Instead of checking your answers for the previous section, you can read the questions ahead that refer to the next section. Then, when the recording instructs you to move on and read the questions of the next section, you will have some more time to continue reading the questions.

Example

You have just finished answering Section 1. The recording announces that your time to check answers has begun. You begin reading the questions for Section 2. The recording announces that now you can read the questions for Section 2. You are continuing reading the questions for Section 2 and that way are already further ahead.

Is it wise to do so? Due to the nature of the Listening test, once a recording has stopped, many students find it difficult to recall what has been said, and therefore it's not likely that you will remember enough to correct your answers. Also, there will be another time slot of 10 minutes when you will be asked to copy your answers from the booklet to the answer sheet—and while copying you can also check the grammar and spelling.

Q. What if I have a problem with spelling?

A. Spelling is a well-known problem, even for people whose first language is English. However, in the IELTS test spelling is very important and your answers may not be considered correct if they are wrongly spelled. For example, if the correct answer is 'calendar' and you wrote 'calender', even though the meaning is clear the spelling is wrong, and so your answer will get zero points.

To overcome this problem the obvious solution is to learn how to spell, but we know that this may take years. People who have to sit the IELTS test are usually in a hurry and have limited time for preparation—months or even weeks—and therefore we propose a shortcut. Our experience with students over the years has taught us that some words are more likely to get misspelled than others.

Please refer to the 'Famously misspelled words list' at the end of this chapter Page 17. By learning the correct spelling of most of the words on that list you will greatly reduce your chances of misspelling an answer in the IELTS exam.

Q. What if I am unsure of an answer?

A. Even if you are unsure what the correct answer is, having listened to the recording you can take a guess. Instead of leaving the answer blank, write your best guess in its space on the answer sheet. This won't hurt your Listening score and, if you're lucky, may even help it.

Q. What if I have a hearing/eyesight problem?

A. If you have a hearing/eyesight problem that can be backed up by a medical certificate, you should contact the test centre where you intend to take the test well in advance. The test centers consider each case individually and make special arrangements, including amplification of the recording or preparing a lip-reading version of the Listening module, or a Braille version of the question booklet for sight-impaired candidates.

Q. What if I get sick on the day of my exam?

A. It is generally a good idea to postpone your exam if you are not well. This is especially true if the sickness makes you sneeze. When we sneeze our ears are blocked, which is why constant sneezing may cause a person (and other candidates nearby!) to miss the key parts of the recording that hold the answers.

Your local test centre can give you the most up-to-date and detailed advice on how to postpone your exam.

7 'Must do' Things for Success in the Listening Test

1. Heard the answer? Write it down straightaway.

A listening test is a very dynamic experience and, simply put, you need to keep up. It is impossible to retain in your memory an answer that you heard, because it will be washed away by the continuous flow of information as the recorded voices keep on talking. This is why, once you've heard an answer to a question, you need to write it down, right there and then. You may think that writing will distract you from listening (and the truth is that initially it might), but with practice you will learn to write and listen at the same time, and writing won't come at the expense of listening.

2. Only look at one group of questions at a time.

You know by now that Listening test recordings are divided into Sections 1 to 4. But you may not know yet that Sections 1 to 3 are divided into smaller subsections, a fact which makes your job a bit easier.

In those sections the recording will refer to a certain group of questions, *not all* of the questions in the section, and it will say what questions you should look at *now*. For example, the recording may say "Now look at the questions 7 to 10" and then be silent for about 20 seconds. This means that in the recorded segment that then follows four answers will be given—
to questions 7, 8, 9 and 10.

So what should you do? Most importantly, read the questions while the recording is silent, but don't read beyond question 10. Underline key words, quickly grasp the main idea of each question and try to understand what sort of answer you will hear— an amount? working hours? a location?

Another excellent consequence of the fact that Listening sections 1–3 are broken down into subsections is that you won't lose a whole section *even if you've missed a couple of answers*. As soon as you hear the recording say "Now look at questions 11 to 13", and you know that you still don't have the answer to question 10, cut your losses—stop looking for the answer to question 10—and move on to the current group of questions. In this way you still have a chance to answer all the questions in the current group and then, at the end of the section/test you can go back and guess the answer to the 'lost' question.

3. Details *are* important.

Any specific information mentioned on a recording, such as names, phone numbers, dates, opening hours, locations, years, colors is usually mentioned for a reason. It is very likely that such details are contained in the answer. When you hear specific information on a recording, have another look at the current group of questions, to see where it may fit.

4. Multiple choice: not all answer options are born equal.

When dealing with Multiple choice tasks not all answer options have the same likelihood of being correct.

Out of three answer options one can almost always be crossed out as plain wrong or as not mentioned by the speaker, and then you will have fewer options to choose from — which will make your job much easier.

5. Summary completion: let sentence structure be your guide.

When completing a summary it is often hard to guess straightaway which word is missing from the blank space. Sometimes it may seem as though no word is missing at all! A trick that always works for this type of task is to look at the words immediately before and after the gap, because they reveal whether the missing word is a noun, an adjective, or a verb.

For instance, consider the summary below

> **Example**
>
> Peter and Mary are planning a **14** _____ together. The **15** _____ they have decided to visit include Canada and USA, where they will be **16** _____ by plane.
>
> It seems that answer 14 should be a noun (such as 'trip'), 15 – also a noun (such as 'countries'), and 16 should be a verb (such as 'arriving' or 'travelling').

How does this help? Once you know that you're looking for a verb, selecting the right one from what you hear on the recording will be easier. You will pay more attention to verbs than to nouns or adjectives.

6. Do not let the use of synonyms confuse you.

It may happen that you will hear a word on the recording, but the question will be worded using its synonym. Test takers whose minds are 'locked' on the exact word the speaker said, may get confused and not realize the question is mentioning the same thing.

Example

The recording may say, "The list of prohibited items inside an airplane includes…" and the question may say, "Passengers are not allowed to take the following items on board a plane".

---

7. The speakers (not just women!) are allowed to change their minds.

Once of the things you are being tested on in the Listening test is whether or not you can follow the *development of the conversation*, AND, just like in a real-life conversation, the speakers on a recording can change their minds.

Example

Peter: "We can book a flight on the 10th of April, what do you think?"

Mary: "My vacation request was approved to start from the 9th, so I am free to go. But hang on, isn't your brother's birthday party on the 10th?"

Peter: "You're right, how could I forget?! Thanks for reminding me. We'd better book our flight on the 11th of April, or he'll never forgive me."

You should pay attention to such unexpected changes of mind, and make sure they don't trick you into giving the incorrect answer.

How to Avoid Problems with Your Answers

You would be surprised how many correct answers get disqualified for 'technical' reasons. To make sure this doesn't happen to you read through the common problems below and make a mental note to avoid making these mistakes.

Problem 1 – not following the task instructions.

You may have noticed how every task type has a clear set of instructions (refer to the table in Figure 1). They specify how many words or numbers you can use, and what you need to do—complete a sentence, answer a question, circle a letter, and so on. It is very important that you do *exactly* as the instructions say. If the instructions say "Circle two letters", do exactly that—don't circle just one or three letters.

Especially important is the word limit, because any answer that consists of more words than the limit allows, will get zero points even if its meaning is correct. If the instructions say, **"WRITE NO MORE THAN THREE WORDS"**, you may write one, or two or three words—but never more than three.

Problem 2 – transferring information incorrectly.

a) Words

When transferring the answers from the question booklet, only the missing words should be written on the answer sheet.

For instance, consider a task that asks you to complete a sentence using **NO MORE THAN THREE WORDS AND/OR A NUMBER.**

Example

The sentence is: "Peter and Mary **are** _____ **to** visit their relatives in Ottawa"

Since the correct answer is 'not going', writing the words 'are not going to' on the answer sheet will mean receiving zero points for your answer.

Note: the definite and indefinite articles 'a', 'the' count as one word each.

b) Symbols and abbreviations

If you are required to complete a sentence that talks about money such as,
"The deposit Peter has to pay for plane tickets is $_____"
write *only the amount* on the answer sheet, without the '$' sign, because it's already written in the question booklet.

In a sentence that talks about time, such as,
"Trading hours of the travel agency are Mon–Fri, _____ **am** to 5 pm."
write only the time on the answer sheet, without the 'am'. The reason is that 'am' is already written in the booklet and you do not need to repeat it.

c) Numbers

Confusing numbers with digits is a common problem. The word 'digit' means any of 0, 1, 2, 3, 4, 5, 6, 7, 8, and 9. A number is a combination of digits, or in other words more than one digit may form a number.

Why is this important? Because when instructions ask to 'answer in **NO MORE THAN THREE WORDS AND/OR A NUMBER**', it is a mistake to think that you are only allowed to write one digit in the space provided on the answer sheet. You are allowed to write one number, which can consist of many digits.

Example

Complete the sentence below using **NO MORE THAN THREE WORDS AND/OR A NUMBER.**

"The address of Peter's uncle is _____ Main street, Moncton, New Brunswick, Canada."

Let's say the correct answer (the missing house number) is '308'. It's a mistake to think that all you're allowed to write just one digit (such as '3'), in fact you are allowed to, and should, write '308'.

---

d) Letters

When the task instructions ask you to circle a letter, this is exactly what you need to transfer to the answer sheet—the letter, not the full answer. There is a whole set of reasons why you shouldn't copy the full answer:

1. It's not what the instructions say
2. You can make a spelling mistake
3. It takes longer to write two or three words than to write a letter.

Example

Circle the correct letter **A–C**.

The reason Mary prefers to stay in this hotel is
A   because of the magnificent view
B   because of the facilities
C   because of the affordable pricing

Let's say B is the correct answer. While you are listening, circle B in the question booklet. When transferring the answers to the answer sheet, write 'B' in the relevant space—don't copy the words 'because of the facilities'.

Famously misspelled words list

Correct	Wrong	Correct	Wrong
A		**C**	
absence	*absense / absance*	calendar	*calender*
acceptable	*acceptible*	career	*carrer*
accidentally	*accidentaly*	careful	*carefull*
achieve	*acheive*	category	*catagory*
acknowledge	*aknowledge*	certain	*certin*
accommodation	*accomodation*	colleague	*collegue*
across	*accross*	collectible	*collectable*
address	*adress / addres*	competition	*compitition*
affordable	*affortable*	completely	*completly*
almost	*allmost*	controversy	*contraversy*
a lot	*alot*		
amateur	*amature*	**D**	
among	*amung*	decide	*dicide*
annually	*annualy*	definitely	*definately*
appearance	*appearence*	description	*describtion*
argument	*arguement*	develop	*develope*
		dilemma	*dilemna*
B		disappear	*dissapear*
balance	*balence*	disappoint	*disapoint*
basically	*basicly*	discipline	*disipline*
because	*becuase*		
before	*befor*	**E**	
beginning	*begining*	embarrass	*embarass*
believe	*beleive*	environment	*enviroment*
benefit	*benifit*	exceed	*excede*
breathe	*brethe / breath*	exercise	*exersize*
business	*bisness / bizness*	experiment	*expiriment*

Correct	Wrong	Correct	Wrong
F		**L**	
familiar	*familier*	leisure	*liesure*
finally	*finaly*	length	*lenght*
foreign	*foriegn*	lesson	*lessen/leson* *
forward	*foreward*	lose	*Loose* *
further	*futher*		
G		**M**	
government	*goverment*	marriage	*marrige*
grateful	*greatful*	minute	*minite*
guarantee	*garantee*	mimic	*mimmic*
		misspell	*mispel*
H		**N**	
happened	*happend*	necessary	*necessery*
happiness	*happyness*	neighbour	*neibor*
height	*haight*	noticeable	*noticable*
hoping	*hopeing*		
I		**O**	
ignorance	*ignorence*	obedient	*obidient*
imitate	*immitate*	occasion	*occassion*
immediately	*immediatly*	occurrence	*occurence*
incur	*incurr*	often	*offen/ofen*
independent	*independant*	opportunity	*oppurtunity*
indispensable	*indispensible*		
interesting	*intresting*	**P**	
interruption	*interuption*	particularly	*particurly*
		pastime	*pasttime*
K		perceive	*percieve*
knowledge	*nowledge/ knolege*	persistent	*persistant*
knives	*knifs*	possession	*posession*
		preferred	*prefered*

Correct	Wrong	Correct	Wrong
R		**U**	
really	*realy*	until	*untill*
receive	*recieve*	usable	*usible*
referred	*refered*	usually	*usualy*
repetition	*repitition*		
ridiculous	*rediculous*		
S		**V**	
separate	*seperate*	vehicle	*vehical*
shelves	*shelfes*	visible	*visable*
similar	*similer*		
sincerely	*sinseerly*		
speech	*speach*		
successful	*successfull*		
surely	*surelly*		
T		**W**	
temporary	*temperary*	weather	*whether* *
therefore	*therefor*	weird	*wierd*
thieves	*thiefs*	whether	*wether* *
til	*till*	which	*wich*
tomorrow	*tommorrow*		
truly	*truely*		
twelfth	*twelvth*		

* These words have correct spelling but their meanings are different from the intended word. However, they have similar pronunciation and are thus easily confused.

LISTENING FITNESS ACTIVITIES

The fitness activities in this section offer you quick practice at the different task types you may encounter in the IELTS Listening test. It's also a chance to use some of the tips from the Listening chapter earlier in our book.

General guidance

- As these are just for practice and not contained within an IELTS Listening test format, it is a good opportunity to experiment with your task strategies.

- Don't forget to read each of the tasks and the instructions carefully before trying to put in your answers.

- If you can wait, check your answers after completing **all** Fitness Activities.

- Later you could also read the transcripts for each activity (See Page 369) to see where the answers were located in the short extracts you listened to.

The recordings for the Listening Fitness Activities listed below, and all other recorded material in later sections can be found on the audio recordings supplied with this book.

Activities	Audio Time
Fitness Activity 1	1 min 53 sec
Fitness Activity 2	1 min 02 sec
Fitness Activity 3	0 min 59 sec
Fitness Activity 4	1 min 02 sec
Fitness Activity 5	0 min 54 sec
Fitness Activity 6	0 min 47 sec
Fitness Activity 7	1 min 06 sec
Fitness Activity 8	1 min 29 sec
Fitness Activity 9	1 min 10 sec
Fitness Activity 10	1 min 59 sec

TASK TYPE » Matching

In this activity you simply have to match the name of the student with the information that they give about themselves. It is important to read the information in the questions first, before listening, so that you know what to listen out for. This is always a good strategy because it gives your listening real focus.

 Listen to Fitness Activity 1

Listen to three students Anna (**A**), Veronica (**V**) and Chris (**C**) introducing themselves. Match each student with their personal information, by writing either **A, V or C**.

1 ____ is Swedish.

2 ____ was a member of a university film society.

3 ____ is studying English literature.

4 ____ wrote for a student publication.

5 ____ has already been in the festival organising committee.

6 ____ will recommend some changes in a written report.

IELTS Listening Fitness Activities

TASK TYPE » Multiple choice

The IELTS Listening test generally uses only three choices in its multiple choice questions – A, B, C. This is simpler than the four-option multiple choice.

An excellent strategy **before** listening is to look through each set of A,B,C choices and cross out any that look (from your common sense or knowledge!) unlikely to be correct. This saves time and gives the task more focus when actually listening.

It may also help you to pick up when a speaker says something which is **opposite** to one or other of the answer choices. It doesn't always work, but see if you can cross out unlikely answers now, before listening to the next extract.

 Listen to Fitness Activity 2

Listen to this short extract on food trends. Choose **A**, **B** or **C**.

1   Mobile meals are:
    A   a form of junk food
    B   Canadian home cooking
    C   foods consumed outside of the home

2   The increase in sales of snack foods in three years could be:
    A   14%
    B   40%
    C   4%

3   Which of these is a nutritious, portable food?
    A   Muesli bar
    B   Cholesterol bar
    C   Food bar

TASK TYPE » Sentence completion

This type of task involves writing not only the appropriate word in terms of meaning but also choosing the correct grammatical form. The best strategy is to:

- Read the task instructions to see what the maximum number of words is for each answer.

- Look through each sentence before listening and decide what type of word is required grammatically (e.g. noun? adjective? verb? adverb?).

- Then when you listen and choose your word try to make sure it is spelled correctly.

 Listen to Fitness Activity 3

Complete these sentences using **ONE WORD ONLY** from the recording.

1   Money for the film festival comes from advertising and charging for _____ .

2   It is necessary to _____ the films by the beginning of March.

3   The deadline for getting sponsors is the _____ of March.

4   The end of March is the deadline for program _____ .

5   During April, posters need to be put together and _____ .

TASK TYPE » Short-answer questions

This type of task is straightforward because it is a conventional Q/A style. In other words, you are listening for the information that actually answers the question.

The best strategy is to read the questions so that you know what you are listening out for and in what order. Remember the maximum number of words you can use for each answer.

 Listen to Fitness Activity 4

Write an answer to each question using **NO MORE THAN TWO WORDS OR NUMBERS** from the recording.

1   What did the invention of the QWERTY typewriter keyboard reduce?
    _____

2   What negative outcome for typists did the layout of the QWERTY keyboard cause? _____

3   On which side are many of the most frequently used typewriter keys?
    _____

4   What happened to typewriter technology after the QWERTY keyboard was invented? _____

TASK TYPE » Form completion

This type of task sort of tests your 'orientational awareness'. In simple terms you need to know where you are, or which part of the form to focus on while listening. So, look at the forms carefully before listening so that you know your way around the forms.

- Often the speaker will make a little mistake with an address or number and then correct it, so listen out for this type of little trick.

- When a speaker reads out a name for you to copy down and spells it out, you need to know how each of the alphabet letters is pronounced in English.

- Don't forget to check the task instructions for the maximum number of words/numbers you can use.

 Listen to Fitness Activity 5

Listen to the airline passenger and complete the form, using **NO MORE THAN THREE WORDS OR NUMBERS**.

Passenger Enquiry Form

Arrival Flight No. **1** _____   Time of arrival: **2** _____

Item lost: **3** _____   Country of flight connection: **4** _____

IELTS Listening Fitness Activities

 Listen to Fitness Activity 6

Listen and complete the address and phone number.

Name: Jenny Lee

Address: 1 _____ , Riverside

Phone: 2 _____

 Listen to Fitness Activity 7

Listen and complete the information about the ATS Office, using **ONE WORD OR A NUMBER**.

ATS Office Regency Theatre

Opening times: Monday – 1 _____ 10–5pm,
                     Friday/Saturday 10 – 2 _____ pm.

Website address: 3 www._____.com

TASK TYPE » Table completion

Again, this type of task requires you to 'know your way around' the table before listening.

A good strategy is to check the headings at the top of each column, and to check the information that is already there so that you can see what type of information is required.

Oh, and don't forget to check the task instructions for the maximum number of words.

Listen to Fitness Activity 8

Complete the table using **ONE WORD ONLY** for each answer.

Student Name	Work Experience Location	Day / Time of Day
Theresa	Uni **1** _____	Friday **2** _____
Manuel	Mainly **3** _____	Friday afternoons
Henry	The **4** _____ Shop	**5** _____ afternoons

IELTS Listening Fitness Activities

TASK TYPE » Summary completion

This task is similar to the sentence completion type (See Fitness Activity 3), but is a little more complex. Sometimes you are given a list of words to choose from for the spaces; sometimes not. If no word list is given use words that you actually hear on the recording.

As with sentence completion you should:

- Read the summary and decide what kind of word is missing grammatically.

- Decide too, what sort of meaning the missing word might have (e.g. is it a positive, negative word, a description, a fact?)

- Check the task instructions for the maximum number of words.

It's worth remembering that summary completion is difficult so it is often used in the later parts of the IELTS Listening test.

 Listen to Fitness Activity 9

Listen to this short talk about the Dvorak typewriter keyboard and complete the summary. Use **ONE WORD ONLY** from the talk for each space.

SUMMARY

Although the Dvorak keyboard is superior it has not been **1** _____ for two main reasons: the Depression, and **2** _____ . Too many people were too accustomed to the QWERTY keyboard. This has prevented improved keyboard **3** _____ for 70+ years.

TASK TYPE » Diagram Labelling

This type of task is similar to forms and tables in the sense that you need to 'know your way around' the diagram BEFORE listening, then you will be more relaxed when listening.

Look at all the information given and what any labels refer to, so that you know more about the topic and about the type of information you will be listening out for. As usual, check the maximum number of words/numbers in the task instructions.

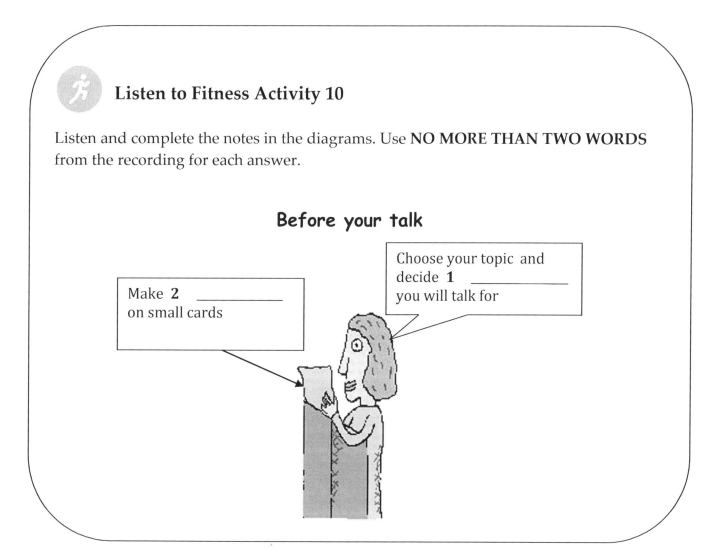

Listen to Fitness Activity 10

Listen and complete the notes in the diagrams. Use **NO MORE THAN TWO WORDS** from the recording for each answer.

Before your talk

Choose your topic and decide **1** _____ you will talk for

Make **2** _____ on small cards

During your talk

3 _____ is vital when talking to an audience

Practise **4** _____ to help pronunciation

5 _____ your voice to reach the person furthest from you

Well done if you completed all the Listening tasks! Tired now? So are we! OK, just one more fitness activity to go! You can do it!

FINAL TASK » Recording your answers on the answer sheet

Finally we'll give you a little practice at transferring your answers to the correct box on a separate, answer sheet. The answer sheet here is not exactly the same as in IELTS but will certainly help you to become careful about putting your answers in the right box, and more aware of spelling.

Put your answers to all 10 Fitness activities in the Answer Sheet below in the correct order.

That's the end of our Listening Fitness section, so after transferring your own answers quickly check the correct answers on Page 356, then relax and make yourself some tea or coffee. When comparing the answers try to understand why your wrong answers are incorrect, and why the ones in this book are correct.

It's important to keep relaxed and sleep as well as you can, before the IELTS test, even if you can't stop yourself from being a wee bit nervous. Everyone who takes the test probably feels pretty much the same.

IELTS Success Formula
Practice Answer Sheet (Listening)

Practise transferring your answers from this Fitness section.
TIME LIMIT: 10 minutes

REMEMBER to keep an eye on:
- where you place each answer
- how you spell any words
- the use of abbreviations (only use well-known ones; write in full if in doubt)
- word endings (e.g. don't forget the final 's')
- any answers that you missed out (write your best guess)

Fitness Activity 1	Fitness Activity 6
1.	1.
2.	2.
3.	**Fitness Activity 7**
4.	1.
5.	2.
6.	3.
Fitness Activity 2	**Fitness Activity 8**
1.	1.
2.	2.
3.	3.
Fitness Activity 3	4.
1	5.
2	**Fitness Activity 9**
3	1.
4	2.
5	3.
Fitness Activity 4	**Fitness Activity 10**
1.	1.
2.	2.
3.	3.
4.	4.
Fitness Activity 5	5.
1.	**Total: 40 answers**
2.	
3.	
4.	

IELTS READING

IELTS Reading Lesson

READING LESSON

First Questions Answered

Q. What is the Academic Reading test like?
A. During the IELTS Reading test you will be asked to read three passages and answer questions on each passage. If you have chosen to do a paper-based test, you will receive a booklet with texts and questions. Alternatively, if you have chosen the computer-based version of the test, you will be reading the texts on a computer screen, and answering questions by selecting the correct answer option with a keyboard/mouse or by typing your answer.

Q. How long is the Reading test?
A. The Reading test takes 60 minutes. During this time you should finish reading the texts and answering the questions. If you are doing a paper-based test, copy your answers on to the answer sheet **during the same 60 minutes**, because you won't be given extra time to transfer the answers. In the computer-based version you won't need to transfer answers.

Q. How is the Reading test structured in the Academic module?
A. Here is what you can expect to see in an Academic Reading test:

Academic module	
Number of texts	Three long texts (maximum overall length up to 2750 words)
Text type	Explanatory or analytical, may include graphs or illustrations
Number of questions	40

Q. How is the Reading test marked?

A. Each of the 40 questions receives one mark if the answer is correct, or zero if the answer is incorrect. The number of marks is then converted to an IELTS score on a nine-band scale.

Q. What kind of questions will I get?

A. All the questions (or, as we call them, 'task types') will be about the information in the texts; however, the way you need to provide your answers can be different. Following the instructions precisely is a big part of success in IELTS, which is why getting familiar with each task type **now** is so important. This will help you concentrate on solving the tasks in the real exam, instead of reading each set of instructions for the first time.

The typical task types are below:

Task type	Example
MATCHING PARAGRAPH HEADINGS — select the appropriate heading to each paragraph of text. **Note: not every heading on the list may be used.**	Questions 1–3 Choose the correct heading for the paragraphs i–iii above from the list of headings below. Write the correct letter (**A–C**) in boxes **1–3** on your answer sheet. **List of headings** A Problems in Paradise? B Benefits outstrip problems C Development of dams in Australia *Need practice? Go to Fitness Activity 1 (Page 59)*

IELTS Reading Lesson

Task type	Example
MULTIPLE CHOICE QUESTIONS — select the correct answer from three or four options. ❗ **Note:** sometimes you may be required to select more than one option.	Question 4 Using **ONLY** paragraph **iii** above, choose the appropriate letter **A,B,C,** or **D**. Write your answer in box **4** on your answer sheet. One of the problems of dams is that …: A new plant species may change the biological balance B they cause more drowning C they lead to changes in salt levels in water further down river D weeds and algae can't survive as easily 🏃 *Need practice? Go to Fitness Activity 2 (Page 60)*
SUMMARY COMPLETION — fill missing words in the blanks. ❗ **Note:** you may or may not be given a list of words to fill in the gaps.	Questions 5–6 Complete the summary below based on paragraphs **ii and iv ONLY**, above. Choose **ONE WORD ONLY** from the paragraphs for each answer. Write your answers in boxes **5–6** on your answer sheet. Dams have benefits and drawbacks. For example, they provide water and **5** _____ but those residing in the dam's path may have to be **6** _____ . 🏃 *Need practice? Go to Fitness Activity 3 (Page 61)*

Task type	Example
DIAGRAM, MAP OR PLAN LABELLING — write short descriptions of up to three words and/or a number for parts of a drawing.	Questions 7–8 Look at the diagrams of types of dams (**A–D**) and read each dam description below. Label each description with the appropriate letter **A–D**. Write your answers in boxes **7–8** on your answer sheet. DAM TYPE DESCRIPTION of DAMS 7 _____ Embankment dams use a long-sloped, massive volume of rock, gravel and sand, with the finest materials in the centre to form a waterproof core. 8 _____ Buttress dams have 45 degree walls that transfer the force downwards. *Need practice? Go to Fitness Activity 4 (Page 61)*

IELTS Reading Lesson

Task type	Example

YES/NO/NOT GIVEN (Identifying Writer's Views) — you will be given a list of statements and asked to decide whether each statement agrees with the author's claim or view, contradicts it, or there is no reference to it in the passage.	Questions 9–10
	
	Do the following statements reflect the views of the writer of the paragraph A above?
	
	In boxes **9–10** on your answer sheet write
	
	   YES if the statement reflects the claims of the writer
	   NO if the statement contradicts the claims of the writer
	   NOT GIVEN if it is impossible to say what the writer thinks about this
	
	9 The deteriorating situation of the lungfish has stimulated public support.
	
	10 The habitat of the lungfish is now restricted to primarily only two rivers.
	
	Need practice? Go to Fitness Activity 5 (Page 64)

Task type	Example
MATCHING INFORMATION — • find a paragraph that has the information in the question, or • match statements to certain items from a list, or • categorise features.	Questions 11–13 Which paragraph (**B, C, D** or **E**) above contains the following information? Write the correct letter **B–E** in boxes **11–13** on your answer sheet. **11** Measures for accommodating likely increases in demand for water. **12** Data illustrating current and projected water demand in Queensland **13** Cost benefit gains and low projected impact of the Mary River Dam *Need practice? Go to Fitness Activity 6 (Page 65)*
FORM/NOTE COMPLETION — enter the appropriate information in the blanks.	Questions 14–15 Using only paragraph **D** above, complete the notes below. Choose **NO MORE THAN 3 WORDS AND/OR A NUMBER** from the passage for each answer. Write your answers in boxes **14–15** on your answer sheet. • Overall cost of the dam = **14** _____ • Reduction of **15** _____ = a goal of building the dam *Need practice? Go to Fitness Activity 7 (Page 65)*

IELTS Reading Lesson

Task type	Example
MATCHING FEATURES — find descriptions in the text and match them to people's names or places on a given list.	Questions 16–17 Which of the individuals mentioned in Australia's Dam Story (Part 3) above has these points of view? Write **A** for Professor **A**rthington, **I** for Kevin **I**ngersole and **P** for Glenda **P**ickersgill in boxes **16–17** on your answer sheet. Which person (A, I or P) believes that…: **16** … most printed material about the dam is really an attempt to promote it? _____ **17** … a large amount of the available documentation outlines the difficulties experienced by river life resulting from dams? _____ *Need practice? Go to Fitness Activity 8 (Page 68)*

Task type	Example
TRUE/FALSE/NOT GIVEN (Identifying Information) — you will be given a list of statements and asked to decide whether each statement agrees with the passage, contradicts it, or there is no reference to it in the passage.	Questions 18–19 Do the following statements agree with the information given in Australia's Dam Story (Part 3)? In boxes **18–19** on your answer sheet, write: **TRUE** if the statement agrees with the information **FALSE** if the statement contradicts the information **NOT GIVEN** if there is no information on this **18** QWI accepts that social problems resulting from purchase of properties have affected everyone. **19** People who have sold their land to QWI may not leave it for some time. *Need practice? Go to Fitness Activity 9 (Page 69)*
MATCHING SENTENCE ENDINGS — complete a sentence according to the passage. **Note: there may or may not be sentence endings provided in a box. If you need to choose words from the passage a word limit will be provided for your answers.**	Questions 20–21 Choose the best endings for the sentences below. Write your answers in boxes **20–21** on your answer sheet. **20** After the QWI announcement, many Mary Valley residents… _____ **21** Glenda Pickersgill is likely to lose her land and property… _____ *Need practice? Go to Fitness Activity 10 (page 70)*

IELTS Reading Lesson

Task type	Example
SENTENCE COMPLETION — complete a sentence according to the passage. ⚠ **Note: words to choose from for sentence completion may or may not be provided in a box**	Questions 22–23 Complete the sentences below. Choose **NO MORE THAN TWO WORDS OR A NUMBER** from the text for each answer. 22 Glenda Pickersgill was _____ when she heard of the government's dam-building plans. 23 Glenda is trying hard to build _____ for the anti-dam protest group. 🏃 *Need practice? Go to Fitness Activity 11 (Page 71)*
SHORT-ANSWER QUESTIONS — answer in one, two or three words and/or a number.	Questions 24–25 Answer the questions below. Choose **NO MORE THAN TWO WORDS AND/OR A NUMBER** from the text for each answer. 24 What has been the overall effect of QWI's property purchase on the community? _____ 25 In what direction is Glenda's land relative to the proposed dam? _____ 🏃 *Need practice? Go to Fitness Activity 12 (Page 72)*

Task type	Example
TABLE/FLOW CHART COMPLETION — fill in the blank cells or blocks.	Questions 26–30 Complete the diagram below, based on the text about how evaporated milk is produced. Choose **NO MORE THAN TWO WORDS** from the text for each answer. Write your answers in boxes **26–30** on your answer sheet. *See diagram in Fitness Activity 13 (Page 74)*

Note: in the real Reading test you won't see task types change after every question or two — normally there is a group of about five questions for every task type.

Q. **Where and how do I write the answers?**

A. You can write the answers in the question booklet or on the answer sheet. One thing to keep in mind is that all your answers must be transferred to the Answer Sheet before the Reading test ends. Nothing written in the question booklet will be marked, and no extra time for copying answers will be given once your 60 minutes have ended.

Please read the section 'How to Avoid Problems with Your Answers' in this book (Page 14), to make sure none of your answers gets disqualified.

Q. **Will I be penalised for writing answers in CAPITAL letters?**

A. When doing any 'completion type' task — a task with missing words such as sentence completion, summary completion, note completion, table completion, etc — you can write in uppercase (e.g. 'AFTERNOON') or lowercase (e.g. 'afternoon') letters, as you wish. It is probably best to choose a particular way, either uppercase or lowercase, and consistently follow it.

Q. Will I need to re-phrase the information from the text in my answers?

A. With 'completion type' questions, use the words just as they are in the text. There's no need to change them in any way, or to use synonyms.

Q. Should I spell words the British or American way?

A. Both British and American spelling versions are accepted. Whichever you adopt, please make sure your spelling is correct, because misspelled answers may be penalised. For example, you can write 'color' (American spelling) or 'colour' (British spelling), but if you write 'calor' the answer will get 0 points.

Q. Will I be penalised for grammatical errors?

A. Grammar is an important part of the Reading test. Any answer with correct meaning but incorrect grammar may get zero points. A common error, for example, is to use a singular form ('apple') instead of plural form ('apples'), or to use the wrong tense or verb form ('he go' instead of 'he goes'). Such ungrammatical answers could receive zero points.

What if I...?   Some Problem Situations

Q. What if I am not familiar with the text topic?

A. It can happen that the text you get will be on a subject you don't know much about. Good news: this doesn't mean you are in trouble.

The truth is that your chances of success don't change much, whether you get a text on a subject you know lots about, or a subject you don't feel confident about. This is because your personal knowledge and life experience **are not needed** to answer IELTS Reading questions—instead you should use the techniques described in more detail in this book.

The techniques you should apply to the text stay the same, regardless of the passage topic, and the outcome depends largely on your effective use of these techniques.

The rule of dealing with texts on an unfamiliar topic is "Don't concentrate on the words you don't know — concentrate on the words you **do** know". Even if you don't understand a few words, guess their meaning from the context.

You can achieve this by reading the words before and after the unfamiliar word, and using them to guess what the word you don't know means.

Q. What if I am a slow reader?

A. Slow reading is a real problem for some people, and it is often caused by:
   a) poor concentration
   b) limited vocabulary
   c) not enough practice in reading long texts (even in your first language!)
   d) poor reading techniques (e.g. reading single words, not phrases)

Slow reading is **not** an incurable disease. To train yourself to become a faster reader you should:

   a) Reduce the level of distraction in the room where you study. Don't sit in front of a window, turn off music/TV/radio, and ask other people near you to keep quiet while you're studying.

b) Learn new words. Every time you practice reading and see a new word, you might try writing it on a flash card (in a sentence!). Spend five to ten minutes a day looking at the flash cards and trying to remember the meaning of each word.

You should also learn how to guess from context — this skill will serve you well in the IELTS Reading test. Guessing from context means using the other words around the word you don't know to help you shape its meaning, without using a dictionary.

c) Read more. Use newspapers, magazines, IELTS practice tests and other sources of reading texts for practice.

d) Stop reading sentences in a word-by-word manner; instead train yourself to read in phrases. This is a skill that fast readers possess, and that you, too, can acquire with practice. Read words in groups, and soon a change in your reading speed will become noticeable.

Example

The sentence below, when read by a slow reader, would perhaps look like this:

> One – of – the – best – known – dolphin – species – the – bottlenose – dolphin – lives – in– every – ocean – of – the – world – except – the – Arctic – and – the – Antarctic – oceans.

Notice how long it takes to read this, when you stop before every word.

Now try reading each of these lines without stopping between words:

> – One of the best known dolphin species, –
> – the bottlenose dolphin –
> – lives in every ocean of the world –
> – except the Arctic and the Antarctic oceans.

Notice how the speed has increased. This is the right way to read in an IELTS Reading test.

Q. **What if I'm almost out of time, and I still haven't answered all the questions?**

A. This can (and probably will) happen to you during the first practice sessions. The IELTS Reading test is time-intensive, meaning there is a lot of reading and answering in the 60 minutes, and anyone who doesn't manage their time can end up in this situation. While it's OK to run out of time at home, in the initial stages of your preparation, try not to let it happen to you during the actual exam. Proper time management will help you avoid such scary moments—please refer to **'7 Fundamentals to Make Your Reading Test a Success'** on page 48.

Q. **What if I have a problem with spelling?**

A. Spelling answers incorrectly may cost you points, so this problem should be addressed early in your preparation. Apart from the obvious solution—to learn how to spell—which may take months, we've come up with a shortcut. Our experience with students over the years has taught us that some words are **more likely to get misspelled** than others.

Please refer to the 'Famously misspelled words list' at the end of the Listening chapter (Page 17). By learning the correct spelling of most words on that list you will greatly reduce your chances of misspelling an answer in the IELTS exam.

Q. **What if I have bad handwriting?**

A. Then you should try writing in block letters, not in cursive script. Block letters are harder to mess up than cursive and are easier to read. It is important that your answers are readable—if they can't be read, they can't be scored.

Q. **What if I am unsure of an answer?**

A. Whenever you are unsure what the correct answer is, you have two options:

Option 1 is to go over the text again, to check your answer is correct or find a different answer.

Option 2 is to guess the answer. Some questions are harder than others, and when there's no time to search the text again, guessing is a legitimate solution. Instead of leaving the answer blank, write your best guess in its space on the answer sheet. There is no penalty for writing incorrect answers, so this can't do any harm—and with some luck you may earn a few points!

7 Fundamentals to Make Your Reading Test a Success

1. Skim and scan instead of reading word by word

Shocking as it may sound, you do not have the time to read the passages entirely. If you try to read and remember every single word in your question paper, you will run out of time well before even getting to the stage where you answer the questions.

The trick is to read only the important and meaningful parts, and that is achieved by skimming and scanning. 'Skimming' means reading fast to get the general idea, and 'scanning' means looking for particular information. Your eyes should be skimming the paragraphs to get the general idea of each, and scanning the paper like radar, looking for keywords, main points and other important information. It is a good idea to circle or underline names, dates and keywords.

How and when to skim

Although this is not the only way, most students of IELTS-Blog.com reported better results when they skimmed the text first. Skimming includes reading the title/heading, looking at pictures (if any) and reading the first sentence of every paragraph. Normally this is enough to harness an overall understanding of the text.

Then it's time to read the questions. Not all of them, of course, but the first group. Questions are broken down into groups, and usually there are questions of just one certain type in each group. There is a set of instructions for every group of questions and an example; read them closely before you begin scanning the text.

How and when to scan

Scanning works best when you have an idea about what you're looking for. When you know what the question is, and you've seen an example answer, you know what sort of information you need to find, and what the answer should look like.

Some questions will require you to scan the text to find the answer; others will require reading in detail. Scanning works best for the following task types:

> **Sentence/Notes/Table/Flow chart/Summary completion**
> **Short-answer questions**
> **Labelling a diagram**
> **Matching features (finding Information in paragraphs)**

Why? Because these question types can be answered by finding a keyword in the paragraph and reading around it, and scanning is the way to find a keyword in text quickly.

Always try to guess what information is missing before you start scanning—this will make finding the answer easier.

Try this in action — go to Reading Fitness Activities 6 and 8, to see how it works (Page 65, 68).

2. Use the text to guide you to the answers

This part we need you to **read closely**, because it may help you find answers to certain types of questions more quickly.

Answers to some types of questions appear **sequentially** in text. This means that the answer to question 2 appears after the answer to question 1, and the answer to question 3 appears after the answer to question 2. In other words you won't have to go back in the text to find the next answer if you do the questions sequentially—you will always be moving forward.

This is important because with each answered question you have less and less text to search— which enables you to find the later answers in a group more quickly.

Here are the task types for which answers appear **in the order of the passage:**

- ➢ **Sentence completion (with or without a list of options)**
- ➢ **Short-answer questions,**
- ➢ **True/False/Not Given,**
- ➢ **Yes/No/Not Given,**
- ➢ **Multiple choice.**

When solving these types of questions, mark the sentence where you found the answer. To find the next answer, you will only need to search **after** that mark.

Try this in action — go to Reading Fitness Activities 10 and 12, to see how it works (Page 70, 72).

Note: when you finish one group of questions and move on to the next group, you may have to go back to the first paragraph and start looking for answers from the top.

3. Use words from the text

Answers to certain types of questions should be copied straight from the passage, exactly as they are. This is great news for you as a test taker—firstly, you don't need to think of an answer from off the top of your head (if it's not in the passage, if you can't copy it exactly as it is—then it's not the right answer). Secondly, when you copy words you won't have to worry about spelling—all you do is copy them as shown.

The task types that require **words to be copied** from the passage **without changing** anything are:

- ➢ **Sentence completion (without a list of options)**
- ➢ **Short-answer questions**
- ➢ **Summary completion (without a list of options)**
- ➢ **Table/notes/flowchart completion**
- ➢ **Diagram labelling**

Try this in action — go to Reading Fitness Activities 7 and 13, to see how it works (Page 65, 74).

4. Read in detail only if you have to

Scanning works fine with some task types—but not all. The trick is to know when you really need to read parts of the text closely. A study that we conducted of IELTS-Blog visitors, helped us to identify these task types that require **reading in detail** to find the correct answer:

> - **True/False/Not Given**
> - **Yes/No/Not Given**
> - **Matching Paragraph Headings**
> - **Matching Information**

5. Pay close attention to task instructions in the test paper

In IELTS, following instructions is not voluntary—it's mandatory. They define the exact way you should answer, and if you deviate, you may lose points.

In particular, the word limit is crucial, so when the instructions ask you to answer '**USING NO MORE THAN THREE WORDS AND/OR A NUMBER**', do the right thing and write one, two or three words, and/or a number, but not more. Don't repeat words unnecessarily (if they already are in the sentence that you're required to complete), and don't write two answers/options if they ask for just one.

 Note: articles (a/an/the) and prepositions (e.g. in/on/by) count as words.

For more information read the section 'How to Avoid Problems with Your Answers' (Page 14).

6. Know when to move on

Let's face it—IELTS is not a 100% kind of test. In our years of working with test-takers through IELTS-Blog.com, from thousands of candidates we have come across only a few people who have answered 100% of the reading questions correctly.

When practicing, you may find that some questions are just harder than others and require more time to find the correct answer. This is why there's no shame in putting a question mark next to the tough question and moving on to the next one—in fact it's much better than getting stuck and losing too much time.

If you have some time left after all the other questions are answered, go back to the tough questions and try to answer them. Or, if you're out of time—just write your best guess.

7. Manage your time

Finding yourself in a situation where there is almost no time left, yet many questions haven't been answered can be very stressful. The good news is that with proper preparation there is no reason why it should happen to you in the actual exam.

Practice with answering questions within firm time limits for each passage can help prevent the loss of points for an entire text and its questions just because you got stuck on the previous one.

How to manage time in an Academic Reading test

In the Academic Reading test there are 3 texts, which usually progress in difficulty. If this wasn't the case, we would suggest dividing the time equally. However, with the first text usually being the easiest and last text being the hardest, it makes sense to allocate about 15 minutes for completion of the tasks based on the first text, around 20 minutes for those based on the second, and 25 minutes or so for those linked to the final text.

Before you begin to read, write when each time allocation begins and ends. When your time is up, move on to the next text. Make sure you transfer the answers to the Answer Sheet within the time limit allocated to that particular text. Don't leave the transferring of answers till the very end—otherwise you will be robbing the last text of all those minutes required to transfer your complete set of answers to the Answer Sheet.

If you find it very difficult, almost impossible to complete the first two texts in 15 and 20 minutes (after you have tried and practiced), then consider a different strategy, more suitable for people with **weaker** reading skills. Concentrate on the first two texts and do them more thoroughly, at the expense of the third text. Yes, you may not have enough time to finish all the questions in the third text, but spending more time on the first two texts can help you get more correct answers there. Experiment with these two alternative strategies and find out which one helps you get a larger number of correct answers.

Techniques for Answering Reading Tasks Quickly & Accurately

TASK TYPE » Matching Paragraph Headings

Technique 1

Matching headings is considered a hard task by some students, but only because they do it the hard way. Here is the easy way: when you match headings, go in the order of **paragraphs**, not in the order of headings. Read paragraph 1, look for a suitable heading in the list, then read paragraph 2, look for a suitable heading, and so on.

In each paragraph, read the first sentence, and then look for a heading. If you can't find the right heading, read the second sentence, then search the list of headings again. If you still can't find the heading, read the last sentence, and then look for a heading. If still you get nothing, then read the whole paragraph before you look for a heading.

This technique is based on the fact that the first sentence of a paragraph often contains its main point. In many cases reading the first sentence will be enough to find the right heading, but even if you need to read another sentence, this method will still save you time because it doesn't require you to read every paragraph in full. What's more, compared to the other, inefficient way students often match headings—when they go in the order of headings, read each heading and try to match a paragraph to it—our way **saves** you from reading the same paragraph over and over again.

The task instructions will tell you when a heading can't be used more than once. In that case, any heading that you matched should be clearly marked as 'taken' on the list (simply by putting a tick '√' next to it). This will save you from considering it again for another paragraph.

Technique 2

If you come across a tricky paragraph that requires a long time for a heading to be found and even then you are still unsure, use the elimination technique. Move on and solve the rest of the paragraphs. After you've done that there will be fewer headings to choose from, and it will be easier to pick the right one. Even if you end up guessing, with fewer options to pick from, your chances of success increase.

> *Try this in action — go to Fitness Activity 1 and see how it works (Page 59).*

IELTS Reading Lesson

TASK TYPE » True/False/Not Given (or Yes/No/Not Given)

This type of task has proven to be problematic for some students, and here is why: apart from testing your English, True/False/Not Given questions test your logical thinking as well.

However with some practice your logical thinking will improve and solving this type of questions will become easier.

Technique 1

The basic rule is that that if the statement clearly agrees with text, the answer is True, if the statement explicitly contradicts the text, the answer is False, and if the statement says something that the text doesn't say, it's Not Given. It works in a very similar way with Yes/No/Not Given.

It is also helpful to keep in mind that the answers to True/False/Not Given and Yes/No/Not Given questions appear sequentially in the passage. This narrows down the search for you, because once you've found the answer to question 1, the answer to question 2 will be somewhere in the sentences that follow, not in the preceding part of the text.

Technique 2

When you practice at home, your work doesn't stop after you've answered all the questions. For this type of task there is a very powerful technique—it helps you turn your weakness into your strength.

Once you've checked your answers against the correct ones in your book/sample test, and you know which of your answers are wrong, go back and try to understand exactly **why** these answers are wrong, and why the ones in the book are correct. This is a very important step, as it enables you to learn from your mistakes.

Then understand why you answered the way you did, what confused you, what tricked you into giving the wrong answer, and try not to make the same mistake the next time. We live, we learn, right?

Try this in action — go to Fitness Activities 5 and 9, to see how it works (Page 64, 69).

TASK TYPE » Summary/Sentence Completion (filling in blanks)

Technique 1

To make filling in blanks easier, quicker and more accurate, try to guess what is missing. Even if you can't guess the meaning of the word, you can still guess whether it's, say, a verb, a noun, or an adjective, by looking at the words around the gap.

Once you know the kind of word that's missing, it is easier to find it in the passage or in the list of options in a box.

While reading the sentence around the gap, also note what it's about, and use that information when you're scanning the text to locate the paragraph where the answer might be.

In the selected paragraph look for words of the same type that could go in the gap. If a verb is missing—look at verbs, if an adjective is missing—look at adjectives, and so on. After you've found the best candidate for the gap, always read the whole sentence, to make sure it makes sense and that grammatically it is correct.

If you find yourself changing the words from the text, or their form, before writing them in the gap, it means that you've got the wrong answer. In tasks such as sentence completion or summary completion you should be able to find the correct answer right in the text, and copy it as is, without changing a word.

Technique 2

Sometimes moving on to the next gap will allow you to use the elimination technique. For example, when you have a list of words to choose from, after you've used most of the options and only have a few left it will be easier to eliminate the wrong ones, and pick the right ones.

Try this in action — go to Fitness Activities 3 and 11, to see how it works (Page 61, 71).

TASK TYPE » Multiple Choice Questions

This type of task may confuse you by offering multiple answer options, so your best way of getting the answer right is by 'shooting down' the wrong options.

First, read the question and find the paragraph that is discussing the same topic. If the right answer is not immediately visible, begin eliminating the wrong answer options one by one, based on the information in the paragraph.

Pretend that each answer option is a statement of the True/False/Not Given type, and decide whether each particular answer option is True, False or Not Given, according to the passage. If the answer option is False or Not Given, cross it out—it's not the answer.

Another helpful observation is that the answers to multiple choice questions are located sequentially in the passage. If you've found the answer to question 1, and the answer to question 3, then the answer to question 2 will probably be between them.

> *Try this in action — go to Fitness Activity 2 and see how it works (Page 60).*

ACADEMIC READING FITNESS ACTIVITIES

Improve your understanding of each of the task types in the IELTS Reading test, by trying these Fitness Activities.

Read the text below and answer Fitness Activities 1–4.

AUSTRALIA's DAM STORY (Part 1)

Section A
Measured across the continent, Australia receives an average of only 465 mm of rainfall a year, compared with Europe's 640 mm and Asia's 600 mm. High evaporation allows just 12 per cent of its rainfall to run off and reach waterways. Even so, there's enough water for everyone—but it's seldom in the right place at the right time.

Section B
European settlers solved this problem with dams. The first two—Yan Yean outside Melbourne and Lake Parramatta, Sydney—were completed in 1857. Dam building continued steadily until after World War II, when it accelerated. Today, 500 large (more than 15 m high) dams store a total  of 93,957 gigalitres (Sydney Harbour holds about 562 GL). There are also countless smaller dams, called weirs, on most Australian rivers—8000 in the Murray-Darling Basin alone—and more than 2 million farm dams.

Section C

Large dams bring quick benefits. They can provide water and electricity, mitigate flooding and create beautiful lakes. But they also have adverse impacts. The first are those on people living in the way of a dam and its lake. They may need to be moved, causing families and communities to fragment. The lake may flood farmland or natural landscape. Many of the drowned river's plants and animals fail to adapt to lake conditions. Alien fish species, introduced into the reservoir accidentally, or for recreational fishing, may further alter the biological make-up of water life, and weeds and algae may thrive in the nutrient-rich water. Downstream, changes in the river's flow and water quality usually cause irreversible effects, often down to the river mouth and beyond. Fish migration and reproduction, siltation and salinity in deltas are altered.

Section D

Once upon a time, these adverse impacts—some of which take years to manifest—weren't really considered before a dam was built. The human need for water, for drinking or to grow food, took precedence. Some people believe they should still. But over recent decades, science has deepened our understanding of natural systems, which we now know can't be broken into discrete pieces, some of which can be exploited and others not. This has given rise to the idea that the environment itself is a legitimate water consumer, with attendant needs and rights. All this calls for careful study of a river's state and function before it's dammed.

Section E

Australia's newest megadam straddles a gentle valley on the Burnett River, 260 km north-west of Brisbane. Apart from a soupy stain low on its upstream face, the concrete is spotless and dazzles the eye under the sharp Queensland sun. This is Paradise Dam, completed in 2005. Impressive though it may be, Paradise, like other large dams, is a mix of good points and bad. For some people, the bad prevail. High among the complaints has been that the rationale behind it was political. Then there are the potential environmental impacts downstream, especially around the river's mouth in Hervey Bay, which worry people such as commercial fishers and tourism operators.

Source: *Australian Geographic, Issue 89 (Jan–Mar, 2007)*

TASK TYPE » Matching Paragraph Headings

 Fitness Activity 1

The reading passage on AUSTRALIA's DAM STORY (Part 1) has five sections, **A–E**. Choose the correct heading for sections **B–E** from the list of headings below.

Write the correct number **i–ix** below. Choose each heading once only.

List of Headings

i	Problems in Paradise?
ii	Benefits outstrip problems
iii	Development of dams in Australia
iv	The importance of water to humans
v	How to solve problems with dams
vi	**Australia's rainfall profile [Example]**
vii	The role of science in the planning of dams
viii	Disadvantages outweigh gains
ix	Meeting Sydney's water needs

1	Section A	vi [Example]
2	Section B	_____
3	Section C	_____
4	Section D	_____
5	Section E	_____

TASK TYPE » Multiple Choice Questions

 Fitness Activity 2

1 Using **ONLY Section C** above choose the appropriate letter **A,B,C,** or **D.**

   One of the problems of dams is that:
   A new plant species may change the biological balance
   B they cause more drowning
   C they lead to changes in salt levels in water further up river
   D weeds and algae can't survive as easily

2 Using **ONLY Section D** above, choose the appropriate letter **A,B,C,** or **D.**

   According to the passage, the negative features of dams:
   A were originally given precedence over the demand for water
   B were at first taken into account before construction
   C have given rise to more sensitivity about the environment
   D have led to national studies of river care

3 Using **ONLY Section E** above, choose the appropriate letter **A,B,C,** or **D.**

   According to the passage, Paradise Dam:
   A has been entirely beneficial
   B is situated beyond a valley
   C has provided environmental advantages for tourists
   D may have been built for political reasons

TASK TYPE » Summary Completion

Fitness Activity 3

Complete the summary below based on **Sections C and D ONLY**, above.
Choose **NO MORE THAN ONE WORD** from the text for each answer.

Dams have benefits and drawbacks. For example, they provide water and **1** _____ but those residing in the dam's path may have to be **2** _____. The reservoir may **3** _____ agricultural land, and biological changes may include unwanted fish species. In recent years better understanding of nature has been helped by **4** _____. The environment is now seen as having rights just like every other **5** _____ of water.

TASK TYPE » Labelling Diagrams

Fitness Activity 4

Look at the diagrams of types of dams (**A–D**) and read each dam description below. Label each description with the appropriate letter (A–D).

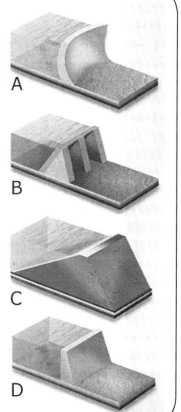

Dam Type	Description of Dams
_____	**Embankment dams** use a long-sloped, massive volume of rock, gravel and sand, with the finest materials in the centre to form a waterproof core.
_____	**Buttress dams** have 45 degree walls that transfer the force downwards.
_____	**Gravity dams** are thick, massive structures with a vertical face that can hold back enormous amounts of water under their own weight.
_____	**Arch dams** have curved sides which redirect a lot of pressure to the valley sides.

Read the text below and answer Fitness Activities 5–7.

AUSTRALIA's DAM STORY (Part 2)

Section A   THREATENED SPECIES

But nothing has galvanised public opinion more than the plight of the endangered Australian, or Queensland, lungfish. Among the last of a group that lived 400 million years ago, this once-abundant fish is restricted mostly to the Burnett and Mary rivers. Biologists believe Paradise Dam has had, and will have, serious consequences for it. A fishway was installed to comply with the Commonwealth's Environmental Protection and Biodiversity Conservation Act (EPBC Act), which lists the lungfish as endangered. The Act requires the fish's spawning and nursery 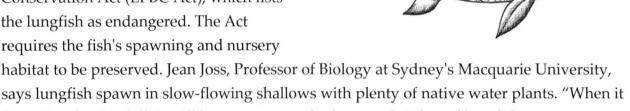 habitat to be preserved. Jean Joss, Professor of Biology at Sydney's Macquarie University, says lungfish spawn in slow-flowing shallows with plenty of native water plants. "When it [Paradise dam] is full, it will have permanently destroyed 42 km of lungfish spawning/nursery grounds," she says.

Section B   GROWTH AND THIRST

Declining water consumption in most of Australia has stalled dam-building in recent years. But not in south-east Queensland. There, the population is set to soar from 2.8 million today to 5 million in 2050, and water consumption is expected to climb with it. The region mirrors not only what has happened historically elsewhere in Australia but also what's happening across the world. Look here and you see humanity's past and its future. South-east Queensland consumes about 440,000 ML a year. The Queensland Government says that by 2050 the region will need 330,000–490,000 ML more, even with water restrictions.

Section C   ALTERNATIVE OPTIONS FOR MEETING WATER DEMAND

Prodded by drought but committed to economic growth, the government has assembled a mix of measures to provide the extra water. Among them are recycling, desalination, raising some existing dams and building two new ones – Traveston Crossing on the Mary River, and Wyaralong nearer to Brisbane.

Section D   THE MARY RIVER DAM PROPOSALS

Queensland Water Infrastructure (QWI) Pty Ltd would build the dam in two stages. Stage 1, due by 2020 and costing $1.6 billion, would flood 3000 ha of farmland and 334 properties; Stage 2, due after 2040, would raise the total cost to $2.5 billion and flood an extra 7135 ha and 265 properties. The dam wall would be made of RCC (Roller Compacted Concrete) at its western end and would merge with an earth-and-rock embankment.

Since one aim of the dam is to limit flooding in Gympie, 20 km to the north, the spillway would have six floodgates. QWI aims to build the dam to Stage 2 height immediately so that the only extra work needed later to raise the water level by another 8.5 m would be the fitting of higher gates. As with Paradise dam, there was talk of political expediency, but the government insisted the looming water crisis allowed no choice.

Section E   SATISFYING THE ENVIRONMENTAL IMPACTS OF THE MARY RIVER DAM

In its Environmental Impact Statement (EIS) on the project, published in October 2007, QWI maintained the dam was the cheapest option offering maximum water returns. On the environment it was upbeat, saying downstream impacts would be negligible and that it could manage the effects around the dam's footprint such that wildlife might even be better off than now. As in the Burnett, the lungfish is central here. But in the Mary it's joined by the Mary River cod and the Mary River turtle. Since all are legally protected under national environmental legislation, the project needs federal approval. A decision based on the final Environmental Impact Statement is due soon.

TASK TYPE » Yes/No/Not Given (Identifying Writer's Views)

 Fitness Activity 5

Do the following statements reflect the claims of the writer in **Section A** above?
Write:

      YES   if the statement reflects the claims of the writer
      NO   if the statement contradicts the claims of the writer
      NOT GIVEN   if it is impossible to say what the writer thinks about this

1   The deteriorating situation of the lungfish has stimulated public support.

      _____

2   The habitat of the lungfish is now limited primarily to only two rivers.

      _____

3   Biologists officially consider the lungfish to be an endangered species.

      _____

4   The breeding grounds of the lungfish have no legal protection.

      _____

TASK TYPE » Matching Information

Fitness Activity 6

Which Section (**B, C, D** or **E**) above contains the following information?

1   Measures for accommodating likely increases in demand for water. ___

2   Data illustrating current and projected water demand in Queensland. ___

3   Cost benefit gains and low projected impact of the Mary River Dam. ___

4   The aquatic life affected by the proposed new dam. ___

5   The likely timing and sequencing of dam construction. ___

TASK TYPE » Form/Note Completion

Fitness Activity 7

Using only **Section D** above, complete the notes below.
Choose **NO MORE THAN THREE WORDS AND/OR A NUMBER** from the passage for each answer.

- Overall cost of the dam = **1** _____

- Reduction of **2** _____ = a goal of building the dam

- **3** _____ to be fitted to enable increase in water level

- Government claimed no alternative due to approach of **4** _____

Read the text below and answer Fitness Activities 8–12.

AUSTRALIA's DAM STORY (Part 3)

For Mary Valley residents, nothing will ever repair damage already caused to families and communities by the dam's announcement and Queensland Water Infrastructure's (QWI) purchase of properties in the dam's footprint. QWI acknowledges that stress, depression, community disintegration and deep mistrust have resulted but says not everyone has suffered.

By late 2007, QWI had reached sale agreements for 65 per cent of the land it needs before it can build the new dam. Many people who sold have leased back their former properties and may continue to live on them for a time. One who hasn't sold is Glenda Pickersgill. Glenda breeds cattle about 1 km upstream of the proposed dam site. Her house and land would vanish under water at Stage 1. The farm has been in Glenda's family for 30 years and she has owned it for 20. Glenda was devastated by the Queensland Government's announcement about planning to build a new dam.

As a member of the Save the Mary River Coordinating Group, an anti-dam residents' coalition, Glenda has thrown all her energy into getting information about the project into the community and rallying support for the campaign against it. Anti-dam protest signs dot the Mary Valley. The signs cluster in greatest quantity and variety at Kandanga's old railway station, used these days only by a historic steam train. There, an airy weatherboard shed has become the headquarters and public information centre of the Save the Mary River Coordinating Group.

The group's chairman, Kevin Ingersole, 63, is a dynamic, semi-retired management consultant who bought a property in the valley five years ago. At Stage 1 he would lose much of his land. Kevin is bitter but, like Glenda, he diverts his emotions into action. He considers the Environmental Impact Statement (EIS) and its associated documents to be a magnificent sales pitch for building a dam, and claims that the government has not demonstrated that the proposed dam at Traveston Crossing is the best long-term solution for south-east Queensland's water-supply needs.

QWI's documents certainly attempt to build a convincing case for the dam's long-term economic importance to the region, emphasising increases in gross regional product, employment and business potential. QWI also claims that the dam's long-term cost will be more than $200 million less than the 'next best' water-supply alternative, a desalination plant. What irks Mary Valley residents most, however, is that water from the proposed reservoir would be pumped out of the area. Of the lake's 153,000 ML at Stage 1, 70,000 ML would go out every year. At Stage 2 the lake would hold 570,000 ML and would yield up to 150,000 ML a year. Professor Angela Arthington says the environmental consequences of such extraction, together with the flooding of a shallow valley, are predictable because they characterise all megadams in similar landscapes. She believes that thousands of publications document the adverse effects of dams on river and estuarine ecosystems.

TASK TYPE » Matching Features

 Fitness Activity 8

Which of the individuals mentioned in Australia's Dam Story (Part 3) above has these points of view? Write **A** (for Professor **A**rthington), **I** (for Kevin **I**ngersole) and **P** (for Glenda **P**ickersgill).

Which person (**A, I** or **P**) believes that

1   ...most printed material about the dam is really an attempt to promote it? ___

2   ...a large amount of the available documentation outlines the difficulties experienced by river life resulting from dams? ___

3   ...it is vital to distribute material about the dam to the local population. ___

TASK TYPE » True/False/Not Given (Identifying Information)

 Fitness Activity 9

Do the following statements agree with the information given in Australia's Dam Story (Part 3)? Answer:

    TRUE   if the statement agrees with the information
    FALSE   if the statement contradicts the information
    NOT GIVEN if there is no information on this

1   QWI accepts that social problems resulting from purchase of properties have affected everyone.

2   People who have sold their land to QWI may not leave it for some time.

3   The majority of the anti-dam signs are near Kandanga Railway station.

4   The EIS discusses the sale of Kevin Ingersole's land to the government.

5   QWI's documents predict that regional wealth will grow.

6   QWI consider that the dam will be less expensive than a desalination plant.

7   People who live in Mary Valley are annoyed about the likely loss of water from their area when the reservoir is in operation.

8   Professor Arthington is unsure about the environmental outcomes likely to arise as a result of the new dam.

IELTS Academic Reading Fitness Activities

TASK TYPE » Matching Sentence Endings

 Fitness Activity 10

Choose the best endings for sentences **1–4** from the **List of Options i–viii** in the box below.

1   After the QWI announcement, many Mary Valley residents
    _____

2   Glenda Pickersgill is likely to lose her land and property
    _____

3   Five years ago, the chairman of the Save the Mary River Coordinating Group
    _____

4   Angela Arthington believes that megadams cause flooding of valleys
    _____

List of Options

i	to her family during the next thirty years
ii	purchased a valley property
iii	which are extracted during construction
iv	suffered traumatic psychological effects
v	can be repaired by avoiding all the damage
vi	was a full-time management consultant
vii	during Stage 1 of the dam's development
viii	that are characteristically shallow

TASK TYPE » Sentence Completion

 Fitness Activity 11

Complete the sentences below.
Choose **NO MORE THAN TWO WORDS OR A NUMBER** from the text for each answer.

1   Glenda Pickersgill was _____ when she heard of the government's dam-building plans.

2   Glenda is trying hard to build _____ for the anti-dam protest group.

3   Kevin Ingersole remains unconvinced that the proposed dam is the optimal _____ to regional water needs.

4   At Stage 2 _____ would be extracted from the lake annually.

TASK TYPE » Short-answer Questions

 Fitness Activity 12

Answer the questions below.
Choose **NO MORE THAN TWO WORDS AND/OR A NUMBER** from the text for each answer.

1   What has been the irreparable outcome of QWI's property purchase on the whole community?

    _____

2   In what direction is Glenda's land relative to the proposed dam?

    _____

3   In what type of dwelling does the Save the Mary River Group have its central office?

    _____

4   Although he remains proactive, how does Kevin Ingersole feel?

    _____

5   In financial terms, what is the economic benefit of a dam compared with a desalination plant?

    _____

TASK TYPE » Flow Chart/Table Completion

Read the text below and answer Fitness Activity 13.

How evaporated milk is produced

First, the raw milk is transported from the dairy farm to the plant in refrigerated tank trucks. At the plant, the milk is tested for odour, taste, bacteria, sediment, and the composition of milk protein and milk fat. The composition of protein and fat is measured by passing the milk under highly sensitive infrared lights. After this, the milk is piped through filters and into the pasteurizers where it is quickly heated in one of two ways: the High Temperature Short Time method (HTST) subjects the milk to temperatures of 71.6°C for 15 seconds; the Ultra High Temperature (UHT) method heats the milk to 138°C for two seconds. The two methods increase the milk's stability, and decrease both the chance of coagulation during storage, and the bacteria levels. Next, the warm milk is piped to an evaporator. Through the process of vacuum evaporation, (a pressure lower than atmospheric pressure) the boiling point of the milk is lowered to 40–45°C. As a result, the milk is concentrated to 30–40% solids and has little or no cooked flavour. The milk is then homogenized by forcing it under high pressure through tiny holes. This breaks down the fat globules into minute particles, improving its colour and stability. Pre-measured amounts of a stabilizing salt, such as potassium phosphate, are added to the milk to make it smooth and creamy. This stabilization causes the milk to turn a pale tan. Finally, the milk is passed under a series of ultraviolet lights to fortify it with Vitamin D. Finally, the milk is piped into pre-sterilized cans that are vacuum-sealed.

Fitness Activity 13

Complete the diagram below based on the text 'How evaporated milk is produced'. Choose **NO MORE THAN TWO WORDS** from the text for each answer.

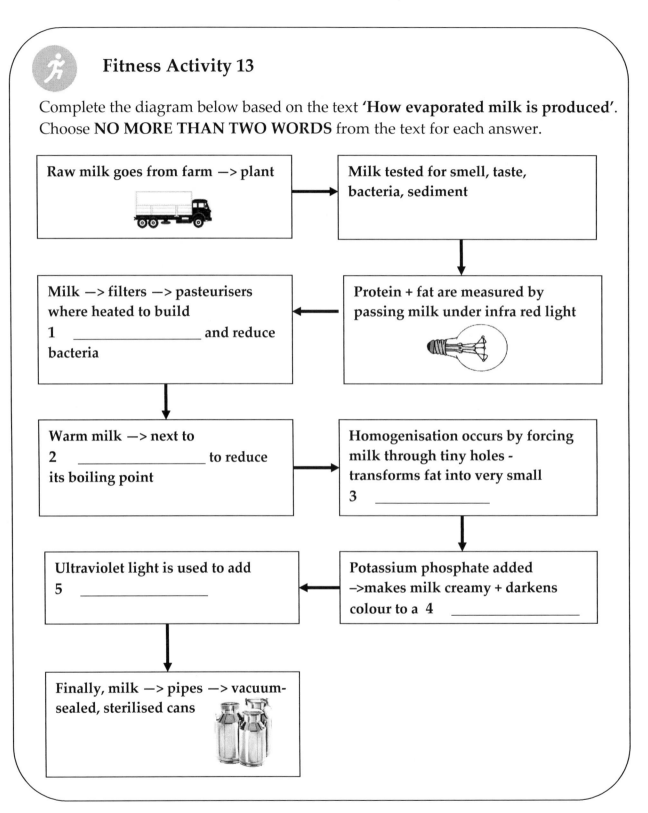

Finished all 13 tasks? You're a hero!

IELTS WRITING

OVERVIEW

Writing Test Basics

Q. How is the Writing test structured?

A. The Writing test has two tasks called Task 1 and Task 2, as briefly described below:

	Writing Task 1	Writing Task 2
Word limit	150 words minimum	250 words minimum
Suggested time limit	20 minutes	40 minutes
Overall Score	On a band scale from 0–9 with half band scores	On a band scale from 0–9 with half band scores

 Note: Task 2 score contributes a little more to the overall score than Task 1.

Q. Where should I write my answers to the Writing tasks?

A. You will be given an Answer booklet in which you should write your Task 1 and Task 2 responses:

> - The booklet has about 20 lines per page and 4 pages.
> - The first page of the Task 1 section has some instructions, leaving only half a full page for writing on that page, plus the following page.
> - The Task 2 section has 2 full pages.
> - It is clearly indicated where to start your answer to both Task 1 and Task 2.

Remember, too:

> - You can do the tasks in **any order**, which means you can decide to do Task 2 first if you prefer, or if you are worried about how best to use the time.
> - You can ask for additional paper if you need it.

Q. How is my writing assessed?

A. By a real person!

Each task is marked by a trained IELTS assessor who reads your answer and gives you a score (from 0 to 9) for different aspects of your performance by comparing what you have written with performance descriptions for different score levels in these four areas:

- **task fulfilment** in Task 1 (Did you do what you were asked to do?) or **task response** in Task 2 (Did you respond to all parts of the task and offer a clear viewpoint?)
- **vocabulary** (How varied, appropriate and extensive is your use?)
- **grammar** (How flexibly and accurately are you able to use different sentence types?)
- **coherence and cohesion** (How well is your answer structured in terms of ideas and paragraphing; how well do sentences link together to build logical movement from one idea to another?)

Note: you may lose marks if you don't write enough words for either answer.

Q. How can I impress the assessor?

A. Well done! This is the **key question** in our book.

There are many ways to manage your answers to each task so that you impress your assessor. These will be discussed and practised extensively later in this section of the book.

Q. How should I begin my preparation?

A. First, have a look at the Task 1 section on Page 78 and the Task 2 section on Page 127.

While going through our advice for Task 1 and Task 2 you may notice that we give several identical suggestions for both tasks. This is because there are **important principles that apply to both Task 1 and Task 2**. It seems a good idea to be reminded of them so you can learn how to apply them while practising, and, more importantly, in the actual IELTS exam.

IELTS Writing Task 1 Lesson

WRITING LESSON – Task 1 Report

First Questions Answered

Q. What kind of task will I be given?

A. For Task 1 you will receive either a **chart**, a **graph**, a **map**, a **process diagram** or a **table**:

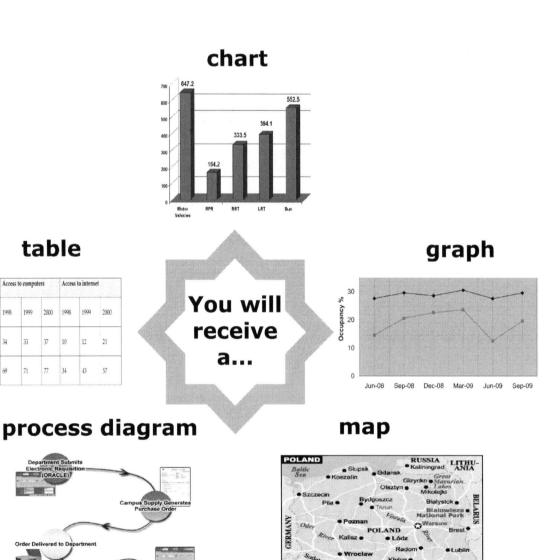

IELTS Success Formula :: Academic

Q. How do I start organising and planning my answer?

A. You need to read the task 1 instructions you receive and then give the accompanying visual a quick overview to identify key features of the data.

Practise this quickly now, by overviewing each of these sample task 1 visuals:

A map: **Fountain Gate Shopping Centre, 1980**

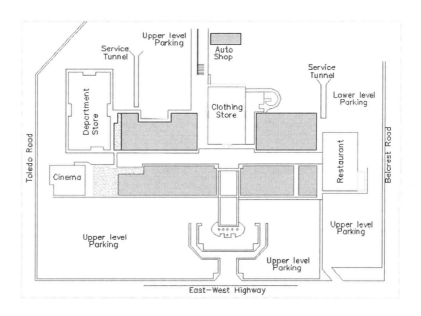

Fountain Gate Shopping Centre, 2008

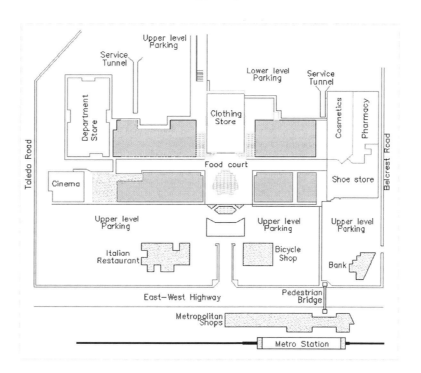

A process diagram:

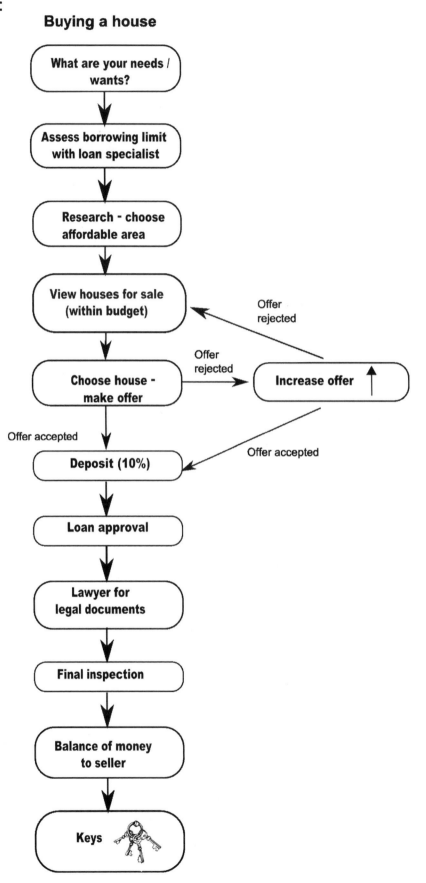

A graph:

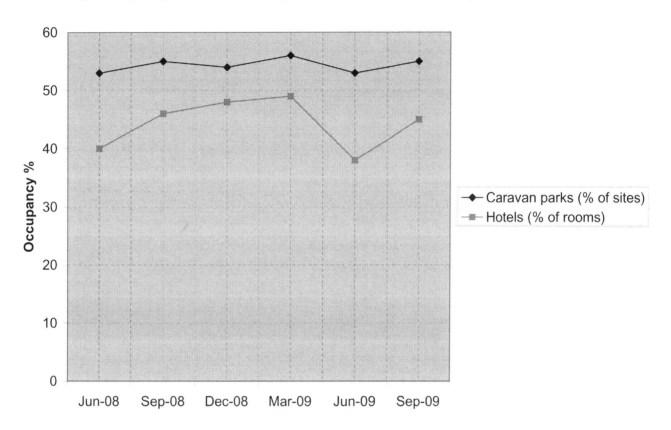

Percentage occupancy rates in caravan parks and hotels Jun '08 - Sep '09

A table:

Percentage of Australian households with access to computers/internet 1998–2000

	Access to computers			Access to internet		
Household income/year	1998	1999	2000	1998	1999	2000
Below $50,000 per year	34	33	37	10	12	21
Above $50,000 per year	69	71	77	34	43	57

IELTS Writing Task 1 Lesson

A chart:

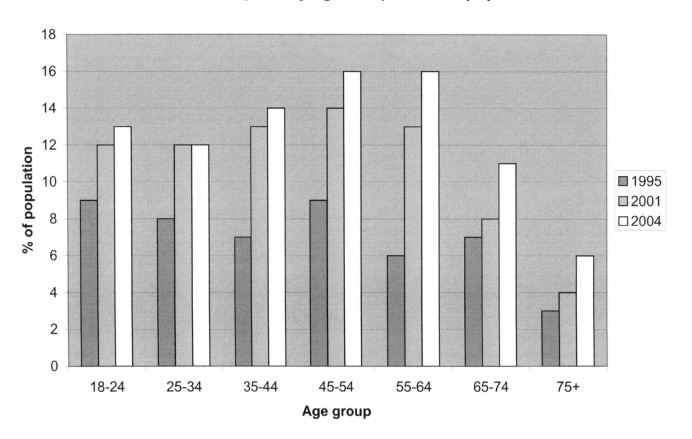

Q. **What do I have to do to respond <u>well</u> to the question?**

A. Your task is to:
  - identify an overview of the data (This means a statement identifying the most obvious main trend),
  - write a well-organised, professional-sounding report in a formal tone, describing and summarising the main features, trends or stages in terms of the data,
  - for detailed statistical information, your task is to select and summarise key trends/stages only by describing categories/figures/numbers/years,
  - write so that a person who doesn't have the visual + information in front of them, is able to understand the report clearly and easily,
  - avoid copying or repeating too many words from the task.

Q. How long do I have to complete Task 1?
A. You have about 20 minutes for this task and must write at least 150 words, but…
- Be careful not to write too much detail or too many words as this may rob you of time for Task 2.
- Try your best to keep to a maximum of about 170 words and a minimum of 150.

Q. How can I be sure to use the time wisely?
A. Practise before the test and follow a systematic routine, like this one:

What you should do:	How?	Why?
Stage 1 — understand the task	By studying the wording and data for one to two minutes	To guarantee relevance of your plan and clear structure of the answer
Stage 2 — plan your answer for about two minutes	By writing a quick outline in logical sections	To organise your answer
Stage 3 — write a systematic answer neatly and with clear paragraphing	By following your plan for about 15 minutes.	To make your answer well structured, clear, and easy to read
Stage 4 — check your work quickly	By skim reading; quick word count by counting number of words in one line and then multiply by number of lines (e.g. 10 words x 15 lines = 150)	To pick up any obvious mistakes

IELTS Writing Task 1 Lesson

Q. Is 15 minutes enough time to write 150 words?

A. Yes, with practice.

Practise writing answers to Task 1 questions with a 20-minute limit.
Get used to following the pattern above. Gradually you will be able to do it, and will feel a sense of professionalism in the way you are approaching this task.

GOLD STAR ADVICE No. 1:
Planning time saves writing time by making writing time structured and managed.

Q. What is a 'clock victim' and why should I avoid becoming one?

A. Some candidates spend too much time counting words or watching the clock and lose connection and focus with the actual task. Practise doing Task 1 questions until you have developed a reliable routine.

Remember, being organised is important because you can then create an organised answer. A relevant, organised answer impresses the assessor because it seems professional even if it still has some vocabulary and grammar weaknesses.

What if I...?   Some Problem Situations

Q. What if I don't understand the chart?

A. Most candidates understand at least some things. So:
a) Look for patterns (trends).
b) Ask yourself questions about the statistical data.
What can I see? What has changed? When did it change? Which group or category changed? What is… bigger? …smaller? …more similar? …less similar? …has increased? …decreased? When did this happen?

Q. What if I don't know how to compare and contrast?

A. Do the fitness activities and study the IELTS Writing Doctor in this book (pages 99, 195). These have useful sections on comparing and contrasting. For example, you need to:
a) Build vocabulary which is used when comparing or contrasting (for example increased/decreased; rose/fell; larger/smaller; more significant/less significant.
b) Build awareness of sentence markers (for example, X on the other hand…; compared with Y, X was…..; similarly, X increased ……; the pattern was similar for Y….; whereas X increased in…., Y decreased during the same period.

Q. What if I'm only half way through and already out of time?

A. This probably means either:
- that you haven't organised and planned your **overall answer** enough before writing,
- or that your language level is low and it takes you a long time either to think of what to write, or to express it clearly.

Either way, you have to decide whether to continue on Task 1 or move on to Task 2. Some options:

Option 1 — if the Task 2 topic looks easy, you might give yourself another five minutes to complete Task 1 before changing to Task 2.

Option 2 — if the Task 2 topic looks tricky and needs full planning time, try to finish the Task 1 paragraph you are writing, then move on to Task 2 and allow yourself five minutes before the end of the test to return to complete Task 1. Aim to write 250 words approximately for Task 2.

IELTS Writing Task 1 Lesson

Q. What if writing about all the details adds up to many more than 150 words?

A. This usually means that you haven't planned your paragraphs well and haven't selected and grouped the information well enough. Before writing, you need to look more carefully at the data and overview it so that you are aware of main trends before writing. Remember there is not time to mention everything so you have to find the main trends and summarise them.

Q. What if I make a mistake, how do I fix it?

A. If it is a factual mistake with numbers, cross out the mistake neatly and write in the correct number. If it is a major mistake, such as misunderstanding the material and then realising your mistake after writing a paragraph or two, cross out the first attempt with a diagonal line, then miss a line and start again but with a tighter plan, and summarise the material more effectively to avoid too much detail. Aim to write at least 140 words in the time remaining.

Q. What if I feel so anxious, my mind goes blank?

A. Stay as calm as you can. This is an opportunity to manage your emotions and become stronger. Follow this 'calming routine': close your eyes and breathe systematically for one minute. To do this:

- count 'one and two and three and four' in your head when you breathe in,
- then hold your breath counting from one to four again,
- and then breathe out counting once more from one to four in your head.

After one minute, return to the question, and make every action systematic and structured. You have to manage panic and not let it control you. This one-minute 'calming routine' is not time wasted but **time managed**!

Secrets of how to impress your assessor in Academic Writing Task 1

Your assessor is a busy person with perhaps 20 Writing tests to score. Perhaps yours is the last one so the assessor could be a little tired. Within the limitations of your English, you need to create a positive relationship with the assessor through the quality of your writing.

 GOLD STAR ADVICE No 2: *Your Writing is YOU.*
Everything you write and how you present your writing represents 'YOU' in the mind of the assessor because you will not meet that assessor in person.

Q. **How can I make a good impression on the IELTS Writing assessor?**

A. There are certain ways to write a report that always create a good impression.

Follow these detailed suggestions and your work will be appreciated by your assessor:

1. Take care with the accuracy of information

Explanation
Whatever material and data are presented to you in Task 1, you need to study it carefully and look at each category or number carefully so that you report on them accurately.

Why is this important?
Accuracy creates a good impression of you as a professional report writer.

2. Write about the important patterns and trends — not everything

Explanation
The Task 1 question usually asks you to **summarise** and **report main trends**. This involves building an overview of the data and then selecting the key information.

Why is this important?
You don't have time to write about everything; a skilful report writer knows how to identify, organise, compare, contrast and synthesise the key information.

IELTS Writing Task 1 Lesson

3. Avoid 'shopping lists', i.e. listing statistics one after another repetitively.

Explanation
Some candidates see information on a graph or table and just repeat it without any selection, comparison or synthesis.

Example

 Report 1

 Report 2

In Belonia in 2001 unemployment was 20%; in 2002 it was 30%, in 2003 it increased to 40%; in 2004 it was steady at 40%; In Celonia in 2001 it was 20%, in 2002 it was 10%, in 2002 it decreased to 5% and in 2004 it rose to 20%.'

Unemployment in Belonia **increased steadily** from 20 to 40% between 2001 and 2003, at which point it **remained steady**. In Celonia, **however**, the percentage without work **halved each year** from 20% in 2001 down to 5% in 2003, then rose again to 20%.

Comment: Report 2 has the better style of reporting as it evaluates the changes, it doesn't simply list them.

Why is this important?
If you identify trends and patterns in statistical data instead of just making mechanical lists, it shows you can interpret information and can evaluate information in terms of what is more/less important. This is not strictly a language skill but it is a sign of mature, critical thinking.

4. Don't make personal comments about the statistical material

Explanation
Some candidates start to give their own explanations for why the data has changed, even though this is not in the graph and not part of the task.

Example

 Watching TV probably increased more for young people in the period 2005–2010 **because parents were too busy** to do other things with their children.

Why is this important?
You have very little time for Task 1 so every word has to count. Bringing in new information that is not in the diagram or graph is considered irrelevant to the task because your task is reporting data not speculating about the causes of it.

5. Use a systematic layout

Explanation
Use an Introduction/body paragraphs/conclusion format, with each body paragraph dealing with a clear and distinct area of information.

Why is this important?
A well-organised and logically structured report seems more professional and makes the task of reading your report much easier for the assessor. This has a strong and positive psychological impact on the assessor.

6. Use a professional writing style and formal tone

Explanation
A professional writing style is formal in tone and economical in style.
It maximises clarity of information and brings together key information effectively by effective use of appropriate formal vocabulary and sentence links.

Why is this important?
The use of an appropriate tone and style adds to the assessor's belief in your professionalism, even if there are still a few grammatical errors. This builds a positive impression. So compare these expressions:

 Expression 1   **Expression 2**

Expression 1	Expression 2
big increase	significant/substantial increase
went up quickly	rose rapidly
got suddenly bigger	increased dramatically
went down a lot	decreased significantly
go a bit higher	increased marginally
stayed the same	remained unchanged/stable
quite a lot of students	a substantial number of students
pretty much the same	broadly similar

Comment: The second expression in each case is more formal and establishes a professional tone for reporting information. The first expression sounds too 'babyish' in this writing context; it seems more like spoken English.

7. Reduce simple grammar mistakes

Explanation
Simple grammar mistakes may seem a little 'babyish'.

Why is this important?
The assessor may think that you should have learnt basic grammar when you first learnt English. Too many basic errors reduce the professional 'feel' of your report and leave a negative impression, even if the assessor can understand what your report says.

Reduce Weaknesses to Maintain a Good Impression

To maintain the good impression you've already created you need to reduce the kinds of weaknesses illustrated in these examples:

Weakness Type #1 — Word Forms (Adjective/Noun/Adverb)

Explanation
In simple terms, **errors that relate to basic rules of English grammar leave a more negative impression than other kinds of mistakes** because the assessor may assume that you learnt about these basic rules when you were younger and have had plenty of time to learn to use them correctly since that time.

Examples of mistakes that create a bad impression

Mistake	What's wrong?
There is some **doubtful** about the data	Noun form **'doubt'** needed
The accuracy of the figures is **doubt**	Adjective **'doubtful'** needed
It is **doubtfully** that the figures are **accuracy**	Adjectives **'doubtful'** and **'accurate'** needed
The population increased **rapid** during 2000	Adverb **'rapidly'** needed

So, **if you still make these basic errors you may give the impression of being like an immature schoolchild,** even if your own native language causes you to make the errors because its verb system is much simpler than the English verb system, or its translated word forms are less varied than those in English. The assessor forms an impression of you from your writing and isn't influenced by such complexities as 'first language interference'. The IELTS test, remember, is based ultimately on comparing performance with a native English speaker equivalent.

IELTS Writing Task 1 Lesson

Weakness Type #2 — Verb Tenses

Explanation

Accurate use of the verb system shows an awareness of how time is marked in English. This is important when reporting graphs and tables with information about past or future years.

Example

Mistake

In 2003 there **is** a major increase in crime

By 2050 the level of crime **has risen**

What's wrong?

should be '**was** a major increase'

should be '**will rise**'

Weakness Type #3 — Subject/Verb Agreement

Explanation

It is becoming more common for students to forget that in English grammar the subject of a sentence often controls the form of the verb. Failure to remember this, leads to elementary grammatical errors, which have a negative effect on the assessor's impression of your level.

Examples

Mistake

Access to computers **are** now increasing

Assessment of your borrowing limits **need** to be carried out

Loan approval **have** to be obtained

What's wrong?

'Access' is the subject word so should be '**is** now increasing'

'Assessment' is the subject so should be '**needs** to be carried out'

'Loan approval' is a singular subject so should be '**has** to be obtained'

Weakness Type #4 — Sentence Boundaries

Explanation
The end of a sentence is shown by a full stop '.' Often candidates forget this and confuse the reader by 'running on' to the next sentence without using any full stops.

Example

 Sentence without boundaries

 Sentences ended by full stops

A loan is usually arranged with a bank the sum borrowed depends on income often actually the bank can refuse a loan application.

A loan is usually arranged with a bank. The sum borrowed often depends on income. Actually, the bank can refuse a loan application.

Weakness Type #5 – Omissions from Sentences

Explanation
IELTS candidates often leave out important parts of a sentence perhaps because they are feeling the pressure of time. Again, this confuses the reader.

Example

 Sentence with omissions

 Complete sentence

Proportion people incomes below $50,000 access to computers 34 percent.

The proportion **of** people **with** incomes below $50,000 **with** access to computers **was** 34 percent.

IELTS Writing Task 1 Lesson

Weakness Type #6 – Not Using Paragraphs Effectively

Explanation

Some candidates forget to use paragraphs to structure their report into clear and logical sections. This makes the information much harder to read.

Example (refer to bar chart at the beginning of this chapter):

The report below has no paragraphing:

The bar chart shows percentage coffee consumption during three years for several different age groups. In 2004, the middle-aged groups drank most coffee at 16%.
Younger age groups drank less than the middle-aged then but almost as much in 2001. The oldest age group (75+) drank the least in 1995, 2001 and 2004. Only 6% of the 55–64 age group were coffee drinkers in 1995 but by 2004 they were equal top at 16%. Generally speaking more coffee was drunk in 2004 than in 2001 and in 1995 in all age groups. The oldest group and the 35–44 age group doubled their coffee consumption between 1995 and 2004 but the 55–64 group more than doubled theirs. Younger people's consumption has not changed very much between 2001 and 2004. Overall middle-aged people have drunk more coffee than other age groups in all three years.

Compare the above with this better version which has clear paragraphing:

The bar chart shows percentage coffee consumption during three years for several different age groups. Generally speaking more coffee was drunk in 2004 than in 2001 and 1995 in all age groups. **(Introduction + overview)**

In 1995 between 7 and 9 percent of the four, younger age groups (18–54) were drinking coffee, with older age groups drinking noticeably less. **(Summary of 1995)**

By 2001, the pattern had changed somewhat with the 55–64 age group more than doubling their consumption to become the second highest consumers at around 13 percent. Increases in the younger age groups were slower. **(Summary of 2001)**

In 2004 two of the middle-aged groups (45 to 64) were clearly drinking the most coffee at 16 percent with the younger age groups increasing less rapidly. There were large increases in the older age groups 65+ relative to previous years. **(Summary of 2004)**

Overall then, middle-aged people's consumption of coffee has risen more than that of other age groups but consumption in all age groups has increased across the three years for which data were provided. **(Conclusion)**

Weakness Type #7 – Leaving Out Important Information

Explanation
Under pressure of time, candidates sometimes leave out important information, which makes their response incomplete.

Example

Using the example above (Weakness Type #6), if a candidate failed to discuss one of the years (2001, say) then the answer would be considered incomplete.

Weakness Type #8 – Using inaccurate information through carelessness or misunderstanding

Explanation
Again, under pressure of time, candidates sometimes write information that is not the same as in the graph or chart or table.

Example 1 – Carelessness (refer to bar chart at the beginning of this chapter):

 Inaccurate information

 Accurate information

In 2001 the 35–44 age group had the highest coffee consumption at 15% with the 45–54 and 55–64 cohorts having the same level at 13 percent.

In 2001 the **45–54** age group had the highest coffee consumption at **14%** with the **35–44** and 55–64 cohorts having the same level at 13 percent.

Example 2 – Misunderstanding of measurement categories

	Access to computers			Access to internet		
Household income/year	1998	1999	2000	1998	1999	2000
Below $50,000 per year	34	33	37	10	12	21
Above $50,000 per year	69	71	77	34	43	57

 Inaccurate information

 Accurate information

In 1998, among men with $50,000 in income 34 lived in houses with access to a computer and 10 to the internet.

In 1998, **34% of households** with an annual salary of **less than $50, 000** had access to a computer, and **10 percent** to the internet.

Weakness Type #8 – Poor presentation (layout, handwriting, crossing out)

Explanation

Poor presentation is very common. Candidates sometimes use writing that is not easy to read, or cross out very frequently, or use a layout that makes their answer look either cramped or unprofessional.

Example

The following are some instances of poor presentation:
- no empty line between each paragraph,
- spacing that is too uneven (too many empty lines, or empty lines of uneven number – sometimes this is done to make a short answer look longer),
- handwriting may be difficult to read, especially the difference between vowels like 'e' and 'o' or 'i' and 'u'; 'l' and 't'; 'u' and 'w'; 'n' and 'h'; 'n' and 'r'; 'm' and 'n'.

Weakness Type #9 – Misspelling Names of Items

Explanation
Candidates often spell incorrectly names given in the data. This could be caused by pressure of time or lack of attention but may create an unprofessional impression.

Example

 Mistake

In 1998, 34% of **Austrian housholds** with a yearly salary of less than $50, 000 had **acess** to a computer, and 10 per**sent** to the internet

What's wrong?

Should be '**Australian**', not 'Austrian';
'**hous**e**holds**', not housholds;
' **access**', not 'acess';
'**percent**', not 'per sent'

Weakness Type #10 – Repetition

Explanation
Some IELTS test takers seem unable to avoid repeating the same expression over and over again. This shows lack of flexibility in use of language.

Example

 Repetition

In 2001 in the 18–24 age group 12 percent **drank coffee**, in the 25–34 age group also 12 percent. In the 35–44 age group 13 percent **drank coffee**, and 14% in the 45–54 age group.
In the 55–64 age group less, 8 percent **drank coffee** and finally only 4 percent of the 75+ group **drank coffee**.

 Less repetition

In 2001, 12 percent **drank coffee** in both the 18–24 and 25–34 age groups. Among those aged 35–44, 13 percent were **coffee drinkers**, while 14% of 45–54 year olds were **coffee consumers**.
In the 55–64 year old cohort the percentage figure was 8. Finally, a mere 4 percent of the 75+ group counted themselves as **drinkers of coffee**.

Weakness Type # 11 – Irrelevant Information

Explanation
Irrelevance can be created by either:
a) too much detailed information which may leave insufficient time for balanced reporting of major trends and important comparisons.
b) personal interpretations which the writer offers but are not included in the data.

Example

 Irrelevant information   Relevant information

a) Too much detail	b) Adding personal interpretations	Better version of a) and b)
In 2001 in the 18–24 age group 12 percent drank coffee, in the 25–34 age group also 12 percent. In the 35–44 age group 13 percent drank coffee, and 14% in the 45–54 age group. In the 55–64 age group less, 8 percent drank coffee and finally only 4 percent of the 75+ group drank coffee.	In 2001, younger and middle aged age groups had similar coffee drinking patterns at 12 percent (younger) and 13/14 percent (middle aged) **perhaps because younger people had less spending money**, while the two older age groups drank much less at 4–8%, **probably to maintain their health.**	In 2001, younger and middle aged age groups had similar coffee drinking patterns at 12 percent (younger) and 13/14 percent (middle aged), while the two, older age groups drank much less coffee at 4–8%.

Enhance the good impression

There are many other ways to enrich your Task 1 response and thus to give the assessor enough reason to lift your score. Often you can make your response sound more professional by good selection of vocabulary and by varied use of the formal sentence styles which are typical of report writing. You will find plenty of examples in our IELTS Grammar and IELTS Vocabulary sections on pages 195 and 232. Good hunting!

WRITING TASK 1 FITNESS ACTIVITIES

Before you start

The fitness activities in this section offer you quick practice at the different task types you may encounter in the IELTS Writing test. It's also a chance to use some of the tips from the Writing chapter earlier in our book.

With the help of these fitness activities you will build awareness of key elements of different Task 1 reports. Work through each section, noting the different aspects of the report being focused on. When you are practising a Task 1 report under exam conditions, try asking yourself similar questions as part of **managing and improving your written response.**

TASK TYPE » Map

Fountain Gate Shopping Centre, 1980

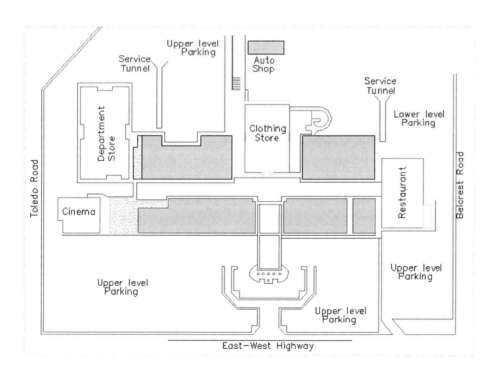

IELTS Writing Task 1 Fitness Activities

Fountain Gate Shopping Centre, 2008

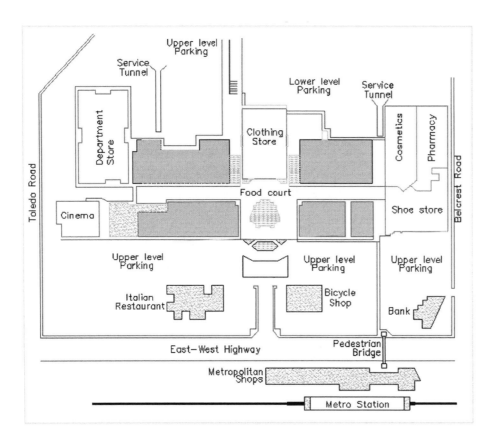

Task Question

The maps show changes to the Fountain Gate Shopping Centre between 1980 and 2008.

Summarise the information by selecting and reporting the key features, and make any relevant comparisons.

Write at least 150 words.

Fitness Activities 1–21 for a Map type task

 Activities 1–6 will help you to get started and build the Introduction:

1 How many paragraphs seem better suited for a good response?

   a) 3
   b) 4
   c) 5

2 What is the function of the first paragraph (The Introduction)?

   a) Introduce the task.
   b) Introduce the task and say how many paragraphs the response will have.
   c) Introduce the task and give an overview of what the maps show.

3 What should you do in the first paragraph?

   a) copy the words exactly from the task
   b) change as many words as you can
   c) change all the words in the task

4 An 'overview' here is:

   a) a sentence summarising the most important changes
   b) an opinion about why the changes happened
   c) a prediction about what will happen in the future

5 A suitable length for the Introduction should be approximately:

   a) 60 words (5-6 sentences)
   b) 30 words (2-3 sentences)
   c) 15 words (1-2 sentences)

6 The verb tense for the first sentence should be:

   a) The maps showed
   b) The maps are showing
   c) The maps show

IELTS Writing Task 1 Fitness Activities

 Activities 7–9 will help you with the language of the Introduction:

7   Use the words in the box to complete this Introduction:

| increased | indicates | essentially | improved |

The map _____ changes by the Fountain Gate Shopping Centre between 1988 and 2000. _____, the centre _____ its range of shops and _____ transport connections.

8   Now correct three mistakes in the Introduction (but not the words you used to complete Activity 7).

9   Complete this summary about Task 1 Introductions, using one word for each space:

The Introduction presents the writing _____ using somewhat different words, and an _____ of the main trends in the data. The first sentence uses the _____ tense and the other sentences use the _____ tense because they describe past events (1980-2008).

 Activities 10–13 will help you to build Body Paragraph 1 (describing the shopping centre in 1980).

10   Circle any of these suggestions that seem a good strategy for Body Paragraph 1:

a) It's a good idea to talk about the map using the logic of directions like north, south, east, and west.
b) It seems helpful to focus on the more important features.
c) It seems important to describe everything.
d) It seems important to write about 90 words.
e) It seems important to try to avoid being too repetitive and mechanical.

11 Put in the missing compass direction words (North/South/East/West):

Body Paragraph 1

In 1980 the Centre has one department store and a cinema on the _____ side, a clothing store situated centrally and a restaurant, with smaller shops surrounding it, and a restaurant on the _____ side. There was auto shop on the _____ periphery, and plentiful parking in both levels. Service tunnels provided access. The central access was from the main East-West Highway on the _____ side.

12 Now find and correct <u>three</u> grammatical mistakes in Body Paragraph 1 (but not the words you used to complete Activity 11).

13 The main function of Body Paragraph 1 is to:

   a) describe one or two key features of the shopping centre in 1980 systematically.
   b) describe all features of the shopping centre in 2008 clearly and systematically.
   c) describe all the features of the shopping centre in 1980 systematically.
   d) describe the key features of the centre in 1980 clearly and systematically.

Activities 14–17 will help you to build Body Paragraph 2 (describing the changes to the shopping centre by 2008).

14 Choose the correct sentence to start the paragraph:

   a) In 2008, numerous development have taken place.
   b) By 2008, numerous developments had taken place.
   c) In 2008, numerous development had taken place.
   d) By 2008 numerous development took place.

IELTS Writing Task 1 Fitness Activities

15 Put the missing prepositions from the box into the paragraph:

| by | on | with | by | to | on | with | to |

Body Paragraph 2

_____ 2008, numerous developments had taken place. _____ the east side of the centre, a shoe store, pharmacy and cosmetic shop had been added, _____ the restaurant having been replaced _____ a food court in the central area. Although the auto shop had disappeared _____ the north, _____ the southern periphery, a bank, Italian restaurant and bicycle shop had appeared. Even more significantly, a metro station had been built south of the East West highway _____ its own shops and pedestrian link _____ the Centre.

16 Which words/expressions in Body Paragraph 2 (Activity 15) could these replace appropriately?

various	(could replace _____)
noticeably	(could replace _____)
walkway to	(could replace _____)
edge	(could replace _____)
been removed	(could replace _____)
constructed	(could replace _____)

17 Choice of tense:

Because the year being discussed is 2008, and because the changes had happened in the period between 1980 and 2008, and thus not necessarily all in 2008, the tense used most often in Body Paragraph 2 is the…

a) simple past
b) present perfect
c) past perfect

Activities 18–20 will help you with writing a short conclusion.

18 Which of these is the main function of the conclusion?

   a) briefly summarise the main changes.
   b) predict what the next changes will be.
   c) give an explanation of why the changes happened.

19 Which <u>two</u> expressions are not suitable to signal the start of the conclusion?

   a) To summarise   b) Overall   c) To sum up   d) In the end   e) Finally

20 Complete this conclusion. Use a maximum of <u>one</u> word or a number for each space.

Conclusion

_____ , by _____ there was more choice at the _____ and better transport options _____ visitors.

21 Now, without looking at the sample answer, write your own report.
Spend no more than 20 minutes and write at least 150 words.

IELTS Writing Task 1 Fitness Activities

Now read this complete sample answer:

> The maps indicate changes in the Fountain Gate Shopping Centre between 1980 and 2008. Essentially, the centre increased its range of shops and improved transport connections.
>
> In 1980 the Centre had one department store and a cinema on the west side, a clothing store situated centrally, and a restaurant, with smaller shops surrounding it, and a restaurant on the east side. There was an auto shop on the northern periphery, and plentiful parking on both levels. Service tunnels provided access. The central access was from the main East-West Highway on the southern side.
>
> By 2008, numerous developments had taken place. On the east side, a shoe store, pharmacy and cosmetic shop had been added, with the restaurant having been replaced by a food court in the central area. Although the auto shop had disappeared to the north, on the southern edge, a bank, Italian restaurant and bicycle shop had appeared. More significantly, a metro station had been built south of the East West highway with its own shops and pedestrian link to the Centre.
>
> Overall, by 2008, there was more choice at the Centre and better transport options for visitors.

 Note: This sample answer is **not** a model answer but only one of many, possible responses to the task. It would probably be awarded Band 9.

 You've made it to the end of these Fitness Activities. Great job!
Give yourself a big pat on the back.
You're on the road to IELTS success!

TASK TYPE » PROCESS DIAGRAM

Buying a house

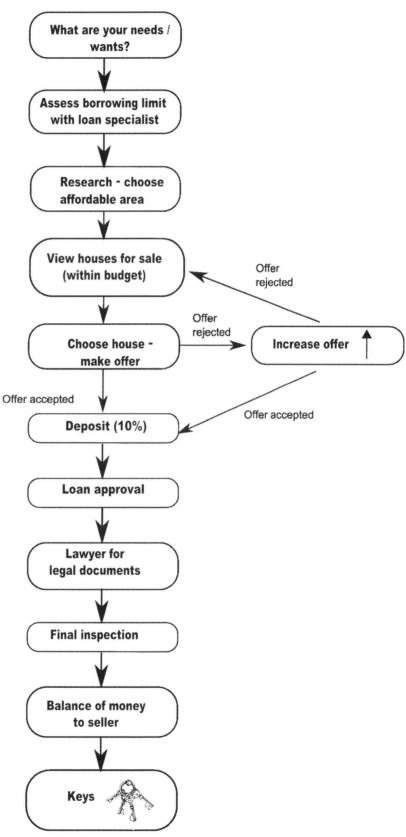

IELTS Writing Task 1 Fitness Activities

> **Task Question**
>
> The diagram shows the stages in buying a house.
>
> Summarise the information by selecting and reporting the key features, and make any relevant comparisons.
>
> Write at least 150 words.

Fitness Activities 1–9 for a Process Diagram type task

 Activities 1–4 will help you to get started and build the Introduction:

1   As there is no past or future time mentioned in the diagram, the main verb tense in the Introduction should be:

   a) present simple (e.g. 'It shows')
   b) present continuous (e.g. 'It is showing')
   c) present perfect (e.g. 'It has shown')

2   Choose <u>two</u> verbs from the box which best complete the Introduction:

tells	shows	demonstrates	outlined	covers

   Introduction

   The diagram _____ the main step in buy a house. It _____ financial and legal issues, view and making offers.

3   Now find and correct the <u>three</u> grammatical errors in the Introduction (but not the words you used to complete Activity 2).

4   Which words in the Introduction (Activity 2) could these replace?

'stages'   (could replace _____)
'purchasing'   (could replace _____)
'aspects'   (could replace _____)

Activities 5–7 will help you to build the Body Paragraph:

5   Describing a process involves identifying stages, often stages that take place one after another in time. Put these 'time sequence' joining words in the correct spaces in the Body Paragraph:

| Once | Then | As soon as | After | After that | The first step | Once |

Body Paragraph

_____ involves establishing your housing needs and then calculating a borrowing ceiling with the help of a loan expert. _____, a prospective purchaser needs to look for affordable areas in their town or city, and go to look at suitable houses, within budget. _____ a house has been chosen an offer is made. If the offer is rejected, the buyer can either increase the offer or choose another house and make a new offer on that one. _____ the offer has been accepted, a deposit of 10% needs to be paid to the vendor. _____ the purchaser's loan has been approved by the bank, a lawyer is required to prepare the legal documents of transfer. _____ a final inspection of the house is carried out and the balance of the selling price is paid to the seller. _____ that money is cleared, the new owner receives the keys.

6   In the Body Paragraph (Activity 5) the writer has avoided using personal pronouns like 'you' 'we', to make the writing more formal.
Look at these 4 sentences. Rewrite them without using 'You':

1) First, you establish your housing needs.   _____
2) Then you look for affordable areas.   _____
3) Next, you choose a house and make an offer.   _____
4) If it is accepted, you pay a 10% deposit.   _____

7   A useful verb form to use in process descriptions is the passive. Find <u>two</u> examples of the present passive and <u>two</u> of the present perfect passive in the Body Paragraph in Fitness Activity 5.

Present passive
Example 1 _____   Example 2 _____

Present perfect passive
Example 1 _____   Example 2 _____

Activity 8 will help you with writing a short conclusion.

8   Only a very short conclusion is needed to round off the process type answer. Underline the new items of vocabulary the writer uses to add variety to the conclusion.

Conclusion

Summing up, those are the seven principal stages in the purchase of a house.

9   Now, without looking at the sample answer, write your own report. Spend no more than 20 minutes and write at least 150 words.

_____
_____
_____
_____
_____
_____
_____
_____
_____
_____
_____
_____
_____
_____
_____
_____

Now read this complete sample answer:

> The diagram shows the main steps in buying a house. It covers financial and legal issues, viewing and making offers.
>
> The first step involves establishing your housing needs and then calculating a borrowing ceiling with the help of a loan expert. After that, a prospective purchaser needs to look for affordable areas in their town or city, and go to look at suitable houses, within budget. Once a house has been chosen an offer is made. If the offer is rejected, the buyer can either increase the offer or choose another house and make a new offer on that one. After the offer has been accepted, a deposit of 10% needs to be paid to the vendor. Once the purchaser's loan has been approved by the bank, a lawyer is required to prepare the legal documents of transfer. Then a final inspection of the house is carried out and the balance of the selling price is paid to the seller. As soon as that money is cleared, the new owner receives the keys.
>
> Summing up, those are the seven, principal stages in the purchase of a house.

 Note: This sample answer is **not** a model answer but only one of many, possible responses to the task. It would probably be awarded Band 9.

 You're doing well! Your efforts will be rewarded in the real test!

TASK TYPE » Graph

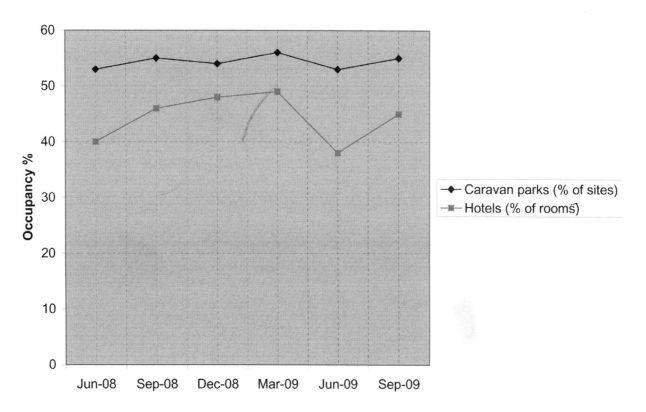

Task Question

The graph shows the percentage occupancy of caravan parks and hotel rooms between June '08 and September '09.

Summarise the information by selecting and reporting the key features, and make any relevant comparisons.

Write at least 150 words.

Fitness Activities 1–10 for a Graph type task

 Activities 1–3 will help you to get started and build the Introduction:

1 What is the best order for the two parts of the Introduction?

   a) First an outline description of the graph, then an overview of the main trends.
   b) First an overview of the main trends, then an outline description of the graph.

2 Correct the tenses of the underlined verbs in this Introduction and then underline the <u>overview</u> sentence:

   The graph <u>indicated</u> levels of occupancy of caravan parks and hotels between 2008 and 2009. Overall it <u>seemed</u> that caravan parks <u>has</u> slightly _____ occupancy rates and _____ fluctuation _____ hotels.

3 Put these three expressions into the empty spaces in the Introduction (Activity 2):

higher	than	less

Activities 4–5 will help you to build Body Paragraph 1
(Describing occupancy rates in caravan parks)

4 Describing graphs involves using verbs or other forms which describe increases and decreases, or no change. Put these verb forms into the correct spaces:

peaking	steady	increased	returned	fell back	recovering

Body Paragraph 1

At the beginning of the period, **in June '08**, the occupancy rate for caravan parks was around 54%. This figure had _____ marginally **by September '08** then _____ a little before _____ at around 57% **in March '09**. **In June '09** it _____ to its original level of 54% before _____ to 56% **by September '09**. Generally, then, occupancy rates were quite _____ across the 15-month period.

IELTS Writing Task 1 Fitness Activities

5   When describing points of time in graphs, correct preposition use is important. Is a, b or c the best definition of the difference between 'by' and 'in' in Body Paragraph 1 (Activity 4)?

   a) 'in' means 'only in that year'; 'by' means in the period of time between two dates.
   b) 'in' means 'only in that year'; 'by' means the specific month of that year.
   c) 'in' means 'only that month'; 'by' means 'before that month'.

Activities 6–7 will help you to build Body Paragraph 2 (Describing occupancy rates in hotels).

6   At the beginning of Body Paragraph 2, the writer signals topic shift with 'Turning to hotels...'. Which 2 of these 4 expressions could also be used?

   a) Moving on to consider
   b) According to
   c) In terms of
   d) About

7   The writer uses the adverbs 'markedly' and 'significantly' to indicate the level of change. Rank these adverbs from smallest level of change (1) to largest (4).

   substantially (__)   noticeably (__)   marginally (__)   massively (__)

Body Paragraph 2

Turning to hotels, a little more variation was evident. 40% was the hotel occupancy rate in June '08, but then this level increased <u>markedly</u> to around 48% by September of the same year reaching nearly 50% by December. Then the rate dipped <u>significantly</u> to 38% by June '09 recovering to 45% by September of the same year.

Activities 8–9 will help you with writing a short conclusion.

8 The use of comparative adjectives helps the writer to summarise efficiently. Choose the two, most suitable and accurate expressions to complete the first part of the conclusion below.

| fewer | higher | more | less |

Conclusion (First part)

To summarise, caravan parks had _____ occupancy and _____ seasonal variation...

9 Writers can sometimes leave out words to save time, without damaging grammar.

Example: '...across the whole period **which was** measured.'
becomes '...across the whole period measured'.

Change these sentence parts in the same way to make them shorter:

a) ...across the period which was surveyed   _____
b) ...across the years which were studied   _____
c) ...across the months which were compared   _____

10 Now, without looking at the sample answer, write your own report.
   Spend no more than 20 minutes and write at least 150 words.

Now read this complete sample answer:

> The graph indicates levels of occupancy of caravan parks and hotels between 2008 and 2009. Overall it seems that caravan parks had slightly higher occupancy rates and less fluctuation than hotels.
>
> At the beginning of the period, in June '08, the occupancy rate for caravan parks was around 54%. This figure had increased marginally by September '08 then fell back a little before peaking at around 57% in March 2009. In June 2009 it returned to its original level of 54% before recovering to 56% by September '09. Generally then occupancy rates were quite steady across the 15-month period.
>
> Turning to hotels, a little more variation was evident. 40% was the hotel occupancy rate in June 08, but then this level increased markedly to around 48% by September of the same year reaching nearly 50% by December. Then the rate dipped significantly to 38% by June 09 recovering to 45% by September of the same year.
>
> To summarise, caravan parks had higher occupancy and less seasonal variation across the whole period measured.

Note: This sample answer is **not** a model answer but only one of many, possible responses to the task. It would probably be awarded Band 9.

Did you get this far? – Great!
Now relax, maybe watch a good movie!

TASK TYPE » Table

Percentage of Australian households with access to computers/internet 1998-2000

	access to computers			access to internet		
Household income / year	1998	1999	2000	1998	1999	2000
Below $50,000 per year	34	33	37	10	12	21
Above $50,000 per year	69	71	77	34	43	57

Task Question

The table shows the percentage of Australian households with access to computers or internet 1998-2000.

Summarise the information by selecting and reporting the key features, and make any relevant comparisons.

Write at least 150 words.

Fitness Activities 1–10 for a Table type task

 Activities 1–2 will help you to get started and build the Introduction:

1 Correct five mistakes in this Introduction and underline the <u>overview</u> sentence:

Introduction

The chart presented data on access to computers and internet for two income levels in Australia 1998-2000. Access levels was greater for the higher income group, but increase generally for both groups across the three year.

IELTS Success Formula :: Academic

IELTS Writing Task 1 Fitness Activities

2   Creating economical expressions is often favoured to prevent repetition. Which shorter expressions describing the income categories are used in the Introduction (Activity 1) instead of these longer ones in a) and b) below?

   a) 'those earning less than $50,000 and those earning more than $50,000 per year'

   What is the shorter expression in the Introduction? _____

   b) 'those earning more than $50,000'

   What is the shorter expression in the Introduction? _____

Activities 3–5 will help you to build Body Paragraph 1 (Describing access to computers)

3   Read Body Paragraph 1. Find the 7-word phrase the writer uses to introduce the data for the $50,000+ group in order to build variety and avoid the same pattern used earlier for the 'below $50,000' group.

   Write it here
   _____

   Body Paragraph 1
   The level of access to computers for those on incomes below $50,000 was 34% in 1998, falling marginally to 33% in 1999 before recovering strongly to 37% in 2000. For the above- $50,000 group, the corresponding percentages across the three years were more than double at 69, 71 and 77% respectively.

4   In Body Paragraph 1, which expressions are used instead of these synonyms?

   'salaries'   (the writer uses _____)
   'dropping'   (the writer uses _____)
   'rising again'   (the writer uses _____)
   'slightly'   (the writer uses _____)
   'equivalent'   (the writer uses _____)
   'twice as large' (the writer uses _____)

5   You need to maintain accuracy of data in your Task 1 report.
    Correct the four data errors in this version of Body Paragraph 1.

    Body Paragraph 1

    Access to computers for those on incomes below $50,000 was 34% in 1990, falling marginally to 33% in 1999 before recovering strongly to 87% in 2000. For the above- $5000 group the corresponding percentages across the three years were more than double at 77, 69, and 71% respectively.

Activities 6–7 will help you to build Body Paragraph 2
(Describing access to the internet)

6   Making the report smooth involves linking data by using linking expressions and commas inside single, long sentences. Put these linking expressions in the correct spaces to complete Body Paragraph 2.

    > 'Starting from'   'then'   'from'   'the figure increased slightly to'   'to'   'and then'

    Body Paragraph 2

    Internet access rates show a slightly different pattern. _____ a low base of 10% in 1998 for the lower income group, _____ 12% in 1999, _____ accelerated to 21% in 2000. For the $50,000 + income group the figures were much higher but the overall increases less dramatic, _____ 34% in 1998, _____ 43% in '99 _____ 57% in 2000.

7   In Body Paragraph 2 the writer offers two general, comparative comments about the data rather than simply listing detailed statistics. This makes the report more mature and less mechanical. Can you find them?

    Comment 1 _____
    Comment 2 _____

Activities 8–9 will help you with writing a conclusion.

8   Which three of these expressions are appropriate to start a conclusion <u>formally</u>?

| 'To sum up'   'I can summarise by saying'   'Summing up' |
| 'In a nutshell'   'To summarise' |

9   Choose the comparative expressions to complete the conclusion neatly.

| upper   more rapidly   much higher   lower |

Conclusion

To summarise, the _____ income group had _____ access to both internet and computers but the _____ income group increased its share of internet access _____.

10 Now, without looking at the sample answer, write your own report.
    Spend no more than 20 minutes and write at least 150 words.

Now read this complete sample answer:

The table presents data on access to computers and internet for two income levels in Australia 1998-2000. Access levels were greater for the higher income group, but increased generally for both groups across the three years.

The level of access to computers for those on incomes below $50,000 was 34% in 1998, falling marginally to 33% in 1999 before recovering strongly to 37% in 2000. For the above-$50,000 group the corresponding percentages across the three years were more than double at 69, 71 and 77% respectively.

Internet access rates show a slightly different pattern. Starting from a low base of 10% in 1998 for the lower income group, the figure increased slightly to 12% in 1999, then accelerated to 21% in 2000. For the $50,000 + income group the figures were much higher but the overall increases less dramatic, from 34% in 1998, to 43% in 99 and then 57% in 2000.

To summarise, the upper income group had much higher access to both internet and computers but the lower income group increased its share of internet access more rapidly.

Note: This sample answer is **not** a model answer but only one of many, possible responses to the task. It would probably be awarded Band 9.

Great work – now as a reward, eat something nice!

IELTS Writing Task 1 Fitness Activities

TASK TYPE » Chart

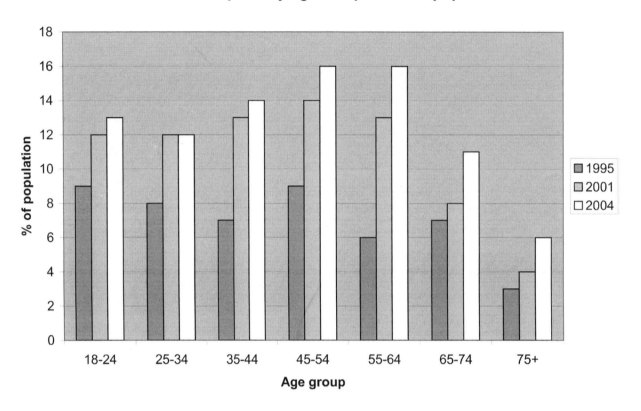

Task Question

The chart shows coffee consumption by age and percentage of population in Australia in three years — 1995, 2001 and 2004.

Summarise the information by selecting and reporting the key features, and make any relevant comparisons.

Write at least 150 words.

Fitness Activities 1–7 for Chart type task

 Activity 1 will help you to get started and build the Introduction:

1 Try to write a completion to this Introduction. Look back at previous tasks to remind yourself of what you are trying to do in <u>an overview</u>.

   Introduction

   The chart shows a three-year, percentage pattern for coffee consumption among different age groups in Australia. In general, _____
   _____
   _____

 Activities 2–5 will help you to build the Body Paragraphs:

2 This time we will look at all three body paragraphs together. What is the writer's way of dividing the paragraphs in Fitness Activity 5. Is it …

   a) by different years?
   b) by different age groups?

3 Avoiding repetition is important. Which 5 general, alternative expressions does the writer use in the three body paragraphs in order to avoid repeating the expression 'age group' too often?

   Alternative expressions used are:

   1) _____
   2) _____
   3) _____
   4) _____
   5) _____

IELTS Writing Task 1 Fitness Activities

4 What do the following expressions mean inside the body paragraphs in Activity 5?

   i) 'predominated' means:
      a) rose the most   b) rose the least   c) rose before the others
   ii) 'accelerated' means:
      a) increased slowly   b) increased rapidly   c) increased more rapidly than before
   iii) 'consumption' means:
      a) drinking coffee   b) buying coffee   c) ordering coffee
   iv) 'steady' means:
      a) reliable   b) unchanged   c) regular increase

5 Task 1 writers should try not only to describe detailed data (facts) but also make descriptive comments about facts. Such comments can establish useful comparisons. In each Body Paragraph which underlined part is a fact (F) and which a comment (C) about the data?

Body Paragraphs

Taking 1995 first, **it is clear that consumption was fairly similar** for those between 18 and 54 ranging from 7% for the 35-44 group to 9% for the 18-24 and 45-54 age ranges. Older age groups drank less with **6% in the 55-64 group and 3% in the 75+ cohort.**

By 2001 increases had occurred. The four younger groups had now been joined by the 55-64 group so that **rates ranged among these five age cohorts from 12% up to 14%.** The **older groups showed some increase but at lower rates** — 8% for the 65-74 and 4% for the 75+ category.

In 2004 further increases took place. **The older, middle age ranges predominated**, with 16% of both the 45-54 and 65-64 cohorts drinking coffee**, followed by 14% of 35-44 year olds and 13% of 18-24 year olds**. The 65-74 year old group had accelerated to reach 11% with the 25-34 group steady at 12% and the over 75s reaching 6%.

Activity 6 will help you with writing a short conclusion:

6   Complete this concluding paragraph in your own words. Look at previous conclusions in order to get a better idea of what you are trying to do.

Conclusion

To summarise, _____
_____.

7   Now, without looking at the sample answer, write your own report.
    Spend no more than 20 minutes and write at least 150 words.

Now read this complete sample answer:

> The chart shows a three-year, percentage pattern for coffee consumption among different age groups in Australia. In general, coffee consumption increased, especially for those in the older age cohorts.
>
> Taking 1995 first, it is clear that consumption was fairly similar for those between 18 and 54 ranging from 7% for the 35-44 group to 9% for the 18-24 and 45-54 age ranges. Older age groups drank less with 6% in the 55-64 group and 3% in the 75+ cohort.
>
> By 2001 increases had occurred. The four younger groups had now been joined by the 55-64 group so that rates ranged among these five age cohorts from 12% up to 14%. The older groups showed some increase but at lower rates — 8% for the 65-74 and 4% for the 75+ category.
>
> In 2004 further increases occurred. The older middle age ranges predominated, with 16% of both the 45-54 and 65-64 cohorts drinking coffee, followed by 14% of 35-44 year olds and 13% of 18-24 year olds. The 65-74 year old group had accelerated to reach 11% with the 25-34 group steady at 12% and the over 75s reaching 6%.
>
> To summarise, coffee consumption increased for all age groups but more rapidly for the middle and older age ranges.

 Note: This sample answer is **not** a model answer but only one of many, possible responses to the task. It would probably be awarded Band 9.

 GOOD JOB – now go and have some FUN!
Maybe not TOO much though! A cup of coffee perhaps!!

WRITING LESSON – Task 2 Essay

First Questions Answered

Q. What kind of task will I be given?
A. For Task 2 you will be given a task prompt, usually on a social issue, and asked to write a response in the form of a short, 250-word essay.

Q. What types of task prompt are there?
A. These are the **four** main types of Task 2 prompt:

Type 1 — Indicate and Support Your Level of Agreement

In a Type 1 essay task you are required to agree, partly agree or disagree with a stated point of view.

Sample task:

"Meeting someone for the first time through the internet is never a good idea. Do you agree?"

How to build your answer

Introduction: Introduce the task issue and say whether or not you agree.
Paragraph 1: Discuss the point of view which is opposite from your own (e.g. if you agree, explain reasons why others might not agree or only partly agree).
Paragraph 2: Give the main supporting point in favor of your view, and provide relevant examples.
Note: If you fully agree/disagree - go to **Paragraph 3**; if you only partly agree, proceed to **Conclusion** and summarise your partial agreement there.
Paragraph 3: [Optional] Give a secondary supporting point in favor of your view, provide relevant examples.
Conclusion: Summarise what you have said (without too much repetition).

IELTS Writing Task 2 Lesson

Type 2 — Present a Two-sided Discussion

In a Type 2 essay task you are required to discuss 2 sides of an argument or 2 points of view, and explain which one they personally agree (or partly agree) with and why.

Sample task:

"Some say you should always marry for love; others say that in an uncertain world it's wiser to marry for money.
Discuss both points of view and give your own opinion."

How to build your answer

Introduction: Introduce the task issue and say what your own opinion is.
Paragraph 1: Discuss one side of the argument **briefly** + supporting examples.
Paragraph 2: Discuss the other side of the argument briefly + supporting examples.
Paragraph 3: Give your own view and explain briefly why you hold that view.
Conclusion: Summarise what you have said (without too much repetition).

Type 3 — Discuss Advantages & Disadvantages

In a Type 3 essay task you are required to discuss the advantages and disadvantages of a given situation or viewpoint.

Sample task:

"In some countries older people are being encouraged to work longer and not to retire.
Discuss the advantages and disadvantages of working beyond retirement age."

How to build your answer

Introduction: Introduce the task issue, say what you will address in your answer.
Paragraph 1: Discuss advantages with supporting examples.
Paragraph 2: Discuss disadvantages with supporting examples.
Conclusion: Summarise what you have said (without too much repetition).

128 IELTS Success Formula :: Academic

Type 4 — Explain & Offer Solutions or Consequences

In a Type 4 essay task you need to explain the reasons why the situation in the task prompt has arisen, and how it can be solved, or what consequences it gives rise to.

Sample task:

"Family life is suffering because of the pressure of work. Why is this happening? What is the most important way to improve the quality of family life?"

How to build your answer

Introduction: Introduce the task issue, say what you will address in your answer.
Paragraph 1: Answer the first question in the task prompt with supporting examples.
Paragraph 2: Answer the second question in the task prompt with supporting examples.
Conclusion: Summarise what you have said (without too much repetition).

Q. What do I have to do to respond <u>well</u> to the question?
A. Your task is to:
- Develop your essay's point of view clearly.
- Write a well-organised, well structured answer in clear paragraphs each with a clear central topic (i.e. a main idea for you to discuss in each paragraph).
- Write legibly and neatly, minimize crossing out.
- Include ideas or information which are relevant, and not repetitive.
- Write accurately and clearly with a variety of grammatical structures and linking words.
- Use a good range of appropriate, formal vocabulary (not just general words).
- Avoid copying or repeating too many words, or expressions, especially from the task wording.

IELTS Writing Task 2 Lesson

Q. How long do I have to complete Task 2?

A. You have about 40 minutes for this task and must write at least 250 words.

Q. How can I be sure to use the time wisely?

A. As we suggested for Task 1, you should practise before the test in order to establish a systematic routine, like this one:

What you should do:	How?	Why?
Stage 1 — understand the task clearly	By studying the wording for one to two minutes, especially the task type and central ideas	To guarantee relevance of your plan and clear structure of the answer and your viewpoint
Stage 2 — plan your answer for about two to three minutes	Build ideas linked to your own view and response type, establish paragraph structure	To organise your ideas into relevant paragraphs; to ensure clarity of answer
Stage 3 — write a systematic answer neatly and with clear paragraphing	By following your plan for about 30-35 minutes.	To make your answer look organized, well structured, clear, and easier to read
Stage 4 — check your work quickly	By skim reading; quick word count by counting number of words in one line and then multiply by number of lines (e.g. 10 words x 25 lines = 250)	To pick up any obvious mistakes

Q. **Is 30-35 minutes enough time to write 250 words?**

A. Yes, with practice.

Practise writing answers to Task 2 questions with a 40-minute limit. Get used to following the pattern above. Gradually you will be able to do it, and will feel a sense of reduced panic and more effective management of this task. It may also be useful to try one or two complete Writing tests within the official, one-hour, time limit so that you learn to combine the writing and time management patterns you have learnt for each task.

GOLD STAR ADVICE No. 1:
Planning time saves writing time by making writing time structured and managed.

Q. **What is a 'clock victim' and why should I avoid becoming one?**

A. Some candidates spend too much time counting words or watching the clock and lose connection and focus with the actual task. Practise doing Task 2 questions until you have developed a reliable routine.

Remember, being organised is important because you can then create an organised answer. A relevant, organised answer impresses the assessor because it seems professional even if it still has some vocabulary and grammar weaknesses.

What if I...?   Some Problem Situations

Q. What if I don't really understand the issue being described in the task?
A. Most candidates understand at least something. So:
a) Focus on those words or ideas that you can understand.
b) Try to guess the meaning of the other parts by using the known words and your own general knowledge of the topic.

Q. What if I can't think of enough ideas?
A. Keep to your planned structure. Sometimes fresh ideas come to your mind as you write. Alternatively, try to think of other examples to support the ideas you do have.
Avoid repeating your ideas if possible; build the other sections a little more (such as the Introduction and Conclusion)

Q. What if I copy most of the words from the task question in my Introduction?
A. If you copy 'word for word' from the task question when you start, then you risk having these words excluded from your essay's total word count. In addition, the first impression you give the assessor will show your limitations.

Solution: try to paraphrase words in the task to show you have flexibility and to increase the word count of your essay.

Q. What if I don't know how to write formal, essay-style English very well?
A. **Before** the test, do the fitness activities and study the IELTS Writing Doctor in this textbook, pages 146 and 204. These have useful sections on how to:
- focus on topic sentences for each paragraph,
- build vocabulary which is appropriate to essay styles, and
- build awareness of how to link sentences to develop your viewpoint.

Q. What if I am only half way through and already out of time?
A. This probably means either:
- that you haven't organised and planned your **overall answer** enough before writing,
- or that you spent too long on Task 1 and didn't follow a time management strategy to cover the whole writing test,
- or that your language level is low and it takes you a long time to think of and/or express ideas clearly in English.

In a real test you may have no options, but, before taking the test again:
- Practise answering Task 2 topics under strict, 40-minute time conditions to learn how to maximize the way you manage the time, and how you balance the time given to each section of the essay.
- Practise making quick plans (two to three minutes) so that the overall structure of your answer, and your main ideas are clear—this saves time later and helps you to relax.
- Learn to use one or two useful expressions which help you to start your answer or to structure paragraphs.

Examples

To start an essay you could use:
'The problem/issue of _____ is a complex one, but one which is receiving more attention. This essay will suggest that _____'

Note: be careful to make the standard of the English in the rest of your response at about the same level as any formulaic phrases.

To start a paragraph:
'One reason why _____ is that _____', or
'There are two main reasons why _____. The first is that ___'

To start a conclusion:
'To summarise, this essay has come to the conclusion that _____'

If the problem is caused by anxiety, then being organized is the best solution. Panic can be caused by a lack of willingness to take responsibility for the situation you are in, when you suddenly have no one to help you. This requires better management of the situation. Planning and organization help you to take more control of how you feel inside this stressful situation.

Q. What if writing just one or two paragraphs takes me close to 250 words?

A. This usually means that you haven't balanced your planned essay structure well enough or haven't had enough practice before the test.

Before writing, you needed to look more carefully at the task, and balance the number of ideas before writing. Remember there is not time to write in too much detail, or to include too many ideas. It's important to complete the essay with a well-balanced paragraph structure. Try to remember at all times that you are communicating with the assessor, not writing to yourself.

Q. What if I make a mistake, how do I fix it?

A. If the mistake involves **lack of relevance** at paragraph level, cross out the paragraph neatly with one diagonal line, and write a more relevant one. If it is a major mistake, such as totally **misunderstanding** the task and realizing your mistake only after writing a paragraph or two, cross out the first attempt with a diagonal line, then miss a line and start again but with a tighter plan to avoid too much detail. Aim to write at least 240 words in the time remaining. Don't panic, because you will probably be able to write more easily once you have realized your mistake.

Q. What if I feel so anxious that my mind goes blank?

A. Stay as calm as you can. This is an opportunity to manage your emotions and become stronger. Follow this 'calming routine': close your eyes and breathe systematically for one minute. To do this:

- count 'one and two and three and four' in your head when you breathe in,
- then hold your breath counting from one to four again,
- and then breathe out counting once more from one to four in your head.

After one minute, return to the question, and make every action systematic and structured. You have to manage panic and not let it control you. This one-minute 'calming routine' is not time wasted but **time managed**!

Secrets of how to impress your assessor in Writing Task 2

As we noted earlier when discussing Task 1, your assessor is a busy person with perhaps 20 Writing tests to score. Usually Task 2 is marked after Task 1. Perhaps yours is the last one so the assessor may be a little tired. Within the limitations of your English, you need to create a positive relationship with the assessor through the quality of your writing.

 GOLD STAR ADVICE No 2: *Your Writing is YOU.*
Everything you write and how you present your writing represents 'YOU' in the mind of the assessor because you will not meet that assessor in person.

Q. **How can I make a good impression on the IELTS Writing assessor?**

A. There are ways to write a Task 2 essay response that always create a good impression. A few of these have been mentioned briefly already, but read these more detailed guidelines.

Follow these detailed suggestions and your work will be appreciated by your assessor:

1. Take care with the layout and appearance of your essay

Explanation
A handwritten piece of writing, even a formal essay, is always a personal reflection of '**YOU**' so you need to take particular care with its layout and appearance, even if you feel under time pressure. Avoid crossing out words too often and make your handwriting crisp and neat. Leave a line between each paragraph, so that the essay's structure is very clear. You are trying to make the assessor's job easier, remember!

Why is this important?
As this is the assessor's very first impression of your management of the task, you need to communicate a positive feeling of competence and care.

2. Try to make your point of view and the direction and structure of your essay clear in the introductory paragraph

Explanation

In Western, academic essay writing, the Introduction often serves not just to introduce the topic but also to signal the writer's intentions or point of view (For example—whether you agree with the topic statement or not and what you are going to discuss).

Why is this important?

If the assessor knows right at the beginning what your opinion and plan is, then this helps in three important ways:

a) It makes you appear well-organised (appearing to be a good essay manager is a good first impression).
b) It enables your reader (the assessor) to predict the likely direction of your essay—this helps the reading to go more smoothly (unless you don't do what you said you were going to do).
c) It forces you to be systematic and relevant in structuring the remainder of the essay.

3. Establish an appropriate level of formality in your essay response

Explanation

The use of language in any written communication reflects the relationship between writer and the **context** of writing (this means the situation in which the writing takes place and the expectations of the person who is to receive it).

Why is this important?

The assessor, who is usually a native speaker, has been deeply immersed since childhood in the culture, and, more specifically, in the education system in which English is used, and is therefore highly developed in terms of the subtle choices and uses of language needed for different purposes when writing.

You should try to build some of these features into your writing to create formality:

- Choose formal vocabulary mostly as this seems more professional to the reader.

- Avoid using clichés, short forms and abbreviations.

- Avoid repetition and over-use of basic verbs like 'is', 'has', 'makes', 'gets', 'does'.

- Vary your use of linking expressions.
  For instance, instead of writing 'For example' all the time, you can write, 'One example of this is….', or 'This is clearly illustrated in….'.

- Enrich your display of vocabulary by using adjectives or other expressions to create greater strength in your written 'voice', as in:
  'One effect of this is…'   —> 'One **striking** effect of this is…';
  'This will lead to…'   —> '**Clearly**, this will lead to…' ;
  'In contrast to this is…' —> 'In **sharp** contrast to this is….'.

- Reduce the use of personal pronouns where possible, by using 'it…' constructions, as in:
  'It seems reasonable to suggest that…' (instead of 'I think that…'), or
  'It is education that is the key to preventing extremism' (instead of 'I believe that education is the best way of stopping extremism').

- Use noun groups instead of lengthy imprecise formulations, as in:
  'There is currently an intensification of **mature age unemployment**' (rather than, 'Now there are many old workers and they don't have jobs and this is getting worse').

To summarise — your task is to try to match the assessor's expectations (as made explicit in the assessment criteria for Writing Tasks) as well as you can. Many younger test takers tend to read less formal English and often feel more comfortable when they speak English. This often limits their vocabulary and reduces their awareness of how to use sentence building to develop and link ideas. The essay produced may then seem immature if it is too 'chatty' or too simplistic, or repetitive in style.

4. Make sure you develop a clear point of view

Explanation
Some candidates can write generally about the task topic but find it difficult to establish a clear point of view or a clear conclusion in terms of their own point of view. This is often related to a lack of experience in either thinking about or discussing social issues, or different cultural thinking styles.

Why is this important?
The clearer your point of view is to your IELTS assessor the better the relationship between writer and reader is in this type of writing. The assessor will be impressed if you are definite about what your standpoint is, even if your overall view is that you are 'undecided'.

5. Use a systematic, paragraph structure

Explanation
The use of clear paragraphs, each with a clear function or a clear central topic (idea) is one of the foundations of clear essay writing. It is a well-established convention in academic writing.

Why is this important?
A well-organised and logically developed essay helps to structure your thinking and at the same time structures the reader's understanding of the point of view you are seeking to develop and support. It reduces 'scatter' of ideas (meaning, when a writer just adds one idea after another, like a shopping list without establishing any link to previous ideas or any support via development, explanation or exemplification of ideas).

6. Reduce simple grammar mistakes

Explanation
Simple grammar mistakes may seem a little 'babyish' to the assessor, who generally expects you to have mastered basic grammar if you are trying to get a higher score.

Why is this important?
The assessor may think that you should have learnt basic grammar when you first learnt English. Too many basic errors in your Task 2 response reduce the natural flow of your essay for the reader, reduce the sense of maturity in your viewpoints, and leave a negative impression, even if the assessor can understand what your essay is communicating.

7. Use modal forms or 'cautious language' to express views on complex issues

Explanation
Even if your point of view is clear, social issues are complex and it is therefore difficult to be 100% certain about anything.

Example

 Sentence 1

Family life is terrible today because work is full of stress and working hours are too long

 Sentence 2

For an increasing number of people family life nowadays seems to be deteriorating, perhaps, in part, because hours of work and levels of stress in many jobs appear to be increasing

Comment: The assessor may think that Sentence 1 is a little too strong and simplistic because it is very general and talks about the situation (family life) as if it is 100% fact (use of 'is' and 'are' generally sound factual). Sentence 2 offers a more considered and cautious formulation, and generates more words.

Why is this important?
The tone of your writing forms part of the relationship you form with the reader. Tone in writing is similar to spoken voice tone. If you speak in a flat tone you may appear bored or sad (and perhaps boring to the person you are speaking to); if you voice has a mix of high and low tones you sound more 'alive', more interesting, warmer. If you write in a tone that seems too confident, too sure, without any caution when discussing complex social issues then you may seem unreasonable, conceited, even naïve or crude in your thinking, even if this is caused by lack of ability in English to write in a different way!

8. Use formal vocabulary to build range and give a more 'serious' tone to your essay

Explanation
The writer of a high scoring Task 2 response is able to select vocabulary which indicates ability both to avoid repetition and demonstrate awareness of which words fit the topic and a formal type of essay writing in this context.

Example

Informal approach	Formal approach
Family life is really bad today	Family life seems to be deteriorating currently
People work too long	Working hours seem to be excessive
Jobs have a lot of stress	Some occupations seem to be generating increasing levels of stress
Something must be done about it	Action is required to tackle this problem
Government should stop all this or there'll be a really bad situation	The government needs to take preventive measures in order to avoid a social disaster
They should do something now	Immediate action seems important

Why is this important?
The ability to draw flexibly on a wider range of appropriate vocabulary convinces the assessor that you share similarities with a native speaker, even if there are still a few grammatical errors. This builds a positive impression and strengthens the psychological comfort that the assessor feels in relation to you (through your writing). Psychological closeness is good.

9. Use appropriate idioms occasionally to enrich vocabulary

Explanation
Occasional idioms or less usual vocabulary extend the range and add to the 'colour' and 'personality' of your writing (so long as they are added sparingly and appropriately).

Example

 Conversational style

 Idiomatic alternative

The government must do something about this problem

The government must **grasp the nettle** in terms of this issue

Teenage kids and parents often get annoyed with each other

Parents and teenage children rarely **see things eye to eye**

It is better to avoid idioms or sayings that seem clichéd and are just used formulaically or inappropriately, rather than in the service of the ideas being expressed.

It's also **not a good idea** to:
- translate idioms from your own language into English, or
- use idioms unless you are really confident that they are currently used, and confident about precisely when and how they are used.

Avoid these over-used idioms or sayings:
'Every coin has two sides'
'To put it in a nutshell'
'Rome wasn't built in a day'

Why is this important?
Although the basic tone of an essay is formal, in the IELTS Task 2 there is room to be occasionally less formal, through use of appropriate idiom (as opposed to just simple conversational forms). This shows the assessor you have a greater range of options in your choices of expression. However, it must seem natural, not forced.

10. Use connectors and referencing pronouns to show relationship between your ideas

Explanation
Ideas need to be connected using appropriate connecting expressions to help the reader follow the way you are building the explanations of your ideas and developing your point of view.

Example

 Paragraph 1
No connectors

 Paragraph 2
Good use of connectors

Marrying for money is rarely a good idea. Money leads to lack of feeling. People live in sadness. They are comfortable, of course. Being comfortable is not enough. People also need to feel loved.

Marrying for money is rarely a good idea **because this** may lead to a lack of feeling and **ultimately** the couple may live together in sadness, **even though** they are comfortable. **This type** of comfort is, **however**, not enough **since** people also need to feel loved.

Why is this important?
The use of connecting expressions helps the reader and seems more mature. It also provides the reader with a better sense of your 'voice' as a writer.

11. Try not to be too repetitive

Explanation
Being repetitive shows your limitations as a writer in two main ways:
    a) It indicates limitations in the range of ideas.
    b) It indicates limitations in the flexibility and range of your vocabulary and grammar.

Why is this important?
Your principal goal is to achieve the highest score you can in IELTS. To do this you need to show flexibility and variety in terms of ideas, vocabulary and grammatical use.

Reduce Weaknesses to Maintain a Good Impression

To maintain the good impression you've already created you need to reduce the kinds of language weaknesses illustrated in these examples:

Weakness Type 1 — Word Forms (Adjective/Noun/Adverb)

In simple terms, **errors that relate to basic rules of English grammar leave a more negative impression than other kinds of mistakes** because the assessor may assume that you learnt about these basic rules when you were young and have had plenty of time to learn to use them correctly since that time.

Examples of mistakes that create bad impression

Mistake	What's wrong?
It is **real** unwise to meet on the Internet	Adverb form **'really'** needed
Marrying for love is always **appropriately**	Adjective **'appropriate'** needed
It is **obviously** that family life is **importance**	Adjectives **'obvious'** and **'important'** needed
Work stress is **certain** a major problem	Adverb **'certainly'** needed

So, **if you still make these basic errors you may give the impression of being like an immature schoolchild,** even if your own native language causes you to make the errors because its verb system is much simpler than the English verb system, or its translated word forms are less varied than those in English. The assessor forms an impression of you from your writing and isn't influenced by such complexities as 'first language interference'. The IELTS test, remember, is based ultimately on comparing performance with a native English speaker equivalent.

IELTS Writing Task 2 Lesson

Weakness Type 2 — Verb Tenses

Explanation
Accurate use of the verb system shows an awareness of how time is marked in English. This is important when writing an essay.

Example

 Incorrect tenses

In the past, family life **is** more important because most people **live** in the countryside and spent more time together, working on the land. In more recent times, the nature of work **is changed**. People nowadays **living** in cities, and **are travel** away from home to work. In the future, this trend **is changing.**

 Correct tenses

In the past, family life **was** more important because most people **lived** in the countryside and spent more time together, working on the land. In more recent times, the nature of work **has changed**. People nowadays **live** in cities, and **travel** away from home to work. In the future, this trend **will change.**

Weakness Type 3 — Subject/Verb Agreement

Explanation
Making the subject and verb agree is a basic aspect of English grammar. It is learnt at the beginner stage but a surprising number of IELTS candidates still make errors, and these create a poor impression.

Example

 Incorrect

Couples who wants to get married should put love first. If **they doesn't** feel love, then their **life together are** going to be unhappy. **Everyone need someone who love** them. As a child it is your parents, but when you are an adult your **partner become** that person.

 Correct

Couples who want to get married should put love first. If **they don't** feel love, then their **life together is** going to be unhappy. **Everyone needs someone who loves** them. As a child it is your parents, but when you are an adult your **partner becomes** that person.

Weakness Type 4 – Run-on Sentences

Explanation
Run-on sentences indicate a lack of awareness of the importance of correct punctuation in showing the boundary between one sentence and another. Assessors get frustrated by this problem as it forces them to re-read sentences in order to make sense of them, and wastes time.

Example

 Run-on sentence

 Improved sentence

Stressful jobs affect psychological health, they reduce energy and motivation as a result, performance is negatively affected.

Stressful jobs affect psychological health. They reduce energy and motivation. As a result, performance is negatively affected.

Weakness Type 5 – Omissions from Sentences

Explanation
Perhaps because many learners of English are more comfortable speaking the language conversationally, written English is often 'telegraphed', which means words are left out but the meaning is still reasonably clear.

Example

 With omissions

 Improved version

One advantage working past retirement age is that keeps you mentally sharp. Those retire early often bored at home. Their brains slow their reactions also slow and results in depression.

One advantage **of** working past retirement age is that **it** keeps you mentally sharp. Those **who** retire early **are** often bored at home. Their brains slow**,** their reactions also slow, and **this** results in depression.

Weakness Type 6... NO, We're sure you've had enough....... for NOW!

WRITING TASK 2 FITNESS ACTIVITIES

Before you start

The fitness activities in this section offer you quick practice at the different task types you may encounter in the IELTS Writing test. It's also a chance to use some of the tips from the Writing chapter earlier in our book.

With the help of these fitness activities you will build awareness of key elements of different Task 2 essays. Work through each section, noting the different aspects of the essay being focused on. When you are practising a Task 2 essay under exam conditions, try asking yourself similar questions as part of **managing and improving your written response.**

TASK TYPE 1 » Indicate and support your level of agreement

Task Question

Shopping is dangerous because it makes people selfish, and careless with money.
Do you agree or disagree?

Write at least 250 words.

Fitness Activities 1–25 for Task Type 1

 Activities 1–2 will help you to understand what kind of response is required.

1   'Do you agree or disagree?' means that you need to:

   a) choose and defend one of these views (Yes I agree OR No I don't agree) based on the nature of your own viewpoint.
   b) write to show you both agree and disagree equally.
   c) do what you like as long as you talk about shopping.

2. The key word in the task wording that communicates you should write in support of only one view is:

   a) money   b) because   c) or

 Activities 3–5 will help you to plan your answer.

3. How many paragraphs will work well in this type of essay?

   a) 4 (Introduction, 2 body paragraphs, Conclusion).
   b) 5 (Introduction, 3 body paragraphs, Conclusion).
   c) 3 (Introduction, 1 body paragraph, Conclusion).

4. What's the best thing to do next?

   a) Start writing.
   b) Write down some key ideas to support and oppose your viewpoint.
   c) Decide on your viewpoint and then write down some ideas.

5. What's a reasonable, approximate number of sentences to aim for in the Introduction?
   a) 2–3 sentences   b) 3–5 sentences   c) 6–7 sentences

 Activities 6–10 will help you to build the Introduction.

6. Look at the Introduction paragraph. What's the main purpose of the first sentence?

   a) To start by talking generally about the overall topic of shopping
   b) To stop the opinion sentence (2) from being the first one.
   c) To raise the topic of shopping and make a 'bridge' into the writer's point of view.

Introduction

Shopping has become a popular leisure activity in many countries in the developed world, but it has hidden risks. This essay **will suggest** that it is indeed dangerous and **is likely to** make consumers more self-centred and less disciplined with their money.

IELTS Writing Task 2 Fitness Activities

7   Which two of these expressions could suitably replace 'will suggest' in Activity 6?

    a) will argue   b) will say   c) will report   d) is of the opinion

8   'is likely to' is a useful phrase in Task 2 essays as it carries more caution than the expression 'will' when making predictions about complex problems.
    Make more cautious predictions by using 'likely' to complete these positive and negative sentences:

    a) Shopping will grow in popularity.   Shopping is _____
    b) Shopping will never die out.   Shopping is not _____
    c) Overspending will cause problems.   Overspending is _____
    d) Shopping will never bring happiness.   It is highly un_____that_____

9   Which synonyms are used in the Introduction in Activity 6 to avoid copying these three words from the task wording?

    people   _____
    selfish   _____
    careless   _____

10 How could you complete these phrases with 'make' so that even with a different verb the meaning doesn't really change very much?

    a) Shoppers are selfish.
       Shopping makes _____ _____

    b) Consumers are dangerous when they go shopping.
       Shopping makes _____ _____

    c) People spend unwisely at the shops.
       Shopping makes _____ _____ _____

    d) Shoppers lack self discipline.
       Shopping makes _____ _____

IELTS Success Formula :: Academic

Activities 11–12 will help you to build Body Paragraph 1.

11 Look at Body Paragraph 1.
    What purpose does the topic sentence (first sentence) achieve?

    a) It enables the writer to establish that not all shoppers are rich.
    b) It enables the writer briefly to discuss his central point of view.
    c) It establishes that there is a point of view that is different from the writer's.

    Body Paragraph 1

    Not all shoppers are poor money managers. As costs and bills are increasing constantly, many families have developed excellent **financial skills, enabling them** to pay their bills and shop fairly for every family member. There are also **financial advisers available** to help develop such skills.

12 The writer economises in the building of sentences in this paragraph.
    Complete the same sentences using these equally effective ways.

    a) Many families have developed excellent financial skills which_____.
    b) There are also financial advisers, who_____.

 Activities 13–16 will help you to build Body Paragraph 2.

13 What is the central idea in the topic sentence (first sentence) which will be developed in Body Paragraph 2?

    a) selfishness   b) reasons   c) advertising

Body Paragraph 2

Advertising is one of the key reasons why people think more selfishly. Many adverts depict glamorous lives where certain products are shown as essential to a sense of being successful, attractive or fashionable. Ordinary consumers are persuaded at a psychological level by advertisers and made to feel inadequate if they don't have products such as cosmetics, brand name goods, new shoes or cars. This creates willing shoppers who put their desire for personal appearance and wellbeing above their sense of community welfare.

14 A useful sentence construction for explaining something in an IELTS Task 2 is: '_____ is one of the key reasons why _____'.
Complete these sentences in an appropriate way:

a) The desire for a good job is one of the key reasons why _____
b) The wish for a more exciting life is one of the principal reasons why _____
c) The hope for more money is one of the major reasons why _____
d) _____ is one of the main reasons why marriage is still popular.

15 Using advanced vocabulary appropriately helps to raise IELTS level. Which words in Body Paragraph 2 (Activity 13) are used instead of these simpler options?

Simpler option	More advanced expression in Body Paragraph 2
show (verb)	
wish (noun)	
look (noun)	
shoppers	
feeling good	
not good enough	
goods	
social good	

16 There are quite a few adjectives in this paragraph. In which two ways do they most help the IELTS candidate's performance?

a) They add variety and interest.
b) They enable the writer to show greater range of vocabulary use.
c) They help build the viewpoint.

Activities 17–21 will help you to build Body Paragraph 3.

17 It's helpful to have options when judging the degree to which something has changed.
    Example in Body Paragraph 3:   'far less cautious')
    Complete these sentences with 'less' or 'more':

    a) Most teenagers read **considerably** _____ than they did in the past.
    b) Women are **far** _____ intelligent than men (You choose!)
    c) Airline fares are **much** _____ expensive nowadays.
    d) IELTS is **considerably** _____ popular than it used to be.

Body Paragraph 3

The advent of the credit card has encouraged consumers to be **far less** cautious about their money. Credit cards are part of the 'cashless society', in which more and more transactions don't require actual cash. **The result is that money becomes** more abstract and, via constantly increasing credit limits, consumers can pretend to have money that they don't actually possess, and can buy things that they want immediately, but before they have really earned the money to pay for them. **This** often results in having to face constant debt and to a sense of life being lived 'here and now' rather than linked to building a stable future.

18 A useful phrase for IELTS Task 2 is, 'The result is that….'
    Which of a, b, c and d could NOT appropriately replace it in Body Paragraph 3?

    a) As a consequence, money becomes...
    b) This results in money becoming…
    c) An outcome of this is that money becomes…
    d) Money becomes a result that…

19 How many sentences are there in Body Paragraph 3? Guess before checking.
    a) 6   b) 8   c) 4

20 'This…' is a helpful referencing word as it prevents the need to repeat an already-used long phrase. What does '<u>this</u>' in Body Paragraph 3 refer back to?

    a) earning money
    b) buying things immediately
    c) pretending to have money

21 Evaluate these effects of long sentences as either + (Positive) or – (Negative)

a) Long sentences can aid reading flow as the writer's ideas are connected more fluently (+ / –)
b) Long sentences put extra pressure on memory (+ / –)
c) Long sentences show more flexible use of connecting expressions (+ / –)
d) Long sentences may reduce clarity of ideas (+ / –)

Review the length and clarity of your own sentences when you practise Task 2.

 Activities 22–24 will help you to build the Conclusion.

22 The purpose of this Conclusion seems to be:
a) to summarise the point of view.
b) to offer some new information.
c) to give the opposite point of view.

Conclusion

All in all then, shopping has become all too tempting for many consumers, who want to feel good and feel rewarded perhaps for their ever-busier working lives. Advertising feeds this desire and credit cards feed instant gratification. The results **may well be** harmful for families and for society.

23 The writer adds expressions to intensify the evaluation of shopping and work. Find the expressions and write them here:

_____ _____ tempting   _____ - _____ working lives

Now put these expressions into the sentences below

all too	ever-growing	far too	never-ending	ever busier

a) It is _____ easy to spend money, and _____ difficult to save it.
b) Internet crime is an _____ problem.
c) Working lives are becoming _____.
d) There seems to be a _____ rise in the price of food.

24 Using cautious language like 'may well be' instead of 'will be' makes opinions in an essay of this type seem more reasonable.
Which three of these expressions are also cautious and could replace 'may well be'?

   a) will definitely be…
   b) could easily be…
   c) might well be…
   d) can't fail but be…
   e) may turn out to be…

25 Now complete your own essay in 40 minutes without looking at the sample essay. Use the 5-paragraph structure and make sure that each body paragraph has a clear topic sentence (that is, a first sentence which establishes the topic to be developed in the remainder of the paragraph).

Now read this complete sample answer:

> Shopping has become a popular leisure activity in many countries in the developed world. **This essay will suggest that** it is indeed dangerous and is likely to make consumers more selfish and less disciplined with their money.
>
> **Not all shoppers are poor money managers.** As costs and bills increase constantly, many families have developed excellent financial skills enabling them to pay their bills and shop fairly for every family member. There are also financial advisers available to help develop such skills.
>
> **Advertising is, however, one of the key reasons why people think more selfishly.** Many adverts depict glamorous lives where certain products are shown as essential to a sense of being successful, attractive or fashionable. Ordinary consumers are persuaded at a psychological level by advertisers and made to feel inadequate if they don't have products such as cosmetics, brand name goods, new shoes or cars. This creates willing shoppers who put their desire for personal appearance and wellbeing above their sense of community welfare.
>
> **The advent of the credit card has encouraged consumers to be far less cautious about their money.** Credit cards are part of the 'cashless society', in which more and more transactions don't require actual cash. The result is that money becomes more abstract and, via constantly increasing credit limits, consumers can pretend to have money that they don't actually possess, and can buy things that they want immediately, but before they have really earned the money to pay for them. This often results in having to face constant debt and to a sense of life being lived 'here and now' rather than linked to building a stable future.
>
> **All in all then**, shopping has become all too tempting for many consumers, who want to feel good and feel rewarded perhaps for their ever-busier working lives. Advertising feeds this desire and credit cards feed instant gratification. The results may well be harmful for families and for society.

Note: This sample answer is **not** a model answer but only one of many, possible responses to the task question. It would probably be awarded Band 9.

TASK TYPE 2 » Present a two-sided Discussion

> **Task Question**
>
> Some say you should always marry for love; others say that in an uncertain world it is wiser to marry for money.
> Discuss both points of view and give your own opinion.
>
> Write at least 250 words.

Fitness Activities 1–20 for Task Type 2

 Activities 1–3 will help you to understand what kind of response is required.

1 This type of essay requires you to:

   a) choose one point of view only.
   b) give your own opinion on both points of view.
   c) talk about both points of view neutrally, then give your own personal view.

2 The main topic is:

   a) marriage as an institution
   b) the basis of marriage
   c) links between love and money

3 The points of view for discussion are:

   a) whether you should only get married because you love someone or whether you should only get married for financial advantage.
   b) whether it's more sensible to get married for love or more sensible to marry for financial benefit given the modern world's uncertainties.

IELTS Writing Task 2 Fitness Activities

 Activities 4–5 will help you to plan your answer.

4   How many paragraphs seems the most logical for this type of essay?

   a) 5   b) 4   c) 6

5   What's the best thing to do next?

   a) Decide which part of the essay will go into which paragraph.
   b) Note some key ideas for the main paragraphs.
   c) Write the introduction.

 Activities 6–8 will help you to build the Introduction.

Introduction

The issue of love and marriage has been part of most cultures for centuries. With economic uncertainties, pure romance is under challenge, but can still find a way to maintain its vital place in marriage.

6   Read this introduction and choose a, b or c.

   The Introduction:
   a) introduces the topic and hints at the writer's own opinion.
   b) talks generally but doesn't hint at the writer's own opinion.
   c) focuses on historical and economic facts.

7   In IELTS writing, candidates sometimes struggle to write economically. Which shorter phrases in the Introduction are more economical than a) and b)?

   a) Some people have jobs but don't have a trust in the future of their jobs or their money.

   Shorter phrase in the Introduction: _____

   b) True and real love has got many things which are trying to make it weaker.

   Shorter phrase in the Introduction: _____

8   Choose the best expression to complete a-d using either 'topic', 'issue' or 'problem'.

   a) Poverty is a _____ facing many nations.
   b) Whether or not to have children is an important _____ these days.
   c) Beauty is a frequently discussed _____.
   d) Climate change is one of the most serious _____ in the world today.

**Activities 9–12 will help you to build Body Paragraph 1.
Read Body Paragraph 1 before trying the activities that follow.**

Body Paragraph 1

Most couples in western societies **would claim that** they still marry for love. **This is because** they are usually free to choose a life partner. Love provides a strong emotional bond between men and women, and continues into adulthood the strong feelings that most children receive from their parents. **It is well known that** a strong marriage based on love gives each partner the strength, stability and emotional security to pursue their careers with confidence. Lonely, unloved individuals, **often seem to** struggle more in every part of their lives.

9   Verb forms that are less direct often seem more mature and considered. Compare:
   'Most couples would claim that they marry for love' **with**
   'Most couples marry for love'

   The first sentence in Body Paragraph 1 seems to hint that the situation is not so simple. Which three of these verb expressions would achieve the same effect in that first sentence?

   Most couples…
   a) want to get…
   b) clearly want to believe…
   c) only get married…
   d) are probably convinced…
   e) would no doubt assert…

10 'This is because...' is a very useful expression and helps the writer give a confident explanation which links to the previous sentence neatly.

Match sentence 1 with its appropriate sentence 2:

Sentence 1	Sentence 2
a) Many women today marry later.	i) **This is because** neither partner can always have their own way
b) The number of divorces is rising.	ii) **This is because** many couples want celebrity-style weddings.
c) Getting married is now very expensive.	iii) **This is because** they want to build their careers first, just like men do.
d) Marriage involves compromise	iv) **This is because** couples get bored too easily and lack commitment.

11 'It is well known that...' helps a writer to claim a general truth.
    Example: 'It is well known that a strong marriage based on love gives each partner...'

    Write your own ending to complete these sentences in a suitable way:

    a) It is well known that women _____.
    b) It is well known that celebrities _____.
    c) It is well known that divorce _____.

12 'often seem(s)' instead of a simple verb stops the writer appearing too assertive.
    Compare:
    'Lonely individuals struggle more in their lives' **with**
    'Lonely individuals often seem to struggle more in their lives'

    Change these verb forms using 'often seem':

    a) Men are less committed to marriage than women.
    b) Women are more romantic than men.
    c) Couples today struggle to keep their marriage alive.
    d) A child knows when parents are not happy.

**Activities 13–15 will help you to build Body Paragraph 2.
Read Body Paragraph 2 before trying the activities that follow.**

Body Paragraph 2

At the same time **it cannot be denied that** economic realities have made everyone more practical. Seeking a partner who has good **career prospects** is a wise and sensible thing to do as it provides a better basis for economic stability within a family. So **it is quite likely that** the modern marriage may unconsciously be based on both love and money, in the sense that a suitable person to fall in love with may tend to be someone with a well-paid job.

13 Writers often use an introductory phrase to strengthen their viewpoint.
    Example: 'It cannot be denied that economic realities have made everyone more practical.'

    Add your own viewpoint about marriage to these introductory phrases:

    a) It cannot be denied that _____.
    b) It is certainly the case that _____.
    c) There is little doubt that _____.
    d) It is undeniable that _____.

14 Using noun + noun is a way to communicate information economically.
    Example: 'Prospects of having a career' = 'career prospects'.

    Put these phrases into a neat, noun + noun form:

    a) A cake eaten at a wedding = _____.
    b) A ceremony in which you get married = _____.
    c) Your partner in marriage = _____.
    d) An opportunity to get a job = _____.

15 Expressing degrees of probability is helpful when making a prediction in writing.
    Example: '…it is quite likely that the modern marriage may…'

    Arrange these predictions from the most likely (1) to the least likely (4):

    a) It is highly likely that   _____
    b) It is very unlikely that   _____
    c) It is quite likely that   _____
    d) There is little likelihood that _____

IELTS Writing Task 2 Fitness Activities

Activities 16–18 will help you to build Body Paragraph 3.
Read Body Paragraph 3 before trying the activities that follow.

Body Paragraph 3

My own view is that love should, as they say, 'conquer all'. Without love we, as human beings, are lost to ourselves and lost to others. **Most surveys show that** happiness is **based on** strong, positive relationships **not on** wealth. Marriage should be based on a strong, emotional relationship **so that** children will grow up being loved, and the cycle of love can continue.

16 It is useful to draw on supporting evidence.
    Example: "Most surveys show that…'

    Which of these phrases seem similar in meaning to the example from Body Paragraph 3?

    a) Much research evidence indicates that…
    b) I have a viewpoint which shows that…
    c) Most of the evidence points to the fact that…
    d) I really believe that…

17 It is often useful to make a contrasting point economically.
    Example: 'Love is <u>based on</u> respect, <u>not on</u> wealth'

    Choose expressions from the box to complete these sentences:

    | proximity | commitment | taste | reputation | infatuation | nutrition |

    a) Marriage should be **based on** _____, **not on** _____.
    b) Choosing a university should be **based on** _____, **not on** _____.
    c) A good diet should be **based on** _____, **not on** _____.

18 Using 'so that' to express purpose is effective in formal writing.
    Example: 'Marriage exists <u>so that</u> children can grow up in a stable family'

    Complete these complex sentences of purpose with your own ideas

    a) Children go to school **so that** they can_____.
    b) Couples get married **so that** they can_____.
    c) Young married couples save **so that** they can _____.

   Activity 19 will help you to build the Conclusion.

19 Which 3 expressions below could replace 'To summarise,...' ?

    a) All in all   b) Finally   c) After all   d) To sum up   e) Lastly   f) Summing up

    Conclusion

    To summarise, marriage is under pressure from the individual's desire for financial security, but ultimately love is still the key to a happy, married life.

20 Now complete your own essay in 40 minutes without looking at the sample essay. Use the 5-paragraph structure and make sure that each body paragraph has a clear topic sentence (that is, a first sentence which establishes the topic to be developed in the remainder of the paragraph).

Now read this complete sample answer:

The issue of love and marriage has been part of most cultures for centuries. With economic uncertainties, pure romance is under challenge, but can still find a way to maintain its vital place in marriage.

Most couples in western societies would claim that they still marry for love. This is because they are usually free to choose a life partner. Love provides a strong emotional bond between men and women, and continues into adulthood the strong feelings that most children receive from their parents. It is well known that a strong marriage based on love gives each partner the strength, stability and emotional security to pursue their careers with confidence. Lonely, unloved individuals, often seem to struggle more in every part of their lives.

At the same time it cannot be denied that economic realities have made everyone more practical. Seeking a partner who has good career prospects is a wise and sensible thing to do as it provides a better basis for economic stability within a family. So it is quite likely that the modern marriage may unconsciously be based on both love and money, in the sense that a suitable person to fall in love with may tend to be someone with a well-paid job.

My own view is that love should, as they say, 'conquer all'. Without love we, as human beings, are lost to ourselves and lost to others. Most surveys show that happiness is based on strong, positive relationships not on wealth. Marriage should be based on a strong emotional relationship so that children will grow up being loved, and the cycle of love can continue.

To summarise, marriage is under pressure from the individual's desire for financial security, but ultimately love is still the key to a happy, married life.

 Note: This sample answer is **not** a model answer but only one of many, possible responses to the task question. It would probably be awarded Band 9.

 You've now completed fitness activities for two task types. Well done. Now go and get married! ...Only joking!
Get a cup of tea... much easier!

IELTS Writing Task 2 Fitness Activities

TASK TYPE 3 » Discuss Advantages & Disadvantages

Task Question

In some countries older people are being encouraged to work longer and not to retire.

Discuss the advantages and disadvantages of working beyond retirement age.

Write at least 250 words.

Fitness Activities 1–10 for Task Type 3

Activity 1 will help you to understand what kind of response is required.

1   In this type of essay you need to:

   a) discuss advantages only.
   b) discuss both advantages and disadvantages.
   c) discuss disadvantages only, if you think there are no advantages.

Activity 2 will help you to plan your answer.

2   What number of paragraphs seems the most logical for this type of essay?

   a) 3   b) 5   c) 4

IELTS Writing Task 2 Fitness Activities

Activity 3 will help you to build the Introduction.
Read the Introduction before trying Activity 3 that follows.

Introduction

The retirement age is no longer fixed in many societies. Some workers prefer to delay retirement as long as possible; others choose to leave while still relatively young. There are pros and cons of prolonging work past retirement age.

3 Good paraphrasing of the task wording is viewed positively by the assessor. Find the wording that paraphrases:

a) advantages and disadvantages   _____
b) working beyond   _____

Activities 4–5 will help you to build Body Paragraph 1.
Read Body Paragraph 1 before trying the activities that follow.

Body Paragraph 1

Some benefit can be easily identified. One clear advantage of delaying retirement is that it enable the maintenance of well-established daily routines. With age regularity seem to become more important psychologically and physically. A second benefit is that most work provide opportunities for social contact with groups and individual. Again, this is beneficial to a sense of wellbeing and usefulness.

4 It is usually a good idea to put all your advantages in one paragraph. How many different advantages are there in Body Paragraph 1?

a) 1   b) 3   c) 2

5 The missing 's'. This writer has started to make a few simple errors. There are five words in the Body Paragraph 1 that need an 's'. Write them correctly below:

1. _____
2. _____
3. _____
4. _____
5. _____

IELTS Writing Task 2 Fitness Activities

 **Activities 6–8 will help you to build Body Paragraph 2.
Read Body Paragraph 2 before trying the activities that follow.**

Body Paragraph 2

On other hand, working past retirement age is not always a good thing. Physically, full time job can be demanding especially these days, and workers of retirement age are starting to lose their physical strength. Secondly, after forty or more years of work, there is less time remaining to pursue those activities and trips for which there was never enough time. Many retired people, for example, undertake ambitious trips worldwide, while they are still healthy. Finally, staying on past retirement potentially robs younger workers of opportunities for promotion, or may prevent young workers from actually entering workforce.

6   Body Paragraph 2 has more ideas than Body Paragraph 1. How many <u>disadvantages</u> can you find? How many of them are supported by <u>examples</u>?

    Disadvantages: a) 5   b) 4   c) 3
    Supporting example(s):   a) 1   b) 2   c) 3

7   'a' and 'the'. The writer has missed two uses of 'the' and one use of 'a'. Can you find them?   Write the complete forms here:

    1. _____
    2. _____
    3. _____

8   The writer chooses some good quality vocabulary to move beyond simple words. Which words does the writer use instead of these simpler possibilities?

    a) hard   _____
    b) left   _____
    c) go on   _____
    d) stop   _____

Activity 9 will help you to build the Conclusion.

9   What does this conclusion achieve? Choose a, b or c:

a) It repeats all the main advantages and disadvantages.
b) It briefly summarises a key point from each paragraph.
c) It offers some new ideas.

Conclusion

Summing up, working past retirement is good for continuity of daily routines but shortens the time available for exciting activities and pursuits during years when health problems may not have surfaced.

10 Now complete your own essay in 40 minutes without looking at the sample essay. Use the 4-paragraph structure and make sure that each body paragraph has a clear topic sentence (that is, a first sentence which establishes the topic to be developed in the remainder of the paragraph).

Now read this complete sample answer:

The retirement age is no longer fixed in many societies. As a consequence some workers now prefer to delay retirement as long as possible; others, however, choose to leave while they are still relatively young. There are pros and cons of prolonging work past retirement age.

Some benefits can be easily identified. One clear advantage of delaying retirement is that it enables the maintenance of well-established routines. With age, regularity seems to become more important psychologically and physically. A second benefit is that most work **provide**s opportunities for social contact with groups and individuals. Again, this is beneficial to a sense of wellbeing and usefulness. Lastly, working for longer enables greater time to build more savings for the post-retirement period. As living costs increase constantly, financial security is vital.

On ᵗʰᵉ **other** hand, working past retirement age is not always a good thing. Physically**,** ᵃ **full time job** can be demanding especially these days, and workers of retirement age are starting to lose their physical strength. Secondly, after forty or more years of work, there is less time remaining to pursue those activities and trips for which there was never enough time. Many retired people, for example, undertake ambitious trips worldwide, while they are still healthy. Finally, staying on past retirement potentially robs younger workers of opportunities for promotion, or may prevent young workers from actually entering ᵗʰᵉ **workforce**.

Summing up, working past retirement is good for continuity of daily routines but shortens the time available for exciting leisure activities and pursuits during years when health problems may not yet have surfaced.

Note: This sample answer is **not** a model answer but only one of many, possible responses to the task question. It would probably be awarded Band 8.5 (**grammar** slightly below Band 9).

TASK TYPE 4 » Explain & Offer Solutions or Consequences

> **Task Question**
>
> Family life is suffering because of the pressure of work.
>
> Why is this happening?
> What is the most important way to improve the quality of family life?"
>
> Write at least 250 words.

Fitness Activities 1–8 for Task Type 4

Activity 1 will help you to understand what kind of response is required.

1. In this task type you should:

   a) Say whether you agree or not with the first statement.
   b) Explain why the situation exists, and what to do to make the situation better.
   c) Talk about ways in which work pressure is increasing and how to improve this problem.

Activities 2–3 will help you to plan your answer.

2. How many paragraphs should you aim for between the Introduction and the Conclusion?

   a) 3   b) 1   c) 2

3   Imagine you are answering this question.
    Write down some ideas under these two headings:

Why is family life suffering?	Most important way to improve family life

Activity 4 will help you to build the Introduction.
Read the Introduction before trying Activity 4 that follows.

Introduction

In many countries both husbands and wives work full time. Unfortunately, this sometimes means that they have less time to spend with their children and may have to put even very young children into care. This essay will seek to offer reasons for this phenomenon and suggest the key to making family life better.

4   The writer avoids copying words from the task too closely. Which phrases replace these from the task question?

In the task question   In the Introduction

a) to say why this is happening   _____

b) the most important way to improve   _____
   the quality of family life

IELTS Writing Task 2 Fitness Activities

 **Activity 5 will help you to build Body Paragraph 1.
Read Body Paragraph 1 before trying Activity 5 that follows.**

Body Paragraph 1

There is a range of reasons why the deterioration in family life can be linked to the work situation. **In the first place**, employers are becoming **so** cost conscious **that** they reduce their workforces as much as they can to reduce costs. **Consequently**, the other workers then may have to work longer hours to cover an increased workload. **Similarly**, workers often feel pressure to get better qualifications in order to remain employable. **As a result**, they enrol for part-time courses which then have to be completed in their leisure time, **thus** robbing them of valuable hours with their children. **Finally**, it seems that work is speeding up. **In other words**, electronic technology saves time in some ways, but increases management's expectations of what employees can be expected to achieve within a working day. **This can mean that** workers have to take work home in order to keep up. **Taken together**, such issues build pressure at home and families spend less time together.

5   Linking expressions. Match each linking expression on the left with one from Body Paragraph 1 on the right that has a similar meaning or function.

Alternative expressions	Expressions from Body Paragraph 1
a) First of all,…	In other words
b) Lastly,…	Taken together
c) All in all…	This can mean that
d) So…	In the first place
e) In the same way,…	Consequently
f) Thereby…	Similarly
g) Putting it another way,…	so…. that
h) The result of this is that…	As a result
i) such that…	Finally
j) This can lead to a situation in which…	thus

**Activity 6 will help you to build Body Paragraph 2.
Read Body Paragraph 2 before trying Activity 6 that follows.**

Paragraph 2

Line
1   There is only one real key to changing the situation. This would involve a big change
2   in social values such that the family and the upbringing of children would be viewed
3   by governments and companies as the biggest social task. Then, work practices and
4   government policies would be built around this good value. As a result workers would
5   be protected and given good time for the big role of socialisation and the building of
6   strong, loving and good relationships with their children.

6   **Improve the level of the vocabulary. The writer has missed an opportunity here to lift the level of vocabulary. Which basic words in the paragraph could these replace?**

   Alternative higher level expression   Word and line number in Body Paragraph 2

   a) fundamental   _____
   b) most significant   _____
   c) vital   _____
   d) sufficient   _____
   e) empathetic   _____

Activities 7–8 will help you to build the Conclusion.

7   **Using 'this' in essays is a good way of making connections economically as a writer. What do the following uses in the Conclusion refer back to?**

   '…and **this** is reducing shared family time'
   a) What is reducing shared family time? _____

   'A major change in social values is the key to changing **this situation**'.
   b) What is the situation? _____

Conclusion

To conclude, economic pressures are leading to harder and longer work and **this** is reducing shared family time. A major change in social values is the key to changing **this situation**.

8. Write a conclusion of your own to this essay in this box. Try to use only two or three sentences.

Now read this complete sample answer:

In many countries both husbands and wives work full time. Unfortunately, this sometimes means that they have less time to spend with their children and may have to put even very young children into care. This essay will seek to offer reasons for this phenomenon and suggest the key to making family life better.

There is a range of reasons why the deterioration in family life can be linked to the work situation. In the first place, employers are becoming so cost conscious that they reduce their workforces as much as they can to reduce costs. Consequently, the other workers then may have to work longer hours to cover an increased workload. Similarly, workers often feel pressure to get better qualifications in order to remain employable. As a result, they enrol for part-time courses which then have to be completed in their leisure time, thus robbing them of valuable hours with their children. Finally, it seems that work is speeding up. In other words, electronic technology saves time in some ways, but increases management's expectations of what employees can be expected to achieve within a working day. This can mean that workers have to take work home in order to keep up. Taken together, such issues build pressure at home and families spend less time together.

There is only one real key to changing the situation. This would involve a **big** change in social values such that the family and the upbringing of children would be viewed by governments and companies as the **biggest** social task. Then, work practices and government policies would be built around this **good** value. As a result workers would be protected and given **good** time for the **big** role of socialisation and the building of strong, loving and **good** relationships with their children.

To conclude, economic pressures are leading to harder and longer work and this is reducing shared family time. A major change in social values is the key to changing this situation.

Note: This sample answer is **not** a model answer but only one of many, possible responses to the task question. It would probably be awarded Band 8.5 (**vocabulary** slightly lower than Band 9).

You should now go and write some Task 2 essays under test conditions! On second thoughts, go and have a nice hot bath or some strawberries, or both! Do some more practice later!

WRITING TASK 1 – RATED SAMPLE

As you may know, IELTS writing task 1s are marked using band descriptors in four categories: **Task Achievement, Coherence and Cohesion, Lexical Resource, and Grammatical Range and Accuracy.** You can find the publicly available performance descriptors on the official IELTS website: www.ielts.org.

This sample report has been analysed to help you understand what score it would perhaps be awarded in each category and some reasons why.

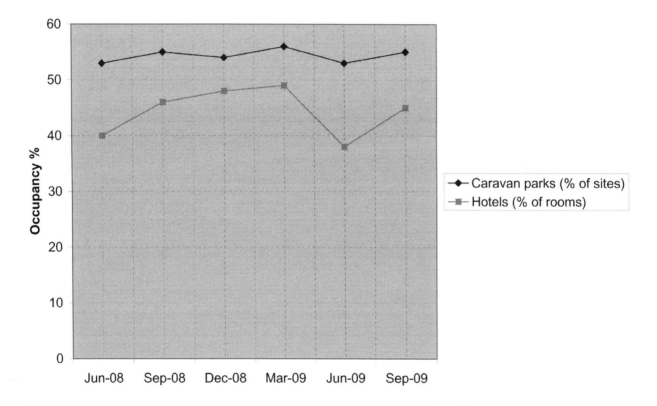

Task Question

The graph shows the percentage occupancy of caravan parks and hotel rooms between June '08 and September '09.

Summarise the information by selecting and reporting the key features, and make any relevant comparisons.

Write at least 150 words.

Writing Task 1 Rated Sample

Analysing Task Achievement

> *The graph compares the proportion of occupancy rates in caravan parks and hotels from June 2008 to September 2009.*
>
> *Obviously, it was observed that there was a constant elevation in the percentage of occupancy rates in hotel rooms, from 40% in June 2008 reaching nearly 50% in March 2009.*
>
> *On the other hand, occupancy rates in caravan parks show a slightly different trend. There was a gradual increase of 2% in June to September 2008, reaching 56% occupancy rate, but, decreased shortly by 1% in December 2008 and went up again in March 2009 to 55%.*
>
> *However, a dramatic drop in the percentage of occupants in both venues was very apparent in June 2009, but managed to gain back in September 2009. The occupancy rate in caravan parks lowered to 53% but increased by 2% after three months. As for the hotels, the rate of occupants significantly dropped to 48% in June 2009, and was able to come up with 7% increase after three months had passed.*

Analysis: This response has a reasonable level of task achievement. It identifies the main trending features of both hotel and caravan occupancy during the period June '08 – March '09, but then seems to mis-apply the word 'dramatic' to the change in caravan occupancy. There is an attempt to include comparisons between the two accommodation types. The statistics quoted (the percentage numbers) seem accurate. One key weakness is that although the answer establishes (in paragraph 1) the subject of the information, it does not establish a broad overview of the data (For example that June is the period of lower occupancy for both, or that occupancy in both types fluctuates, or that caravans overall have a better occupancy rate).

<u>Impression score for Task Achievement</u>: The report seems to be between **5** and **6** level.

Writing Task 1 Rated Sample

Analysing Coherence and Cohesion

> *The graph compares the proportion of occupancy rates in caravan parks and hotels from June 2008 to September 2009.*
>
> *[Obviously], it was observed that there was a constant elevation in the percentage of occupancy rates in hotel rooms, from 40% in June 2008 reaching nearly 50% in March 2009.*
>
> *[On the other hand], occupancy rates in caravan parks show a slightly different trend. There was a gradual increase of 2% in June to September 2008, reaching 56% occupancy rate, but, decreased shortly by 1% in December 2008 and went up again in March 2009 to 55%.*
>
> *[However], a dramatic drop in the percentage of occupants in both venues was very apparent in June 2009, but managed to gain back in September 2009. The occupancy rate in caravan parks lowered to 53% but increased by 2% after three months. [As for] the hotels, the rate of occupants significantly dropped to 48% in June 2009, and was able to come up with 7% increase after three months had passed.*

Note: Brackets [ ] show the connecting expressions.

Analysis: The response to this task in terms of coherence and cohesion is only reasonable. Cohesive expressions are used appropriately (Obviously/On the other hand/As for…) but there is insufficient signalling of the report's parts. For example, there is no final paragraph starting with a connector such as 'Overall' or 'In conclusion'. The expression 'however' is used in English more often as a link between sentences and is not so commonly used as a paragraph starting device. There are no clear topic sentences (meaning the first sentence of a paragraph that is used to establish what the paragraph will talk about) within the two larger paragraphs. The paragraph structure of the report lacks clarity for these reasons. There is very little use of referencing (such as 'This trend…,', 'it', 'this') as an aid to cohesion and as a means of avoiding over-repetition.

<u>Impression score for Coherence and Cohesion</u>: Possibly **5** or **6**.

Analysing Lexical Resource

> The graph compares the **proportion (#1)** of occupancy rates in caravan parks and hotels from June 2008 to September 2009.
>
> Obviously, it was observed that there was a **constant (#2) elevation (#3)** in the percentage of occupancy rates in hotel rooms, from 40% in June 2008 reaching nearly 50% in March 2009. On the other hand, occupancy rates in caravan parks show a slightly different trend. There was a gradual increase of 2% in June to September 2008, reaching 56% occupancy rate, but, decreased **shortly (#4)** by 1% in December 2008 and went up again in March 2009 to 55%.
>
> However, a **dramatic (#5)** drop in the percentage of occupants in both venues was very apparent in June 2009, but **managed (#6)** to **gain back (#7)** in September 2009. The occupancy rate in caravan parks **lowered (#8)** to 53% but increased by 2% after three months. As for the hotels, the rate of occupants significantly dropped to 48% in June 2009, and was able **to come up (#9)** 7% increase after three months had **passed (#10)**.

Note: '**#**' **(+ number)** is used to mark each vocabulary item that seems faulty or inappropriate.

Analysis: The response communicates effectively but the use of vocabulary indicates lack of precise understanding of when and how to use certain forms, with the result that inappropriate choices are sometimes made. Occasionally a lack of grammatical knowledge is exposed at the same time as poor word selection. There is also a slightly repetitive quality which tends to indicate lack of lexical flexibility.

<u>Impression score for Lexical Resource</u>: **6** would probably be awarded for this criterion.

Corrections

#	Explanation of problem	More appropriate forms
1	The graph is not comparing proportions but percentage occupancy.	'occupancy levels' 'rates of occupancy as percentages'
2	'constant' suggests an unceasing quality rather than steady movement or change.	'marked'; 'noticeable'; 'gradual'

Writing Task 1 Rated Sample

#	Explanation of problem	More appropriate forms
3	'elevation' is not commonly used in his way, and is more appropriately used in contexts such as reporting blood pressure, or building.	'increase'; 'rise'
4	'shortly' is generally used in conversation as a time expression, as in, 'I'll be back shortly' (meaning, 'soon', 'after a short time'), or as in 'shortly afterwards' (often when discussing past time). However, it seems more likely that the writer was probably trying to say that the decrease was small or insignificant.	'decreased slightly…' 'decreased a little'
5	The rise in percentage terms is not dramatic (certainly not for caravan occupancy), so this expression is too strong.	'noticeable'; 'marked'; 'significant'
6, 7	'managed' generally suggests human involvement (as in 'I managed' or 'the company managed'); 'gain back' is not a common expression ('win back' is used more). In this instance the grammar is also faulty so a different approach is needed in terms of lexis.	'this reduction was in large part reversed' 'this drop in occupancy was largely regained'
8	The expression 'lowered' is a verb form (past tense of 'to lower') and is transitive, so usually 'someone lowers something'. Not used in this sense with preposition 'to'.	'fell back down to' 'decreased to' 'slid down to'
9	The choice of vocabulary seems to be associated here with a confusion between 'come' and 'go'.	'went up by 7% after three months…' ' to claw back 7%' 'increased again by 7% 'managed to increase by 7%' 'to recover an additional 7%'
10	'passed' is more commonly used in accounts of events through time, or in stories in which the passage of time is charted to structure the narrative.	'after a further three months' 'after another three months had elapsed' 'by the end of the period surveyed'

Analysing Grammatical Range and Accuracy

> *The graph compares the proportion of occupancy rates in caravan parks and hotels from June 2008 to September 2009.*
>
> *Obviously **it was observed(#1)** that there was a constant elevation in the percentage of occupancy rates in hotel rooms, from 40% in June 2008 reaching nearly 50% in March 2009. On the other hand, occupancy rates in caravan parks show a slightly different trend. There was a gradual increase of 2% **in June (#2)** to September 2008, **reaching 56% occupancy rate(#3)**, but, **decreased (#4)** shortly by 1% in December 2008 **and (#5)** went up again in March 2009 to 55%.*
>
> *However, a dramatic drop in the percentage of occupants in both venues was very apparent in June 2009, **but managed to (#6)** gain back in September 2009. The occupancy rate in caravan parks lowered to 53% but increased by 2% after three months. As for **the hotels (#7)**, the **rate of occupants (#8)** significantly dropped to 48% in June 2009, **and (#9)** was able to come up 7% increase **after three months (#10)** had passed.*

Note: '#' (+ number) is used to mark parts of the answer that contain grammatical problems.

Analysis: The use of grammar is this response shows reasonable range and reasonable accuracy but there are probably insufficient sentences overall without error to warrant a higher rating.

<u>**Impression score for Grammatical Range and Accuracy:**</u> Possibly **6**.

Corrections

#	Explanation of problem	Correct form
1	When talking about graphs <u>before</u> talking about the past time frame of the data, present tense forms are used (as in 'The graphs shows…').	'it can be observed…'
2	When discussing a period between two dates the prepositions 'from….to' are used.	'from'

Writing Task 1 Rated Sample

#	Explanation of problem	Correct form
3	'rate' is a count noun and needs an article	'reaching an occupancy rate of 56%' 'reaching a 56% occupancy rate'
4	The verb 'decreased' has no subject or subject-replacing referencing word (such as 'this') and is therefore grammatically incomplete	'but this decreased by 1% shortly after' 'but there was a 1% decrease in this level soon after…'
5	The information before 'and' contrasts with the information after 'and' so a contrastive conjunction is needed, or a contrastive linking expression	'but it went up'; '…; however, it went up…'
6	The verb 'managed' needs a subject to be grammatically complete and clear	'the rate managed to recover…'.
7	'the hotels' suggests there are a definite number of hotels under discussion; however it is hotel occupancy that is the core topic, or the hotel industry as a whole, not specific hotels.	'the hotel sector' 'hotel occupancy'
8	'occupants' are those who occupy (usually people), so the wrong word form has been selected here.	'occupancy rate' 'rate of occupancy'
9	See #5 above – same error	
10	Although it is not a conventional grammatical mistake, by omitting an expression like 'the final' the time reference is left unclear and unspecific.	'after **the final** three months had elapsed'

Impression-based <u>Overall</u> Score for the Sample Report: 5.5 or 6.0

Improving the report to achieve an IELTS 7

The same report now at around a 7 level might look something like this. Read it carefully and compare it with the original:

The graph compares occupancy rates in caravan parks and hotels from June 2008 to September 2009. Overall, occupancy rates for caravans were higher and the rates for both forms of accommodation showed some difference.

In terms of hotel sector, it is observed that there was an increase in percentage occupancy, from 40% in June 2008 to nearly 50% in March 2009. On the other hand, occupancy rates in caravan parks show a slightly different trend. There was a gradual increase of 2% from June to September 2008, to 56% but shortly, in December 2008, the rate decreased by 1%, but went up again in March 2009 to 55%.

Later, a noticeable drop in the percentage of occupants in both venues was very apparent in June 2009, but the rate recovered in September 2009. The occupancy rate in caravan parks lowered to 53% but increased by 2% after three months. As for the hotels, the rate of occupants significantly dropped to 48% in June 2009, but was able to come up 7% after three months had passed.

To summarise, there is different occupancy for both hotels and caravan parks.

Writing Task 1 Rated Sample

Improving the report to achieve an IELTS 8

To turn the level 7 report into a level 8 would basically require further improvement in accuracy of grammar, better flagging of paragraph topics, more assured expression of data, and a slightly wider range of appropriate, higher level vocabulary.

So the same report now at around an 8 level might look something like this.
Once again, read it carefully and compare it with the original:

> *The graph compares occupancy rates in caravan parks and hotels from June 2008 to September 2009. Overall, occupancy rates for caravans were higher and the rates for both forms of accommodation showed some fluctuation across that time period.*
>
> *Comparing occupancy levels in the two types of accommodation, it can be seen that there was an increase in percentage occupancy of hotel rooms, from 40% in June 2008 to nearly 50% in March 2009. On the other hand, equivalent rates in caravan parks show a slightly different trend. There was gradual increase of 2% from June to September 2008, to 56% but shortly after that, in December 2008, the rate decreased by 1%, only to go up again in March 2009 to 55%.*
>
> *In the latter part of the period surveyed, a noticeable drop in the percentage of occupants in both venues was very apparent in June 2009, but the rate recovered in September 2009. The occupancy rate in caravan parks dropped to 53% but increased by 2% after three months. As for the hotels, the rate of occupants significantly dropped to 48% in June 2009, but recovered by 7% after the final three months had elapsed.*
>
> *To summarise, there is fluctuating, seasonal occupancy for both hotels and caravan parks.*

 Note: please remember that these re-written reports are only samples of those levels for guidance, not official scores. Neither are they models of task responses at those levels.

WRITING TASK 2 – RATED SAMPLE

Task 2 is also marked using band descriptors in four categories: **Task Response, Coherence and Cohesion, Lexical Resource, and Grammatical Range and Accuracy.** You can find the publicly available performance descriptors on the official IELTS website: www.ielts.org. As you may have noticed, the first band descriptor category is different from that used in task 1: task 1s are rated for **Task Achievement**, whereas task 2s are rated for **Task Response**. This is because in task 2 you are required to present a well-developed point of view in answer to the question with relevant, fully extended and well-supported ideas.

This sample essay has been analysed to help you understand what score it might be awarded in each category and some reasons why.

Task Question

Some say you should always marry for love; others say that in an uncertain world it is wiser to marry for money. Discuss both points of view and give your own opinion.

Give reasons for your answer and include any relevant examples from your own knowledge or experience.

Write at least 250 words.

Analysing Task Response

> *Nowadays, money is one of the most significant materials in our lives. To many people, it is appropriate to marry for money rather than love. However, I believe that both love and money should be bounce together in any marriages.*
>
> *Certainly, money is an important part in our lives. It is hard for any persons to accept a partner which does not have money or at least a job to take care of future family. Hence, said "marry for money" also has its right in some extent.*
>
> *However, love should be the root of any marriages. Firstly, it is because love is such a glue to connect two persons which have their own lives, become one. So, they can share each other's the sadness, happiness to overcome any difficulties in daily lives. Moreover, love makes people growing up because they do not only have responsibility to themselves, but also to their partners as well. That is why marrying with love is always encouraged.*
>
> *In my opinion, I think that both love and money is both necessary. Marriage relying on money would be rapidly disintegrated when unfortunately the money is run out. In contrary, marriage relying on love would sometimes come to end when they could not earn money to carry out family, such as paying bills, buying food, etc. Therefore, love and money should stand together in marriage even though their contribution could be unbalanced.*
>
> *As we have seen, marriage without either money or love would come to an unhappy ending. So I believe that they both have their own contribution to a merry family.*

Analysis: This essay follows the task requirements quite well. Both points of view are discussed (in paragraphs 2 and 3) and the writer's personal opinion is offered (in the introduction, paragraph 4 and the conclusion). The opinion is clear. The paragraph on money is not very well developed and not entirely clear.

Impression score for Task Response: The essay seems to be good enough for a **7** level.

Analysing Coherence and Cohesion

[Nowadays], money is one of the most significant materials in our lives. To many people, it is appropriate to marry for money rather than love. *[However]*, I believe that both love and money should be bounce together in any marriages.

[Certainly], money is an important part in our lives **(TS)**. It is hard for any persons to accept a partner *[which*]* does not have money or at least a job to take care of future family. *[Hence]*, said "marry for money" also has its right in some extent.

[However,] love should be the root of any marriages **(TS)**. *[Firstly]*, it is because love is such a glue to connect two persons which have their own lives, become one **(NC)**. *[So]*, they can share each other's the sadness, happiness to overcome any difficulties in daily lives. *[Moreover]*, love makes people growing up because they do not only have responsibility to themselves, but also to their partners as well. *[That is why]* marrying with love is always encouraged.

[In my opinion], I think that both love and money is both necessary **(TS)**. Marriage relying on money would be rapidly disintegrated *[when]* unfortunately the money is run out. *[In contrary*]*, marriage relying on love would sometimes come to end *[when]* they could not earn money to carry out family **(NC)**, such as paying bills, buying food, etc. *[Therefore]*, love and money should stand together in marriage *[even though]* their contribution could be unbalanced **(NC)**.

[As we have seen], marriage without either money or love would come to an unhappy ending. *[So]* I believe that they both have their own contribution to a merry family.

Note: Brackets [ ] show the connecting expressions, **(TS)** denotes topic sentences, **(NC)** denotes sentences where ideas are not clear.

Analysis: Most linking expressions are appropriate but two are not (See asterisk *). Coherence is concerned with the effectiveness of what the essay is trying to communicate. The essay is well structured – each paragraph announces its topic clearly (TS) and the introduction announces the opinion of the writer. Sometimes the ideas are not entirely clear inside the paragraphs (see NC). Also the writer has a tendency to be repetitive.

Impression score for Coherence and Cohesion: Possibly 7.

Analysing Lexical Resource

> *Nowadays, money is one of the most significant materials in our lives. To many people, it is appropriate to marry for money rather than love. However, I believe that both love and money should be* **bounce (#1)** *together in any marriages.*
>
> *Certainly, money* **is (#2)** *an important part in our lives. It is hard for any persons to accept a partner which does not have money or at least a job to take care of future family. Hence,* **said (#3)** *"marry for money" also has its right in some extent.*
>
> *However, love should be the* **root (#4)** *of any marriages. Firstly, it is because love is such a* **glue to connect (#5)** *two persons which have their own lives, become one. So, they can share each other's the sadness, happiness to overcome any difficulties in daily lives. Moreover, love makes people growing up because they do not only have responsibility to themselves, but also to their partners as well. That is why marrying with love is always* **encouraged (#6)**.
>
> *In my opinion, I think that both love and money is both necessary. Marriage relying on money would be rapidly disintegrated when unfortunately the money is run out. In contrary, marriage relying on love would sometimes come to end when they could not earn money to carry out family, such as paying bills, buying food, etc. Therefore, love and money should* **stand together (#7)** *in marriage even though their* **contribution could be unbalanced (#8)**.
>
> *As we have seen, marriage without either money or love would come to an unhappy* **ending (#9)**. *So I believe that they both have their own contribution to a* **merry (#10)** *family.*

 Note: '#' **(+ number)** is used to mark each vocabulary item that seems faulty or inappropriate.

Analysis: The use of vocabulary seems quite reasonable but attempts to use a wider range are not always successful (see corrections #1–10 on the next page). Probably not quite good enough for a 7.

Impression score for Lexical Resource: Possibly **6** or **6.5**.

Corrections

#	Explanation of problem	More appropriate forms
1	'bounce' is usually used with 'ball' as in 'bounce a ball'	'love and money should **combine together** in any marriage' 'love and money **should both be present** in any marriage' *It's possible, too, that the writer meant to write* '**bound together**', *which is also fine.*
2	'the expression 'part' is usually preceded by its 'word friend' 'play' as in 'play a part'	'money plays an important part in our lives'
3	'said' is a verb in the past tense and cannot be used without a subject word, so a better lexical option is needed	'Hence the saying, "Marry for money"…' *(Or, alternatively, changing the grammar):* 'Hence it is sometimes said, "Marry for money"…'
4	'root' is often used to talk about 'cause' as in 'root cause of'… but not just about marriage	'love should **be the basis** of any marriage' 'love should **form the foundation** of every marriage' 'love should **underpin** every marriage' 'every marriage should be **built on** love'
5	'glue' sounds rather unusual here and doesn't normally go with 'connect'	'love **cements** the relationship between two people' ' love is a kind of glue that **bonds** two people' '…love **bonds** two people' '…love is the bond that **holds** two people together'
6	'encouraged' seems incomplete *(encouraged by whom?)* and may not be what the writer is trying to mean	'That is why marrying for love is always an **advantage**' 'For these reasons, marrying for love **should always be encouraged**'

#	Explanation of problem	More appropriate forms
7	'stand together' makes sense but is not a standard usage	'For the above reasons, love and money **should co-exist** within marriage' 'For these reasons, love and money **should both be present** in a marriage' 'For these reasons, a marriage needs a **felicitous blend** of love and money'
8	'unbalanced' here is ambiguous and could mean 'mentally unstable'; the overall meaning could be made more precise	'…even though their relative contribution to it could be **uneven**' '…even though they **may not each contribute evenly** to it'
9	'ending' is used usually to describe the conclusion to stories, films or plays	'…would come to an unhappy end'
10	'merry' is not usually used as a description of a family; most often used with 'Christmas' as in 'Merry Christmas'	'…their own contribution to a **happy** family' '…their own contribution to a **well-balanced** family' '…their own contribution to a **successful** family';

Writing Task 2 Rated Sample

Analysing Grammatical Range and Accuracy

*Nowadays, money is one of the most significant materials in our lives. To many people, it is appropriate to marry for money rather than love. However, I believe that both love and money should be bounce together **in any marriages (#1)**.*

*Certainly, money is an important part in our lives. It is hard for **any persons (#2)** to accept a **partner which (#3)** does not have money or at least a job to take care **of future family (#4)**. Hence, **said "marry for money" (#5)** also **has its right in (#6)** some extent.*

*However, love should be the root of **any marriages (#7)**. Firstly, **it (#8)** is because love **is such a glue to connect (#9)** two persons **which (#10)** have their own lives, **become one (#11)**. So, they can share each other's **the (#12) sadness, happiness (#13)** to overcome any difficulties **in daily lives (#14)**. Moreover, love makes people **growing up (#15)** because they do **not only have (#16)** responsibility to themselves, but also to their partners as well. That is why **marrying with love (#17)** is always encouraged.*

*In my opinion, I think that both **love and money is (#18)** both necessary. Marriage relying on money would **be rapidly disintegrated (#19)** when unfortunately **the money is run out (#20)**. **In contrary (#21)**, marriage relying on love would sometimes **come to end (#22)** when they could not earn **money to carry out family (#23)**, such as paying bills, buying food, etc. Therefore, love and money should stand together in marriage even though their contribution could be unbalanced.*

*As we have seen, marriage without either money or love would come to an unhappy ending. So I believe that they **both have their own contribution (#24)** to a merry family.*

Note: '#' (+ number) is used to mark parts of the answer that contain grammatical problems.

Analysis: Although the essay is quite easy to follow, it has too many grammatical errors in too many sentences to merit a 7 score (see corrections #1-24 on the next page). The range of grammatical constructions used seems quite good.

Impression score for Grammatical Range and Accuracy: Possibly **6** or **6.5**.

Writing Task 2 Rated Sample

Corrections

#	Explanation of problem	Correct form
1	'any' takes a singular noun	'any marriage'
2	'any' takes a singular noun	'any person'
3	'which' is used to refer to things (not a person)	'partner **who** does not have money'
4	'future family' needs further specification to establish whose family it is	'take care of **their** future family' 'take care of **their** family in the future'
5, 6	After a subject noun phrase ('the saying, 'marry for money') the verb should be 'is + right' and the preposition should be 'to' because 'right' means 'correct' (adjective) here, not 'a right' (noun)	'the saying, 'marry for money', **is** also **right** to some extent'
7	The writer repeats this same error frequently and should try to use alternative forms to reduce mistakes	'any marriage' 'all marriages' 'every marriage'
8, 9	'it' is not the most appropriate backward reference word here, when adding an explanation, and neither is 'such'	'**This** is because love is a glue connecting two persons…'
10	'which' is not used when the preceding noun is a person;	'This is because love is a glue uniting two persons **who** have their own lives…'
11	'become one' no longer fits with the whole sentence and needs to be replaced by a more suitable vocabulary word 'uniting'	'This is because love is a glue **uniting** two persons who hitherto have had their own, independent lives…' *(makes the sense more precise)*

#	Explanation of problem	Correct form
12	'the' is not needed here	'…share each other's sadness **and** happiness to overcome any difficulties in **their** daily lives'
13	the comma between 'sadness, happiness' is not correct as there are only two items listed; conjunction 'and' is required	
14	a word needs to be inserted before 'daily…' to complete the sense *(whose lives?)*	
15	'makes' takes bare infinitive form 'grow up'	'love makes people **grow up** because they have responsibility **not only to themselves** but also to their partners'
16	'not only' could be positioned better	
17	preposition 'with' is not correct here	'marrying for love…'
18	'love and money' is plural; 'both' is repeated unnecessarily	'both love and money are necessary' or, 'love and money are both necessary'
19	The passive form is not normally used with 'disintegrated'	'Marriage relying on money would **rapidly disintegrate**'
		'Marriage relying solely on money would **rapidly disintegrate**' *(completes the sense more precisely)*
20	Use of hypothetical 'would' in the preceding part of the sentence ('would disintegrate') means that the verb form in this later clause requires a 'simple past' verb form	'when unfortunately the money ran out'

#	Explanation of problem	Correct form
21	'In contrary' isn't used as a linking expression – this form is a confusion of two other forms: 'In contrast to…' and 'On the contrary…' In any case the writer doesn't need a discourse marker of contrast here.	'**Similarly**, marriage relying on love would sometimes come to **an** end' *(This sentence parallels the writer's previous one, it is not in contrast to it)*
22	'to end' requires an article	'Similarly, a marriage relying on love alone would rapidly disintegrate' *(marriage is being used in a countable sense; 'alone' completes the sense using an alternative form to 'solely', used above in #19)*
23	'money' needs to be given more precision; 'carry out family' is not complete *(family what?)*; use of 'etc' is not to be encouraged in formal writing as it seems lazy	'enough money to carry out **family duties** such as paying bills or buying food.'
24	'have' is not used to form the expression 'have a contribution' unless the words 'to make' are added as in, '…have a contribution to make'; otherwise 'make' is used	'…they both make their own contribution…' '…they both have their own contribution to make…'

Impression-based <u>Overall</u> Score for the Sample Essay: 6.0 or 6.5

Improving the essay to achieve an IELTS 7

The same essay now at around a 7 level might look something like this.
Read it carefully and compare it with the original:

Nowadays, money is one of the most significant materials in our lives. To many people, it is appropriate to marry for money rather than love. However, I believe that both love and money should be combined in any marriage.

Certainly, money plays an important part in our lives. It is hard for any persons to accept a partner who does not have money or at least a job to take care of their future family. Hence, it is said, "marry for money" is right in some extent.

However, love should be the root of any marriage. Firstly, it is because love is such a strong bond between two persons who have their own lives, and become one. So, they can share each other's sadness, happiness to overcome any difficulties in their daily lives. Moreover, love makes people grow up because they do not only have responsibility to themselves, but also to their partners as well. That is why marrying for love is always encouraged.

In my opinion, I think that love and money are both necessary. A marriage relying on money would rapidly disintegrate when unfortunately the money ran out. In contrary, a marriage relying on love would sometimes come to end when they could not earn money to carry out family duties such as paying bills, buying food, etc. Therefore, love and money should stand together in marriage even though their contribution could be unbalanced.

As we have seen, marriage without either money or love would come to an unhappy end. So I believe that they both make their own contribution to a merry family.

Improving the essay to achieve an IELTS 8

To turn the level 7 essay into a level 8 would require further improvement in range and accuracy of grammar, greater clarity and better connection of ideas, and a wider range of appropriate, higher level vocabulary.

So the same essay now at around an 8 level might look something like this.
Once again, read it carefully and compare it with the original:

> *Nowadays, money is one of the most significant elements in our lives. So, for many people, it may seem appropriate to marry for money rather than love. Certainly, money plays an important part in our lives. It is challenging for any persons to accept a partner who does not have money, or at least a job to take care of their future family. Hence, the expression, "marry for money" seems appropriate, in some extent, at least. However, I believe that marriage should involve a combination of both love and money.*
>
> *Clearly, love should be the foundation of any marriage. This is because firstly, love is such a strong bond between two persons, who have their own lives, yet become one. They can share each other's sadness or happiness in order to overcome any difficulties in daily lives. Moreover, love fosters maturity because each member of a couple no longer has responsibility only for themselves, but also for their partner. These are just two, key reasons why marrying for love should always be encouraged.*
>
> *In my opinion, love and money are equally necessary. A marriage relying solely on money might rapidly disintegrate in the unfortunate event of the money running out. Similarly, a marriage relying on love alone might sometimes come to an end if the couple could not earn enough money to manage their family's obligations such as paying bills, or buying food. Therefore, love and money should stand together in marriage, even though their contribution might often be somewhat unequal.*
>
> *To summarise, marriage without either money or love could come to an unfortunate end. For that reason, I would claim that they both make their own, vital contribution to the creation of a merry family.*

 Note: please remember that these re-written essays are only samples of those levels for guidance, not official scores. Neither are they models of task responses at those levels.

IELTS WRITING DOCTOR

IELTS GRAMMAR — WRITING TASK 1

Task 1 answer — Introduction paragraph

> Grammar can sometimes make you feel a bit sick, right? But, it's so important in IELTS. In Academic Task 1, often the problem is in choosing suitable language that allows you to describe statistical data in a formal yet clear and easy-to-understand way.
>
> This first section shows some of the different ways to start your Task 1. Why not take a look! You might even feel better afterwards!

Starting your Task 1 answer

Getting off to a confident start is important. Remember, too, that wherever possible you need to avoid copying all the words from the task prompt! Check out these possible starts:

The graph **shows…/presents data on…/compares…**
The table **shows…**
The bar graph **shows…**
The map is a diagram **representing…/which represents…**
The flow chart **shows…/illustrates the process involved in**…
The process diagram **shows…**
The bar chart **compares…/presents a comparison between…**

Overview sentences

An 'overview' is a sentence indicating the most dominant overall feature of the statistics or information presented—it can be written as an additional sentence in your introductory paragraph, or possibly as part of your summary at the end.
For examples of complete overviews refer to Fitness Activities section, Page 99.

Possible starts to an overview sentence:

Generally, the graph/information shows that…
It is clear from the graph/statistics that…
In broad terms, the chart indicates that…
The main trend/pattern displayed indicates that…
It is clear from the graph/table/map/flow chart/bar chart that…
The dominant trend represented indicates that…

Task 1 answer — Body and Conclusion paragraphs

> To write a good Academic Task 1 answer you need to know quite a few things: how to compare and contrast data, which tenses to use, how to describe a process, how to link the events or time periods you are describing, how to vary sentences, how to create a formal tone, and how to avoid sounding repetitive or boring!
>
> Here are some suggestions that will help you write an Academic Task 1 in a way that will impress your assessor:

Comparing/Contrasting two different pieces of information

In Task 1 it is almost impossible to avoid making comparisons or contrasts between different pieces of information. You need to be able to control the language of comparison and contrast, and to vary it. Look at a few examples below:

Compared with women, men drink 10% **more** coffee.
In comparison with the USA, per capita coffee consumption is **lower** in New Zealand.
Coffee drinking is increasing among younger age groups. **Similarly**, older age groups are showing a growth in coffee consumption.
In contrast to younger age groups, middle-aged coffee drinkers consume most coffee before noon.
Men drink coffee mainly in the morning; women, **however**, consume more in the evening.
While men drink their coffee mainly in the morning, women consume more in the evening.
Whereas men drink their coffee mainly in the morning, women consume more in the evening.
Men drink their coffee mainly in the morning; women, **on the other hand**, consume more in the evening.

Comparing the level or rate of increase or decrease

Coffee consumption increased **more/less noticeably/rapidly/significantly** in the 1990s.
The percentage of coffee drinkers was **greater/larger in** the USA **than in** the UK.
The speed of the increase in coffee consumption **was greater between** 1970 and 1980 **than between** 1990 and 2000.
The increase was **greater for** the higher income group **than for** the lower income group.

Using tenses properly

Being careful with verb tenses is crucial in IELTS report writing. You need constant awareness of the sense of time because it can change during a report, as these examples show:

Describing the present

Tense/Verb Form	Example of use
Present	The table **shows** the consumption of coffee from 1970 to 2010
Present continuous	Currently/At present coffee consumption **is rising** in all the countries in the table
Present perfect	So, overall, consumption of coffee **has increased** since the 1970s
Passive	Next, the milk **is transported** from the farms to the processing plant

Describing the past

Tense/Verb Form	Example of use
Past	In 1990 the consumption of coffee **reached** its highest point. Between 1990 and 2010 coffee consumption **rose** by 10%. In January, coffee consumption **declined** but it **recovered** in February.
Past Perfect	By the following year coffee consumption **had jumped** by 15%, and by 2000 **had reached** 60% among the younger age group.
Passive	Coffee **was consumed by** 25% of 18-30 year old males.

Describing the future (predicting)

Tense/Verb Form	Example of use
Future	In 2050 coffee drinkers **will increase** by…
Modals	Coffee consumption **may decline.** The number of coffee drinkers **might decrease.** The number of coffee drinkers **could fall.** *(Modals are used to express future probability/possibility)*
Other verb forms	In the next decade coffee consumption **is likely to/unlikely to** increase/**will probably increase/decline** The number of coffee drinkers **is expected** to increase by 20% by 2040.

Here is a sample paragraph showing an accurate and appropriate combination of some of these tenses:

> The table **shows** coffee consumption from 1970 to the present. In 1970 consumption **stood** at 30%. After that it **rose** sharply and **has now reached** 45%. In the next 5 years it **is likely to** increase by about 5% but after that it **could fall**. More coffee **was consumed** in 2010 than in any other year.

Developing commentary on time-based data

Sometimes the task asks you to report on changes across a sequence of time markers. You need to be able to use the time indicators accurately in order to link the sequence together. Take a look at this paragraph showing a progressive commentary on data from the earliest point in time to the most recent:

> **In 1979** the level of coffee consumption was 30%. **One year later/By the following year/A year later**… it had risen to 35%. **During the next ten years** it increased steadily. **After another decade**, it had reached 45%. **By 2000** it had risen to 50%. **Between 2001 and 2005** it grew by a further 5%. **In the next ten years/By** 2020 it is expected to rise to 60%.

Building a process description

In Task 1 questions that ask you to describe how something is made or some other process, you need to link sentences together using simpler 'step' markers.

> **First of all,** you take/**The first stage/step involves** taking the toothpaste out of the cabinet. **Then** you unscrew the cap of the toothpaste. **Next,** you squeeze the toothpaste on to the toothbrush. **After that,** the brush is placed in the mouth and moved in a circular movement across all the teeth and gums. **Once** the teeth have been cleaned, the mouth is rinsed with water. **Following that** the toothbrush is also rinsed. **The penultimate stage** involves replacing the toothbrush in its holder. **Finally** the teeth are checked in a mirror.

Sentences to express ranking of countries, information or age groups

If you are given a list which is ranked from first to last, you may need to report on this ranking. These types of expression are useful in this case:

The most noticeable trend…, **the most important** factor…
The second most…/The next most… noticeable feature…
The least significant statistic/trend/change/figure/country…
The country **with the most/least/highest/lowest** (percentage/number of…/level of…/) was…

Now, have a look at a paragraph showing how to rank a list of countries:

> France **was** the country **with the lowest** percentage of unemployed men/**the lowest level of/least** unemployment. **Following** France **was** Germany with 7%/Germany **came next** with 7%. **Next came** Sweden with 9% and then Turkey with 10%. The (country) **with the highest** unemployment **was** Spain with 12%.

Ways of avoiding repetition

Repetition shows that you lack the language resources to write in a more varied and flexible way. It can hold down your IELTS score. You can avoid repetition from sentence to sentence using little pronouns or other expressions. At the same time this increases the flow and economy of words.

Examples: This is…
            It is…
            This (+ noun)…
            Such (+noun)…
            The same pattern is evident/can be observed/emerges
            A similar pattern/trend/increase/decrease
            The same group
            This group/pattern/trend/increase/decline/figure/percentage

Now take a look at these two, sample paragraphs, one showing a repetitive style and then a better one showing how to use some of these referencing expressions.

Repetitive style

Coffee consumption is rising in Australia. Coffee consumption is rising in other countries too. Coffee consumption is rising because of clever marketing of coffee.
Coffee consumption trends seem to be global. Coffee consumption is helping the coffee-producing countries. Coffee-producing countries, however, need to be treated fairly by the multinational corporations.

 Using referencing words to avoid repetition

Coffee consumption is rising in Australia. **It is** rising in other countries too. **This is** because of clever marketing of coffee. **Such trends** seem to be global. **This increase** is helping the coffee-producing countries. **Such** countries, however, need to be treated fairly by the multinational corporations.

You can also use **synonymous expressions as referencing** to avoid repetition of lengthy expressions. Look at this example about 'people staying in caravans/units':

In June '08, 50% of people stayed in caravans with 45 percent of people staying in holiday units. In August '09 **the figures were** 60% in caravans and 30% in units. By 2010, **the percentages** had jumped to 70 and 35, **respectively**.

Changing from one graph, diagram, table or category to another

It is really important to 'mark' your writing with clear expressions which tell the reader when you are moving from one part to another in the body of your report. Take a quick look at these:

Turning to…(the second/next/middle… table/graph/diagram/group/category**), it can be seen that**…

Moving to the next/other/second graph/country, it can be seen that…/it is clear that…/it is apparent that…/the situation is different/a very different picture emerges.

Final paragraph (starting a conclusion)

It is common to use the final paragraph to summarise briefly the main points of your report as a sort of final overview. Here are some useful ways of starting off:

Overall then, the table shows that coffee drinking increased in popularity between 1970 and 2010, especially for younger age groups.

To summarise,…

Summing up,…

To sum up,…

Improving Sentence Formation

> It is important that you use complex sentences in an Academic Task 1. Often a small change to your sentence structure can improve it and demonstrate to your assessor the variety of sentence patterns you are using in your writing.
>
> Here are some helpful suggestions on how to improve your sentences:

Use of 'which...' and 'who...' to extend sentence length or avoid repetition

It sometimes helps if you can combine information to extend a sentence successfully. Take a quick look at these pairs and the way the single sentence (**A+B**) avoids repetition:

A	The older age group increased coffee consumption during the first decade
B	The older age group changed its drinking habits after that
A+B	The older age group, **which** had increased coffee consumption during the first decade, changed its drinking habits after that.
A	These age groups increased their coffee drinking in the period 1990-2000.
B	The (same) age groups increased coffee consumption between 2000 and 2010.
A+B	The age groups* **which** increased their coffee drinking in the period 1990-2000 also increased consumption between 2000 and 2010. (**not all age groups increased coffee drinking so no comma after 'groups'*)
A	Full-time working men drink more coffee than part-time working men.
B	Part-time working men drink less coffee than full-time working men.
A+B	Men **who** work full time drink more coffee than men with part-time jobs.

Using 'although', 'even though' and 'despite' to compare data

In Academic Task 1 good sentences are ones that enable you to report flexibly on differences you notice in statistical or visual data. The so-called 'concessives' can be helpful here and are a good alternative to the over-use of 'but'. Have a look—you probably recognise some of these sentence-connecting expressions:

A	Coffee consumption increased throughout the period shown.
B	Coffee consumption increased more rapidly in the decade, 2000-2010.
A+B	**Although/Even though/Despite the fact that** coffee consumption <u>increased</u> throughout the period shown, **it** increased more rapidly in the decade, 2000-210.
A+B	**Despite*** <u>the increase in coffee consumption</u> throughout the period shown, **the increase** was more rapid in the decade, 2000-210. * **Note** that if you use just 'Despite', it must be followed by a noun or noun phrase only, not by a verb phrase.

A	By 2008, the auto shop had disappeared to the north.
B	By 2008, a bank and restaurant had appeared to the south.
A+B	By 2008, **although/even though/despite the fact that** the auto shop had disappeared to the north, a bank and restaurant had appeared to the south.
A+B	By 2008, **despite*** the disappearance of the auto shop to the north, a bank and restaurant had appeared to the south. * **Note:** again, 'Despite' is only followed by a noun phrase, not a verb.

Advanced grammar tools

> If you are looking for a really healthy IELTS score, then it doesn't hurt to try to use some slightly more advanced language, such as 'voice' adverbs as sentence starters, and passive or '–ing' forms to create a formal report style. Read through these ideas:

Use of adverbs to add precision / clarification / commentary

Using adverbs such as the ones below is not strictly necessary in your Task 1 answer; however, occasional, well-judged use gives your report a slightly more natural 'writing voice'.

Examples: **Specifically**, the figure for men was…
Generally speaking, men drink more coffee than women.
Similarly, women drank more coffee in the morning than in the evening.
Interestingly, retired men drank more coffee than young men.
Gradually, the situation changed, with coffee consumption increasing every year of the next decade.
Actually, the figures suggest otherwise.
Comparatively fewer younger men than women eat breakfast regularly.

Using the passive to make your report less personal

Writing reports involves trying to avoid personal language. Some students like to use the word 'people' as a general start to a sentence, but the passive can help you to avoid using and repeating such 'person' words and can also put the focus of the sentence on the information, often more economically.

Compare these sentence pairs:

30% of 70-80 year olds accessed the internet daily.
The internet was accessed daily by 30% of 70-80 year olds.

According to the table, people seem to like to drink coffee mainly in the morning.
According to the table, coffee is drunk mainly in the morning.

People had built a new shopping centre by 2000.
A new shopping centre had been built by 2000.

Next, the lessee signs the contract.
Next, the contract is signed.

Using the 'fast' passive voice

Sometimes the passive form is reduced to aid flow of writing, but still remains grammatically correct. Take a look at the differences between these pairs. Note, too, that there is no difference in the meaning.

Once the contract <u>has been signed</u>, it is legally binding on both parties.
Once <u>signed</u>, the contract is legally binding on both parties.

If the table <u>is taken</u> as a whole, it shows an increasing preference for caravans.
<u>Taken</u> as a whole, the table shows an increasing preference for caravans.

Coffee consumption increased across all age groups during the period <u>which is covered</u> by the graph.
Coffee consumption increased across all age groups during the period <u>covered</u> by the graph.

'-ing' forms

Use of –ing forms aids variety and also reduces personalisation in writing reports. It also changes the focus of the sentence somewhat by putting attention more on the activity. Have a little look at these:

In 2000 more <u>people</u> <u>liked to stay</u> in caravans than in tents.
<u>Staying</u> in caravans was more popular than camping in tents in 2000.

<u>People</u> in the younger age groups <u>like to drink</u> coffee at any time of day.
<u>Drinking</u> coffee is popular with younger age groups at any time of day.

As the next important step in the process, <u>the couple go to view</u> suitable houses.
<u>Viewing</u> suitable houses is the next important step in the process.

Use of 'It'/'There' sentences to make your writing more formal

Sentences beginning with 'It' or 'There' may help to make your style of writing more formal and less personal. This helps the overall tone to sound appropriate to a report. Read one or two examples:

There was an occupancy rate of 50% for caravans and 45% for holiday units in June 08. This rate increased to 60% for caravans, but decreased to 30% for units in Aug. 09

It can be seen that occupancy rates were generally higher in caravans than in units
In June 08 for example 50% were accommodated in caravans, rising to 60% in Aug 09. In units, on the other hand, the occupancy rates for the same dates were only 45% and 30% respectively.

There was an increase in coffee consumption across all age groups during the period covered by the graph.

It is the younger age group which consumes most during the next ten-year period.

Having a late night IELTS prep. session? Yes?

Well, now that you have read so many sentences about coffee drinking in this section, I'm prescribing a REAL cup of coffee for you right now! Only a small one, though!

IELTS GRAMMAR — WRITING TASK 2

Writing Task 2 places different kinds of demand on your language skills. It involves careful understanding of what the task prompt requires, and then an ability to develop and justify your own point of view, using ideas and examples based on your own knowledge of social issues. The importance of accurate and appropriate grammar needs to be respected, especially as Task 2 carries more weight than Task 1. Let's have a little look at how to use grammar more effectively. Are you ready?

Essay Type 1 — Indicate and Support Your Level of Agreement

In a Type 1 essay task you are required to agree, partly agree or disagree with a stated point of view.

> **Sample task**
>
> *"Parents are totally responsible for the bad behaviour of their children.*
> *Do you **agree**?/Do you **agree** or **disagree**?/To what extent do you **agree**?"*

Language for introducing your essay (Introduction paragraph)

Usually an essay starts with a general statement linked to the IELTS Task 2 topic. Then the introduction usually proceeds with a statement of intention, telling the reader what your essay is going to do and/or what your general point of view is. Future tense form 'will…' is often used in this part of the essay.

After writing your general statement related to the task topic, you could express your intentions for this type of essay using language such as shown in these examples:

Examples

- This essay **will suggest/argue that** … is …
- Although/Even though … is …, **it will be argued** here that …
  This essay **will express full agreement** with this view **and will offer** reasons for this position.
- This essay **will agree in part** with this view, and **will offer reasons** for this position
- This essay **will express complete disagreement** with this view and **will justify** this viewpoint.
- I totally agree that…/I largely agree that…/I partly agree that…/I totally disagree that…

> **Here is a sample Introduction:**
>
> *Parenting is a complex and challenging role in the busy, modern world and it seems to be the case that some children are behaving less thoughtfully. There are those who believe that the responsibility lies fully with parents. This essay will agree in part with this view.*

Improving grammar in the early sentences of body paragraphs

In a Type 1 essay your body paragraphs will probably involve firstly a shorter paragraph explaining reasons for holding the point of view which is opposite to your own (either agreeing or disagreeing), then a longer paragraph justifying the other side (your own view)

Using 'There is/there are'

- **There is** a range of/**There are** various agencies other than parents which **share** some responsibility for a child's behaviour…
- **There are** various ways in which parents should shoulder the greatest responsibility for the way their children behave.

  Or, more simply,

- Various other social agencies **share** responsibility for the way children behave.

Starting body paragraphs with extended topic sentences
(using 'Even though…', 'Although…', '…who…', '…that…')

Using subordinate clauses helps to create longer, more detailed sentences.

Example

Although it can probably be agreed that other agencies have some role in shaping children's behaviour, **it must be** parents **who** carry the most responsibility.

Replacing simple connectors when developing paragraph ideas/examples

It's really tempting to use simple connectors like **'Firstly/Secondly/Thirdly/Finally'** especially when you are under time pressure but usually this merely indicates a list rather than a commentary. Look at some alternative options for connecting different essay points:

Alternative options   Parents clearly **have/carry** the primary **responsibility** for the way their children **behave. It seems undeniable that** they are the child's first teachers, and… **Linked to this is the fact that** parents are crucial to the development of identity and personality. … **What is more** … **Overall then** …

Finishing off your essay

A short conclusion helps to round off your essay, but sometimes the final paragraph in a Type 1 Essay is used to express your personal opinion.

Starting off the conclusion appropriately

These are the usual ways of beginning/signalling your concluding paragraph:

In conclusion, …/**Summing up,** …/**To conclude,** …/**To summarise,** …/**All in all,** …

Using tenses appropriately in the conclusion

See how a conclusion might continue for Essay Type 1 using **Simple Present**:

Summing up, from a personal perspective it **seems** *reasonable to suggest that parents* **are** *largely rather than totally responsible for their children's behaviour because ...*

Or you might prefer **It + Present Perfect Passive + clause with Simple Present**:

Summing up, **it has been argued** *in this essay* **that** *parents* **are** *largely, rather than totally responsible for their children's behaviour because ...*

 For more tips on how to add fluency to your writing, give examples, form complex sentences and much more, go to:
'Grammar suggestions for all IELTS Task 2 essay types' on page 213.

Essay Type 2 — Present a two-sided Discussion

In a Type 2 essay task you are required to discuss 2 sides of an argument or 2 points of view, and explain which one you personally agree (or partly agree) with, and why.

> **Sample task**
>
> *Some people think that parents are responsible for their children's bad behaviour; others say that schools are responsible.*
>
> ***Discuss*** *both views and give your own opinion.*

Language for introducing your essay (Introduction paragraph)

You would probably first write a general statement linked to task topic, then express your intentions for this type of essay by using language like the following:

Use of basic 'will' form
This short essay **will explore** both perspectives and then offer a personal viewpoint.

Use of passive form
Both perspectives **will be explored** and then a personal view **will be offered**.

Use of '-ing' forms
After exploring/discussing both viewpoints, this essay **will suggest/argue that**…
Having explored both viewpoints, …

Noun form + 'will' future
After an exploration/discussion of both viewpoints, this essay **will offer** the view that…

> Here is a sample Introduction:
>
> *The relative influence of home and school on a child's behaviour changes with time. These days everyone seems to be busy. After an exploration of the respective responsibilities of both agencies this essay will offer the view that…*

Improving grammar in the early sentences of body paragraphs

In a Type 2 essay, you will recall, your body paragraphs are expected to discuss two different viewpoints and then, in a final paragraph, give your own opinion.

Using present tense forms to start body paragraphs

Parents clearly **have/carry** the primary **responsibility** for the way their children **behave** (* **for a number of reasons…**).
Note: if you add * '**for a** <u>number</u> **of reasons**' then you would normally continue by using connecting signal expressions like, '**First of all …/Another reason why … is that…/Finally…**'
at the beginning of each sentence which is offering a new reason.

Starting body paragraphs with extended topic sentences
(using 'Even though...', 'Although...', '...who...', '...that...')

Using subordinate clauses helps to create longer, more detailed sentences.

Examples

- **Although it seems reasonable to suggest that** schools are responsible for their pupils, parents are the prime agent of socialisation.
- **Even though parents have the primary responsibility, schools probably share** at least some responsibility for behaviour.

Replacing simple connectors when developing paragraph ideas/examples

It's really tempting to use simple connectors like '**Firstly/Secondly/Thirdly/Finally**' especially when you are under time pressure but usually this merely indicates a list rather than a commentary. Look at some alternative options for connecting different essay points:

Alternative options

Schools also **have/carry** a key responsibility for the way children behave. **It seems incontrovertible that** they have many years of contact with each child. ...**Allied to this is the fact that** schools set and impose their own rules of behaviour for pupils at school... **Furthermore**... **To sum up**,...

Finishing off your essay

In Essay Type 2 the final paragraph can be used to offer your own opinion on the topic, so it may be developed differently.

Starting off the conclusion appropriately

These are the usual ways of beginning/signalling your concluding paragraph:

In conclusion, .../**Summing up**, .../**To conclude**, .../**To summarise**, .../**All in all**, ...

Using tenses appropriately in the conclusion: Present Perfect Passive

Look at this example of the use of an 'it + present perfect passive' sentence, followed by the personal opinion with a present tense form:

Example

*To conclude, **it has been shown/suggested/argued** that both parents and school seem to share responsibility for shaping the behaviour of children. **My own opinion/view/perspective is that... Personally, I believe/think that** responsibility for behaviour can never be in the hands of parents only, except, perhaps, in the very early years of life. It is only during those early years that the parents are the sole agents of socialisation patterns. At this time, they lay the vital foundations for the child's future, successful adaptation into the wider society.*

For more tips on how to add fluency to your writing, give examples, form complex sentences and much more, go to:
'Grammar suggestions for all IELTS Task 2 essay types' on page 213.

Essay Type 3 — Discuss Advantages & Disadvantages

In a Type 3 essay task you are required to discuss the advantages and disadvantages of a given situation or a viewpoint.

> **Sample task**
>
> *It is widely believed that a child who behaves badly should be punished. What are the **advantages** and **disadvantages** of punishing a child?*

Language for introducing your essay (Introduction paragraph)

You would probably first write a general statement linked to the task topic, then express your intentions for this type of essay by using language like the following:

Example

- This response **will explore** the relative advantages and disadvantages of …
- This essay **will compare** the advantages and disadvantages of …

    Or, a passive

- Both pros and cons of …**will be discussed** in this short essay.

> **Here is a sample Introduction:**
>
> *No child is perfect, but the long process of socialisation enables parents and other agencies to shape children's behaviour so that they can fit into their culture and society effectively. This essay will explore the relative pros and cons of punishing…*

Improving grammar in the early sentences of body paragraphs

In a Type 3 essay your two body paragraphs will probably examine the pros, and then the cons of the situation described in the task prompt.

Use of complex sentences with 'that…'

There are several advantages of punishing a child's inappropriate behaviour. One clear benefit **is that** … Another advantage **lies in the fact that**…

Starting body paragraphs with extended topic sentences (using 'Even though…', 'Although…', 'who…', 'that…')

Using subordinate clauses helps to create longer, more detailed sentences.

Example

Although many parents would advocate the judicious use of appropriate punishment, there are some parents who believe that all punishment brings negative consequences for a child's healthy development.

Replacing simple connectors when developing paragraph ideas/examples

It's really tempting to use simple connectors like **'Firstly/Secondly/Thirdly/Finally'** especially when you are under time pressure but usually this merely indicates a list rather than a commentary. Look at some **alternative options** for connecting different essay points:

Alternative options

A variety of advantages can be put forward for punishing a child's poor behaviour. **Foremost among these** is the establishment of clear rules for right and wrong… **A further benefit** involves the building of awareness about consequences of one's actions… **Yet another advantage** comes from the reinforcement of parental authority…

Finishing off your essay

A short conclusion helps to round off your essay, summarising what was previously said without too much repetition.

Starting off the conclusion appropriately

These are the usual ways of beginning/signalling your concluding paragraph:

In conclusion, …/Summing up, …/To conclude, …/To summarise, …/All in all, …

Using appropriate tenses in the conclusion: present perfect

To summarise, this essay **has outlined** *a range of advantages and disadvantages of punishing children.* **It has suggested** *that punishment enables a child to acknowledge wrongdoing, and acts as a deterrent. In contrast, it* **has argued** *that punishment always risks resentment and rebellion if not administered sensitively.*

 For more tips on how to add fluency to your writing, give examples, form complex sentences and much more, go to:
'Grammar suggestions for all IELTS Task 2 essay types' on page 213.

Essay Type 4 — Explain & offer Solutions or Consequences

In a Type 4 essay task you need to explain the reasons why the situation in the task prompt has arisen, and how it can be solved, or what consequences it gives rise to.

> **Sample task**
>
> *Children's behaviour seems to be getting worse.*
> ***Why** is this happening and **what** can be done to improve it?*

Language for introducing your essay (Introduction paragraph)

You would probably first write a general statement linked to the task topic, then express your intentions for this type of essay by using language like the following:

Example

- This essay **will explain why**… and **will suggest what** can be done…/**will suggest what** X should do…?
- **After explaining why**…, this essay **will suggest what**…
- This essay **will suggest that the reason why**…is that…
- It will be argued that the best way to… is to…/… that the best solution to this problem is to…

> Here is a sample Introduction:
>
> *There seem to be more incidents involving bad behaviour at school and in society generally than was the case fifty years ago. This essay will try to explain why this is happening and suggest measures which might improve the situation.*

Improving grammar in the early sentences of body paragraphs

Use of passive

In response to 'Why' part of task:
- Various reasons **can be offered to explain** falling behaviour standards in children.
- Falling behaviour standards **can be explained** in terms of these key reasons. Firstly…

In response to 'What' part of task:
- A number of solutions **can be offered** with respect to changing children's behaviour.
- Improvements to a child's behaviour **can be achieved** in a variety of ways.

There is…/There are…

- **There are** numerous reasons/explanations **for** the deterioration in children's behaviour.
- **There is** a variety of **reasons why** children's behaviour is worsening/…**explanations for** the worsening behaviour of children.

Note: it is excellent if you can change the word forms/vocabulary given in the task wording when building your paragraphs. All of the above examples illustrate this.

Starting body paragraphs with extended topic sentences
(using 'Even though…', 'Although…', 'who…', 'that…')

Using subordinate clauses helps to create longer, more detailed sentences.

Example

There are many parents **who believe that** kindness is by far the best way to improve behaviour among children.

Replacing simple connectors when developing paragraph ideas/examples

It's really tempting to use simple connectors like '**Firstly/Secondly/Thirdly/Finally**' especially when you are under time pressure but usually this merely indicates a list rather than a commentary. Look at some alternative options for connecting different essay points:

Alternative options

There are various courses of action that can be taken to improve behaviour among children. **First and foremost,** children need to be taught firm boundaries of what is or isn't acceptable. **Another, important factor** concerns/involves/is… **Also of some significance** is… **All in all then**…

Finishing off your essay

A short conclusion helps to round off your essay, summarising what you have said without too much repetition.

Starting off the conclusion appropriately

These are the usual ways of beginning/signalling your concluding paragraph:

In conclusion, …/**Summing up**, …/**To conclude**, …/**To summarise**, …/**All in all**, …

Using tenses appropriately in the conclusion

For Essay Type 4, the present continuous/progressive can work well if the topic is a **current** issue. When summarising the second part of the task a tense change is needed to mirror the task wording.

Example

- To summarise, children's behaviour **is worsening** largely because…
- In order to improve the situation, parenting skills **need to/should** become a compulsory school subject because…

Or, with a passive

- To improve the situation, better parenting skills **are required/are needed**.

 For more tips on how to add fluency to your writing, give examples, form complex sentences and much more, go to:
'Grammar suggestions for all IELTS Task 2 essay types' on page 213.

Grammar suggestions for all IELTS Task 2 essay types

The advice below may help with any of the four essay types.

Using 'reduced' clauses

This is a device for making your writing a little more fluent. Look at one or two examples and note that passive forms and '–ing' forms work best. The words in brackets are left out of the sentence but the grammar is still considered correct.

- **Parents** *(who are)* **looking after** more than one child often have to be more careful to treat each child similarly.
- **Children** *(who are)* **cared for** in families which are unstable, are more likely to develop poor behaviour.
- **Grandparents, if** *(they are)* **used** wisely, can be good models of appropriate behaviour.
- **The children** *(who were)* **given** sugary drinks were found to behave worse than other children.

Note: clauses are not usually reduced when the verb is in the present simple tense, the future tense, or the present/past perfect.

Referencing

In Task 2, referencing skills (meaning the use of little words to replace or 'refer back to' words used in previous sentences) are another effective way of maintaining fluency and economy, while avoiding repetition. Compare these two texts:

 Text 1 - without referencing

Parents are responsible for their children's bad behaviour. Bad behaviour is learned, not genetically transmitted. Bad behaviour has negative, social consequences. The negative, social consequences often lead to a child feeling isolated or too 'different' from peers. Feeling isolated from peers may reduce the desire to fit in even more. Feeling isolated may reduce desire to 'fit in', and even worse behaviour may occur.

 Text 2 - with referencing

Parents are responsible for their children's bad behaviour. **Such** behaviour is learned not genetically transmitted. **It** has negative, social consequences. **These** often lead to a child feeling isolated or too 'different' from peers. Feelings **like these** may further reduce the desire to 'fit in', **which** may lead to even worse behaviour.

Giving examples

It is a good idea to offer examples to illustrate your ideas/points/opinions; however, it's not a good idea to introduce every example repetitively, using 'For example' every time.

IELTS Grammar Writing Task 2

Read this range of options:

- Parents mould their children's behaviour by the way they conduct their own lives. **For instance**, parents who argue regularly may find that their child both imitates them and sees arguing as a successful life strategy.
- Parents shape their children's behaviour unconsciously, too. **For example**, a parent who never hugs a child, may unconsciously be communicating to the child that physical affection is not important.
- A young child can develop poor behaviour if parents fail to set and apply clear boundaries in areas **such as** bed times, eating times, and times for getting up in the morning.
- **Examples of** poor parenting might include failure to make clear to children the difference between right and wrong, and failure to model good behaviour.
- **One example of** poor parenting might involve punishing a child without explaining the reason for the punishment or without any consistency.
- Poor parenting **is easily exemplified in** the practice of inconsistent punishment.

Using modal forms to communicate a cautious viewpoint

Modals like **'may'**, **'might'**, **'could'** are really helpful in preventing your own viewpoint from seeming over-confident, or even unreasonable. But, if you have a strongly-held opinion, writing directly is sometimes more honest.

Look at these:
- Parents **may well be** the most important shapers of a child's behaviour.
- Children **might behave** better if **there were** real consequences for poor behaviour.
- Schools **could teach** parenting skills as part of the core curriculum.

Now, compare with these:
- Parents **are** the most important shapers of a child's behaviour.
- Children **behave** better if there **are** real consequences for poor behaviour.
- Schools **must teach** parenting skills as part of the core curriculum.

Developing your ideas using other subordinate clause types

When time permits it helps your grammar score if you can use a variety of complex sentence forms appropriately and accurately to express, when, for example:

Giving Reasons

Children need good parenting **because/as/since** they too may be parents eventually.

Expressing Result

- Parents should teach their children good behaviour consistently **such that** they become responsible and caring adults.
- Good parenting is considered **so** important in some countries **that** it is now taught in schools.
- **As a result of** poor parenting, children often lack awareness of what is appropriate.

Expressing Purpose

- Children need to behave well **so that** they can learn how to fit into social groups.
- Parents need to learn parenting skills **in order to** raise standards of behaviour.

Expressing contrast

- Well-behaved children fit into society, **whereas/while** poorly-behaved children always struggle to be accepted.
- Well-behaved children fit into society; poorly behaved children, **however,** rarely do.
- Well-behaved children fit into society; **however**, poorly behaved children rarely do.
- Well-behaved children fit into society; poorly-behaved children, **on the other hand/in contrast,** rarely do.

Expressing degrees of similarity

- **Just as** well-behaved children need love, it is even **more likely that** poorly-behaved children also need to feel loved.
- All mothers need support; **equally,** all fathers need to feel supported in their role.
- Being a good parent is **as** vital **as** being a good son or daughter.
- Being a good parent is **(much/somewhat/considerably/a little) more** vital **than** being a good son or daughter.
- Having a polite child is **(much/somewhat/considerably/a little) less** important **than** a successful child.
- Being rich is **not (at all/quite/nearly) as** important **as** being a good parent.

Using 'if' clauses

'if' clauses can be useful when you need to state the conditions under which something might improve.

Read these:

- **If schools teach** parenting skills as an obligatory part of their curriculum then bad behaviour amongst children **will gradually decrease.**
- **If parents are taught** the most important principles of child rearing, then the behaviour of their sons and daughter **will obviously improve.**
- **If parents were forced** legally to guarantee financially the good behaviour of their children, then obviously careful parenting **would increase.**

Using 'unless' constructions

'Unless' is similar in meaning to 'If not' but useful for expressing the wish to avoid a negative situation in the future. Take a little look at this **example:**

Example

Unless children **are** shown good models of behaviour, it may well be that standards **will deteriorate** even further.

Using 'whether' constructions

'Whether' or **'whether or not'** are very useful especially in the introduction or conclusion of an essay which asks you to discuss two points of view.

Look at the examples below:

- It is undeniably difficult to assess **whether** parents **or** schools are more responsible for the bad behaviour of children.
- **Whether or not** children's behaviour is getting worse is in itself probably debatable, but this essay will assume it to be so.
- **Whether** parents **or** schools should be held responsible for bad behaviour in children is an issue that relies very much on cultural context.

Developing your essay's ideas in other ways

As you develop your ideas and viewpoints, you may want to connect sentences using other expressions in order to signal what the sentences are doing. This shows variety and flexibility. Perhaps you want to…

…add something

- Parents could **also** apply their rules consistently.
- **In addition/Additionally/In addition to that/Moreover/Furthermore/What is more,** they could give their children real punishments for disobedience.

…express levels of probability

- **Without** better parenting, behaviour levels are bound **to/almost certain to/very likely to/likely to/quite likely to/perhaps likely to** deteriorate further.
- **Without** better parenting, **there is every likelihood/a major possibility/some likelihood/a small possibility that** behaviour levels will deteriorate further.
- **With** better parenting **there is little likelihood/no possibility/absolutely no likelihood that** behaviour levels will deteriorate further.

…express doubt and uncertainty

- **It seems unclear whether or not** behaviour will improve in the next decade.
- **It is doubtful that** behaviour will improve in the next decade.
- **There is uncertainty** about whether behaviour will improve in the future.
- **It is difficult to determine whether** bad behaviour is increasing in schools.
- **A lack of certainty surrounds** predictions of future behaviour.

Using adverbs as emphasis or as indicators of attitude

Adverbs (when used sparingly) are a really helpful way both of adding a sense of your own attitudes to ideas, and of adding emphasis. Compare these:

Without an '–ly' adverb

Parenting is one of the most important tasks you'll ever have in your life.

With an '–ly' adverb

- **Obviously/Surely/Clearly/Actually/Certainly** parenting is one of the most important tasks you'll ever have in your life.
- Parenting is **arguably/possibly/unquestionably/probably/definitely/indubitably/undeniably** one of the most important tasks you'll ever have in your life.

This was a really detailed section, wasn't it?

Time for a break! Do something relaxing now, and then tomorrow practice a Task 2 essay. As you practice more essays, try, little by little, to add some of the grammatical features here that fit each Task type. But, use the grammar to develop your own style of writing; don't imitate the samples in this book too closely.

You WILL get better at writing, but please be patient. It's better not to have unrealistic expectations or you might end up being 'a patient'!

IELTS GRAMMAR — ARTICLES: INDEFINITE ('A'/'AN') AND DEFINITE ('THE')

In English the expression '**articles**' means either '**a**', '**an**', or '**the**'. Is that a deep sigh I can hear? If your first language doesn't have these little words, you will be finding them really tricky to learn. You have my full sympathy!

Articles are used in English to identify something or someone that can be counted (countable). A person or thing being talked about generally is usually considered **indefinite**; if being talked about in a more detailed or particular way then is usually considered **definite**.

Basic differences

'a' versus 'an'

Article	is used	for example
a	before nouns beginning with a consonant or consonant sound	a car, a number, a date, a hotel *(more natural than 'an hotel')*, a one-dollar coin *(consonant sound 'w')*
an	before a word beginning with a vowel sound	an export, an MP3 player, an economic problem an hour

'a' / 'an' versus 'the'

Article	is used	for example
a/an	to identify a thing or person that can be counted (e.g. **1,2,3 apples**) but is not a particular (*i.e. is an 'indefinite'*) one	I want **an apple** *(any apple, or not a particular apple)*
the	with things that can usually be counted **but** to identify the object or person as a particular one *(a defined or 'definite' one)*	I want **the apple** in the fruit bowl. *(There's one fruit bowl, and it only has one particular, definite apple in it)* I want **the green apple** *(There's only one green apple (so it is a particular one); the other apples may be red)*

When to use 'a' / 'an'

1. If you want to mention a particular person or thing without detailed identification.

Examples: They live in **a new apartment.** *(I mention a simple, general fact for the first time)*
He gave me **a watch**. *(I'm less interested in the make, more in the gift itself)*
She married **an Ethiopian** *(I don't know his name, only where he's from)*

2. If you want to talk in a general way about a member of a professional or other group.

Examples: **A teacher** must be patient *(meaning all teachers/any teacher)*
A cow is more useful to humanity than **a dog** is. *(as a general rule, I believe this)*
She's **an actress** *(she's a member of that profession; it's her job)*

3. Numbers.

'a' is used with 'round' numbers or with duration of time – such as 'a thousand', 'a hundred', 'an hour'.

Note: when the number is more complex 'one' is often preferred:

Examples: Three thousand one hundred *(not 'three thousand and a hundred')*.
One thousand, six hundred and two *(not 'a thousand six hundred and two')*.

4. To specify things even if you don't normally count them.

Something you don't usually count is called 'uncountable'. For example, words like 'cream', 'heat', 'consumption', 'globalisation' are uncountable *(we don't say 'two consumptions' or 'two heats')*. Most uncountable words don't usually need articles.

Examples: I like cream in my coffee; Heat is necessary in order to boil water;
Globalisation has increased international interaction

But... if the same expressions are **described in more detail**, 'a' or 'an' is sometimes used.

Example: The heater gives off **a heat** <u>which is very dry</u>.

IELTS Writing Doctor Articles

'the' is usually necessary...

1. When two people both know the specific item or person they are talking about.

Examples: Did you remember **the sunscreen**? *(the one usually in the bathroom at home)*
Could you pass **the water**? *(the water jug is on the table at which they are sitting)*

2. When something has been previously mentioned (and thus is defined).

Examples: He has **a brother in Spain** and another in Thailand. **The brother in Spain** is a flamenco guitarist.
There was **an increase** in 2012, but **the increase** that year was very small.

3. When there is only one.

If you write about something that is unique, use 'the'.

Examples: The earth, the moon, the world

Note: with countries 'the' is **not** normally used even though they are unique, unless they are **made up of letters**.

Examples: I love Japan and Korea (*not* the Japan and the Korea)
I love **the UAE**, more than **the USA**.

4. When information is added that makes something more defined.

Examples: **The beauty** of a summer's day in Paris is unsurpassed.
(the non-count noun 'beauty' is described more definitely and so attracts 'the')
The group with incomes below $50,000...
The economic problems of 21st century America are complex.

Even short expressions with 'of' require 'the', as in:
the number of passengers, **the length** of stay

5. When talking about the familiar, natural environment in which you live, and weather.

Examples: **The sea** is rough today.
I can hear **the wind**.
We live near **the mountains**.
The countryside is festooned with wild flowers at the moment.
The weather seems to be unusual for this time of year.

6. With most..., least..., ...–est.

When you use a superlative form, use 'the' before it.

Examples: **The largest** room has three windows.
Older people seem to have **the least free time** on average.
The most significant change in our shopping centre has been...

7. When talking about the peoples of particular nations or particular groups of people.

Examples: **The French** are often more outspoken than **the Finns**.
              The blind receive more support than either **the deaf or the elderly**.

8. To identify a plural thing that is particular (defined).

Examples: She was supposed to deliver **the strawberries** this morning
              (the particular strawberries ordered for delivery)
              Those are not **the prices** we were given on the phone
              (the prices that were previously specified)

Note: If you talk **generally about plural things** 'the' is not necessary.

Examples: **Strawberries** are good for you. *(all strawberries)*
              Prices are going up *(prices of many things in general)*.

IELTS Writing Doctor Articles

DON'T use articles

1. After fixed expressions, often with prepositions.

Examples: I first met him **at university**
He's **at work** every day until 5pm
I travel **by train** every day.
I **left home** when I was 20

2. After 'both' or 'all'.

Examples: Both kinds (*not* usually *'both the kinds'*)
All three groups (*not* usually *'all the three groups'*)

3. With possessive expressions.

Examples: John's coat (*not* *'the John's coat'*)
Spain's economy (*not* *'the Spain's economy'*)

4. With street names, towns, cities, states, lakes, famous town or city buildings.

Examples: Oxford Street, Wall Street
Bristol, Paris, British Columbia
Lake Titicaca
Cambridge University, Sydney Airport, London Zoo
Westminster Cathedral

Note: art galleries take 'The' as in **The** National Gallery, **The** Louvre.

Typical examples of 'a' / 'the' in Academic Task 1 answers

In task 1 Academic answers use of articles is important. Overall 'the' is used far more than 'a' basically because statistical information is usually particular and defined.

1. Usually 'the' is used to announce the type of data displayed.

Example: **The** graph/chart/table/map/flow diagram/diagram shows...

2. When describing age groups, 'the' is generally used.

Examples: **the** over 75s, **the** upper income **group**, **the** 25-34 **group**, **the** four younger **groups**

3. When describing time periods shown in the data, 'the' is usually used.

Examples: across/during/over/throughout **the** ten-year **period**, ...**the** three **years**,
...**the** whole **period**, between **the years*** 2000 and 2010, ...but **the months** June and October were different...

* Note: articles are <u>not</u> used when discussing years or months only.

Examples: Between 2000 and 2010, In 2010..., June and October were different...

4. When making a second mention of something, 'the' is generally used.

Examples: The table presents <u>information/data/statistics</u> on…
            The <u>information/ data/statistics</u> shows/show that…
            Once a house has been chosen <u>an offer</u> is made. If <u>**the** offer</u> is rejected…

5. When paraphrasing time periods to avoid repetition, 'the' is often used.

Examples: In 2012… **The same year**…during **the same** 12-month **period**…
            In May the figure increased… Also, in **the same month**…
            Between 2000 and 2010…During **the same period**…During **the same decade**…During **the same, ten-year period**…

6. Other time markers also use 'the' because they refer to specific data shown visually.

Examples: **The** following/preceding year… **The** following/preceding period…
            The year after that/before that…
            At the end of the period shown/**at the beginning** of the period shown…
            During **the middle of** the overall period…, for **the remainder** of that period…

Note: 'One year later/A year later the pattern had changed' *('the' is not used)*

7. When using compass direction words to orient the reader to a map or diagram, 'the' is usually used.

Examples: In **the southern part** of the town… , **to the north** it is clear that…
            Changes were different **between the east and the west**.

8. After the introductory expression 'There is/was…' the indefinite article 'a' is often used.

Examples: In 2010, <u>there was</u> **a** dramatic increase in…
            <u>There was</u> only **a** slight change during the next, three-year period.
            <u>There was</u> **a** levelling off for the remainder of that decade.

9. For noun groups or nouns involving non-count elements, usually articles are <u>not</u> used.

Examples: **Consumption** increased steadily throughout that period…
            Coffee consumption remained steady…
            Spending on computers…
            Household expenditure was unchanged across the decade…

But, note these differences:

            The level of coffee consumption increased…
            The rate of spending on computers went down…
            The proportion of household expenditure allocated to food…

IELTS Writing Doctor Articles

10. When describing processes, sometimes 'a' is preferred but 'the' is also sometimes acceptable.

Examples: Next the chocolate passes to **a/(the)** grinder where it is...
             After that the chocolate is transported to **a/(the)** warehouse where it is stored...
             Once **a house** has been chosen **an offer** is made and **a deposit** needs to be paid to the vendor.

11. Before adding the detail which makes a description more particular, 'a' is often used.

Example: Internet access rates show **a** slightly different pattern *(Then the writer goes on to describe the pattern).*

12. Expressing numbers, proportions or percentages.

Note these differences in the use of articles:

98 per cent
The percentage increase was 98.

The number of people fined for speeding in 2012 was 1500. *(The information is defined)*
A number of changes can be seen in the pattern of expenditure. For example.... *(The information is not yet defined)*

The proportion of time taken to read to children increased by 10% *(The information is defined)*
A small proportion of the older age groups did not participate *(The information is insufficiently defined so 'a' is used)*

Do you now know your 'a' from your 'the' now?
The only acceptable answer is **a** cautious 'yes', **an** affirmative.
The IELTS test will be **a** chance to show what you have learnt!

IELTS GRAMMAR – PREPOSITIONS

Prepositions in English are a real nightmare, aren't they?!

Whether you are writing an IELTS Task 1 letter or a Task 2 essay, you need to be as careful as you can with prepositions.

Prepositions and time expressions

'At' — for times and night/dawn
At 5.30pm/at midnight/at noon/at night/at dawn

'Between' — for years
Between 2010 and 2012, for the years **between** 1990 and 2010, the statistics were…

'By' — for months/years/seasons/most parts of the day
By 2012/By September/2012 *(when writing about a series of months/years)*

'In' — for months/years/seasons/most parts of the day
In April/In 2012/In Spring/In the evening/…morning/…afternoon

'On' — for days/dates
On Monday/on the 6th

Prepositions (and one or two adverbs) for STRETCHES of time

She has been in France **since** 1999. *(She went there in 1999 and has not returned)*
I'm going on holiday to Florence **for** three weeks. *(I will spend three weeks in Florence)*
The exhibition lasted **from** September **to** December. *(It began in September and ended in December)*
The construction program lasted **from** summer **until** spring. *(It started in summer and ended in spring)*
I fell asleep **during** the performance. *(I was asleep for some part of the performance)*
He has to pay the fine **within** a month. *(No longer than a month)*

'A kaleidoscope' of prepositions with the word 'time'

I was **in time** for my interview.
At that time I was unemployed.
I always try to be **on time** for appointments.
Pain heals **with time/over time**.
From time to time/At times I get bored with my job.
I'll keep working **for the time being/for a long time**.
By the time you read this, I'll be in Istanbul.

Prepositions and statistics

The figure for men was very different, **with** 50% not eating breakfast
40 **to** 50% of the 25-30 age group didn't eat breakfast **on** working days
Up to 50% **of** men and close **to** 40% of women ate breakfast regularly
rose **to** 50%/fell **to** 30%/decreased **from** 45% **to** 40%

Prepositions and groups/categories

The figure **for** men/**for** France/**for** older age groups/**for** consumption of coffee …
Consumption **in** Spain was very different, **with** 50%...
With the older age group.../**In terms of** the older age group, the data were different
The rate **of**/the growth **of**/an increase **in the percentage of**/a decrease **in the level of** coffee drinking among the middle-aged group continued **in** the next, ten-year period.
Men **with** part-time jobs ; countries **with** high incomes; cities **with** increasing populations
A slow down **in** the growth **of** coffee consumption occurred **in** 2012

Prepositions of location

Most shops are located **on** the east side…
…is located **in** the northern part of the town/shopping centre…
to the north **of** the cinema, there is…
in the centre **of** the town the market is situated…

Prepositions that are followed by "–ing" expressions

About
I'm **excited about** start**ing** my new job.
They're **pleased about** mov**ing** to a new house.
She's **sad about** leav**ing** her family.

At
I was **disappointed at** fail**ing** the driving test again.
I'm afraid I'm **not very good at** keep**ing** my own accounts.
He's **useless at** cook**ing** Italian food.
She's really **good at** mak**ing** speeches.

By
He paid for it **by** work**ing** every night for 3 months.
By concentrating on prepar**ing** for the test, I improved my score.
I think it was **by** liv**ing** cheaply that I was able to stay overseas for so long.

For
Thank you for lett**ing** me stay.
He's **responsible for** arrang**ing** the accommodation.

In
I'm **interested in** buy**ing** your car.

Of
I don't like **the idea of** travell**ing** by plane.
I'm **fed up of** argu**ing** with you.
I'm **tired of** go**ing** to the same restaurant.
He's **frightened of** los**ing** his job.

On
They always **insist on** giv**ing** us meat to eat.
She's so **keen on** mov**ing** to New Zealand.

To
I **look forward to** hear**ing** from you soon.

Preposition sandwiches

There are many useful expressions for letter writing which have a preposition at both ends!

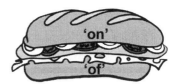

She's **in trouble with** her boss.
She's **in fear of** losing her job.
He knows she's **on good terms with** her colleagues.
He wants her to be **in charge of** the redundancy program.
She's **at odds with** her colleagues on this issue.
But she's **in tune with** management on the need for greater efficiency.
I joined the company's social club **in the hope of** making new friends.
The manager was **at pains to** remind me of the poor salary.
But later he said I was **in line for** promotion.
Because of the low salary, I was **on the verge of** leaving.
But **for the sake of** my colleagues, I stayed.
Also I was **in love with** one of my co-workers.
Later, I got **in touch with** an old friend, whom I had always been **in awe of** because of his great ambition.
Out of respect for this friend I sent my resume.
He wrote back saying: **In answer to/With respect to/With reference to/With regard to** your letter and **by virtue of/on account of** our friendship, and **for reasons of** expediency I want you to work for me. You'll soon get **on top of** things here and become **up to date with** our processes, even though right now, you may feel a bit **out of touch with** the new technology. Welcome aboard.

Two colloquial examples: That dress is **to die for**.
I'm pretty much **in synch with** the way they do things.

Common verb forms + prepositions

Preposition	Examples of use
On	
To stand on	You should learn to **stand on** your own two feet.
To rely on	We **rely on** my wife's income.
To spend on	I **spend** very little **on** luxuries.
To	
To listen to	It's better if you **listen to** instructions carefully.
To complain to	I **complained to** the police.
To attend to	I'll **attend to** your problem in a moment.

Preposition	Examples of use
In	
To live in	Many people **live in** poverty.
To settle in	It didn't take long to **settle in** to our new house.
To send in	Please **send in** your resume.
With	
To play with	I often **play with** my mobile phone applications.
To help with	She **helps with** the cooking at the retirement home.
To assist with	The government **assists with** relocation costs.
By	
To stand by	I'll **stand by** the entrance and wait for you there.
To travel by	We always **travel by** train.
To get by	Although we are not well paid, we manage to **get by**.
For	
To ask for	I'm going to **ask for** a pay rise.
To look for	I've been **looking for** my passport everywhere.
To come for	I've **come for** the money you owe me.
About	
To talk about	We must **talk about** this new problem.
To hear about	I **heard about** your accident.
To worry about	I'm **worried about** my health.
To know about	I **know about** your situation.
At	
To laugh at	It's too easy to **laugh at** other people.
To stare at	It's not polite to **stare at** others.
To glare at	When I overtook him in my new car, he **glared at** me.
From	
To suffer from	This country **suffers from** too much unemployment.
To hear from	I haven't **heard from** my brother for ages.
To leave from	The train **leaves from** the main station.
Of	
To remind of	This town **reminds** me **of** home.
To think of	I'll be **thinking of** you when I'm on the cruise/What do you **think of** the new iPad? (*Note:* the second example means 'What is your opinion of…'?)

Prepositions for ways of getting around

By plane/by car/by train/by bicycle/by taxi/by boat/by camel/on foot/on horseback

Some useful adjectives + prepositions

Expression	Example of use
angry with	I'm not **angry with** you, but I am annoyed.
annoyed about/at	I'm **annoyed about** the damage to my computer.
aware of	You may not be **aware of** the problem.
blind to	I'm certainly not **blind to** your abilities as a manager.
comfortable with	I'm not **comfortable with** the way they treat their customers.
concerned about	I'm **concerned about** your behaviour.
confident in	We are **confident in** your ability to give us sound financial advice.
crazy about	I'm **crazy about** Russian folk music *(informal)*.
curious about/to	I'm **curious about** the origin of your name/I'm **curious to** know more about it.
dependent on	I'm still **dependent on** my parents for financial support.
hungry for	I'm **hungry for** new experiences.
interested in	I'm **interested in** doing a PhD at Harvard.
keen on	I'm **keen on** travelling to Antarctica to study the penguins.
mad about	I'm **mad about** tennis *(informal)*.
nice to	She's seldom **nice to** her little brother.
pleased with	I'm **pleased with** the new dress I bought.
polite to	He's always **polite to** the customers.
rude to	It's not a good idea to be **rude to** your work colleagues.
satisfied with	Overall, they were **satisfied with** my progress.
sorry about/for	We are **sorry about** the delay you experienced/I feel **sorry for** his wife.
surprised at	I'm **surprised at** your attitude.
tired of	I'm **tired of** your constant complaints.
wrong with	There's something **wrong with** my computer.

Prepositions and passive forms

The most common preposition with passive forms is 'by'.

Examples: I **was taught** the piano **by my mother**.
This novel **was written by Steinbeck**.

But there are **other examples:** I don't like being **laughed at**.
He was **operated on** last night.
This bed looks **slept in**.
The movie star was tired of being **looked at**.

Other common uses of prepositions

What's **on TV**?
He is **under age**, and can't watch this movie, I'm afraid.
I feel a bit **under the weather**, so I'd like to postpone our meeting until next week.
I was **under the impression** that you had gone overseas.
She didn't break the plate **on purpose**.
On balance, I'm satisfied with my job.
The photo is **on page 10**.

A few, common phrasal prepositional forms

I don't **get on with** my parents because they are always critical of my lifestyle.
I'll **look out for** you when I arrive.
She tries **to get by on** less than $300 a week.
I need **to find out about** accommodation options in Bulgaria.
I can't **go along with** your analysis of the situation, I'm afraid.

Describing objects in detail, using prepositions

It's possible you may be asked to describe an article that you lost or was damaged and so you need to use prepositions carefully.

Examples: It is a green suitcase **with** a black leather handle.
There is a grease mark **on the front of** the jacket.
On the back of the parcel is my address.
Down the side of the sofa is a large tear.
In the corner of the room **just below** the ceiling there is a damp mark.
The vase is in the entertainment unit, **right beside** the TV.
The hotel was located **right opposite/right next to** a noisy night club.

Prepositions of position

Q. Where's your ball?

A. It's... **on** the table, ...**under** the table, ...**on top of** the cupboard, ...**inside** the bag, ...**behind** the door, ...**in** the hedge, ...**next to** the tennis racket, ...**at the corner** of the street, ...**over** the road. Actually, I've lost all eight of them! Pretty careless, eh?!

Q. Where do you live?

A. I live... **opposite** the shopping centre, ...**next** to the church,...**between** the hotel **and** the park, ... **among** the trees, ...**near** the school, ...**by** the police station, ...**below** the water in a submarine, ...**beneath** the branches of that huge tree, ...**underneath** that huge umbrella. In fact, I suppose I live just about anywhere and everywhere!

Position of prepositions

Position of prepositions can sometimes affect the level of formality.

Examples: **With whom** did you go? *(more formal)*
Who did you go **with**? *(less formal)*

About which person are you **talking**? *(more formal)*
Which person are you **talking about**? *(less formal)*
It's a great place **in which to live**. *(more formal)*
It's a great place **to live in**. *(less formal)*
(**Note:** 'It's a great place to live' is also used)

Feeling better now? Oh dear, so you're still feeling sick…I see…but only sick of grammar! Oh well, never mind. Have an early night and then practice writing IELTS reports or essays using some of the grammar in my various 'Writing Doc' sections. This will make you better prepared for the IELTS writing test. Write accurately and appropriately, of course! Trust the writing doctor!

IELTS VOCABULARY — WRITING TASK 1

Hello again. Using appropriate vocabulary is an important part of writing a good IELTS answer.

Expressions like 'nice', 'big', 'got bigger', 'got worse', all of which communicate effectively in some general situations, need to be replaced when you write a formal report in English, otherwise the assessor may judge you to be very limited as a user of English. We hope that some of the expressions below will be of help to you when practising Academic Task 1 Writing. Enjoy! Or is it Endure!!??

Appropriate, formal expressions for a report

In writing a report it is important to use an appropriate level of formality. Report writing requires a formal choice of vocabulary, not everyday, conversational choices. Compare these:

Achieving Appropriate Level of Formality

A ![child] might write…	An ![adult] would write…
In the picture is…	The graph/chart/diagram shows…
was the same	levelled off, remained the same, didn't change, remained unaltered/stable
numbers	figures/statistics/data
got bigger	increased
went up	rose
at the time in the table	during the period shown
got money	earned/received an income
got worse	deteriorated, worsened
got smaller	decreased, diminished, reduced
went up fast	increased rapidly, jumped
went up a lot	increased dramatically, markedly, significantly
went up and down	fluctuated
was at its biggest	reached its high point of…, peaked at/in…
I can see that…	It can be observed that…/it is clear that…
It's a…/It'll be a good thing	This is bound to be/may well be a positive development
had	owned, bought, consumed, enjoyed
had the same…	experienced, owned the same…
went to…	visited/attended…
made	manufactured
going to/gonna	highly likely to…
got better	improved, recovered
was different	altered, changed
big	significant, major, large

A might write…	An would write…
very big	huge, extremely large, major
little	small, minor
very small	minor, barely significant, hardly noticeable, tiny
I can see that…	It can be observed that…/it is clear that….
it's a/it'll be a good thing	This is bound to be/may well be a positive development
was/were good	was/were impressive/beneficial/favourable
eat/drink	consume
things are not good	the situation is unfortunate
nearly all people	the vast majority
just a few	only a minority
is pretty much the same	virtually identical to…
is quite like	is broadly similar to…
every place	everywhere/ubiquitous
all over the place	widespread
every place in the world	worldwide/globally

Sample paragraphs contrasting some of these expressions

 Informal

In the picture is numbers of drinkers of coffee in 1970-2010. Coffee drinking went up fast at the time in the table and was at its biggest in 2010. Australia was big coffee drinking country. Situation in America was pretty much the same. I can see that in future a big increase is gonna happen. It'll be a good thing for coffee makers.

 Formal

The graph shows data for coffee consumption from 1970 to 2010. Consumption rose rapidly during the period shown, and peaked in 2010. Australia was a major consumer of coffee. The situation was virtually identical in America. It is clear that in future significant growth is highly likely, which will be a positive development for coffee manufacturers.

Avoiding other, general expressions

It is important to write precisely, especially in Task 1 so you need to avoid general expressions that may either be incorrect or lack precision. Here are some examples:

Incorrect	Use this instead
do swimming	swim/go swimming
do the making of cars	carry out the production of cars/manufacture cars
do leisure time on sport	spend their leisure time playing sport
it is big cost	it is very expensive/costly/the cost is enormous
it is more percent older age groups spend lot of income on clothes	A higher proportion of older age groups spend a considerable amount of their income on clothes.
a lot of no work time, 80%, is time spent do sport	A high proportion of available leisure time, 80%, is devoted to various sports
from table, poor money from job is cause of lack of savings	According to the table, lack of income/insufficient income is the most significant cause of inadequate savings.
a big number of 30-40 years spent over 20% of income after tax on themselves	The majority of 30-40 year olds spent over 20% of disposable income on personal items

Talking flexibly about percentages and numbers

Graphs and tables often use percentages. It helps if you can use expressions which reduce the number of times you repeat the same style, such as, 'forty per cent', or 'twenty per cent'. Take a look at some possibilities.

Figure	Alternative expressions
0%	zero per cent/none of/absolutely no one/…failed to register anything
5%	five per cent/a twentieth/only a minority/a small proportion/percentage/a very low level of…
10%	ten per cent/a tenth/only one in ten
20%	twenty per cent/a fifth/less than a quarter
25%	twenty-five per cent/a quarter/one in four
30%	thirty per cent/slightly more than a quarter/nearly a third of…
40%	forty per cent/two fifths/between a third and a half of/somewhat less than half
50%	fifty per cent/half/the whole number was evenly divided…
60%	sixty per cent/almost two thirds/more than half/the majority
70%	seventy per cent/a good majority/nearly three quarters
75%	seventy-five per cent/three quarters/a clear majority
80%	eighty per cent/four fifths/a very sizeable majority
95%	ninety-five per cent/nearly all/the vast majority/all but 5%
100%	a hundred per cent/all/the whole group/everyone in that group
1-5	a few/only a few
10	a small number
101-105	just over a hundred
12	twelve/a dozen
24	two dozen
50,000 dollars	the same amount/half that amount (25,000 dollars)
50,000 litres	fifty thousand litres/the same volume
50,000kg	fifty thousand kilos/the same weight/half that weight (25,000kg)

IELTS Vocabulary Writing Task 1

Years and months

Year/Period	Alternative expressions
1949	previous year/the year before that/the preceding year
1950 (base year)	1950/that year/the same year
1951	the following year/a year later/a year after that
1700	seventeen hundred (During the seventeen hundreds/during the 18th century)
1800	following century/the 19th century/during the eighteen hundreds
1900	1900 the century after that/the 20th century/during the nineteen hundreds
2000	a century later/this century/the 21st century
January	the previous month, the month before, the month prior
February	that month/the same month
February 1st (base)	**the beginning of February/the first day of the month**
February 2nd	the next day/the following day/a day later
February 5th	later that month/four days later/a few days after that
February 25th	towards the end of the month
February 28/29	at the end of the month/on the last day of the month
1950-60	between 1950 and 1960/that decade/the same decade/that ten-year period
1960-70	the following decade/the next decade/the decade after that

Income, Population, Volume of production

These are also popular measures for statistical displays and each requires its own appropriate expressions.

%	Income ($)	Expression to describe each group
45%	20,000	Those on the **lowest incomes** comprised 45% of the population. Those earning the **lowest incomes** made up 45% of the population The group on/those earning $20,000 occupied 45% of the population
38%	40,000	the **middle-income earners**/those earning middle-range incomes
17%	60,000 or more	the **high–income earners**/those earning high incomes/salaries

Population in 2000	City	Expression to describe each city
5 million	Sydney	the least populous city was Sydney with 5 m./the city with the smallest population was...
10 million	Mumbai	the second most populous city/the next most populous city was Mumbai with 10 million
15 million	Shanghai	the most populous city/the city with the greatest population was Shanghai

IELTS Vocabulary Writing Task 1

Production in 2000	Country	Expression to describe each country
5 billion tonnes	India	the country with the lowest volume of production was India with 5 billion tonnes
7 billion tonnes	Russia	the country with the second highest volume was Russia with…
10 billion tonnes	China	the country with the highest volume of production was China with…

Word forms

Although this is also a grammatical issue, we have decided to mention word form in our vocabulary section. It is vital for students to know the different forms of base words and select the appropriate one.

Much / many

These are popular expressions; however, you should try:
a) to use them appropriately and b) not over-use them – try to use alternatives

Not good	Better
Many jobs is too much stress	A **large number** of occupations are too stressful/cause excessive stress
Very many people surveyed like free time	**Most** of those surveyed would prefer additional/more leisure time
Too much smoking make much lung cancer	**Excessive** smoking leads to increased chances of lung cancer

Big / little

Expressions in the left column are just too easy to use and rarely impress an assessor, especially if over-used.

Not good	Better
Big amount of coffee drinkers are young people.	A **high proportion** of coffee drinkers are young people.
Biggest number of holiday makers like better stay in the holiday units.	The **majority** of holiday makers prefer to be accommodated in holiday units.
A big reason for absence from work was boring.	A **major** reason for absenteeism was boredom.
A big cause of sickness among the 40-50 year olds was diet.	An **important** cause of sickness among the 40-50 year olds was diet.
Younger age groups have only a little time for family life.	Younger age groups have only **a small amount of** time to devote to their family.
Only little number of people prefer to stay home at weekend.	Only **a minority** prefer to stay in at the weekends.
Little volume of coals produced in 1995 in Wales	Only **a low volume** of coal was produced in Wales in 1995.

Almost / Almost all

😠 Not good	🤔 Better
Almost young people drink coffee in the morning.	**The vast majority** of young people drink coffee in the morning.
Almost the 20-30 year olds prefer drive car to work.	**Almost all** of the 20-30 year olds prefer to drive their cars to work.

Paraphrasing by using synonyms to avoid repetition

It helps the quality of your writing, especially your vocabulary score, if you are able to avoid repetition by using synonyms for key expressions or categories. Please note, however, that synonyms are not usually 100% interchangeable. In other words there may be contexts where the one word doesn't quite work as a replacement. Look down this list for some helpful options.

a wide range/a broad range/a wide variety
according to the data/the figures indicate that
According to the table/graph/chart/map/diagram…/From the evidence/data in the table/graph/chart/map/diagram
age group/age range/category
amount/volume/level
annually/every year
ate/consumed
babies/infants
bought/purchased
buyers/purchasers
charge/payment
children/youngsters
clothes/garments
company/business/commercial enterprise
consisted of/comprised* (*no preposition!)/was made up of
consumers/customers
country/nation
daily/every day/per day
declined to/by/decreased to/by/fell to/by/dropped to/by
dominated/were dominant/were predominant
dramatic decline/sharp decline/major decline/steep decline
dramatic increase/sharp increase/major increase/steep increase
drank/consumed
drop/decrease/fall/decline/reduction
every two years/biennially/once every two years
fell dramatically to/by/plummeted to/by/dropped sharply to
figures/data/statistics
fluctuation/variation/uneven pattern/uneven movement
grew faster/accelerated its growth/speeded up its growth
In terms of…/with respect to…
income/salary/pay

increased/rose/went up
increasing/growing
men/males/the same* gender (*used only after an earlier sentence which has 'men/males' as subject)
monthly/every month/per month
noticeably/significantly
one hundred years/a century
passengers/travellers
peaked at…/reached a high point of…
per capita/per person/per head
produce/yield
production/output
proportion/percentage
rate/speed
recovered/regained its level/rate/position
remained steady/stayed the same/maintained its level/stabilised
shoes/footwear
slight increase/modest increase/marginal increase
spent on/devoted to/allocated to…
spent their time/used their time/occupied their time
step/stage
steps/stages
ten years/a decade/a ten-year period
the 40-50 age group/the same* age group/the same* group/the same* cohort
the cost of/price of/charge for…
The figures show/indicate/demonstrate that…
tourists/holidaymakers/holiday travellers/visitors
trend/pattern
twice-yearly/bi-annually/every six months
very slightly/marginally/minimally/barely
visited/went to/frequented
weekly/every week
went down a little/dipped
went on holiday to/holidayed to/spent their vacation in…
women/females

IELTS Vocabulary Writing Task 1

Language for Graphs and Tables

Graphs and tables are commonly used in Task 1.
These formulations/items of vocabulary will be helpful:

In 2000 the **level/number/proportion/percentage of...** stood at...
In 20005 **it increased/rose sharply/suddenly/dramatically**
By 2005 **it had increased/had risen to**...
...**fell/went down/declined/dropped/dipped by** 5%/**to** 10%
...**fell/went down marginally/significantly/markedly/sharply/dramatically**
During the decade 1990-2000 the... **gradually rose/rose slowly/started to rise.../remained stable at.../remained low/high**
...**rose/fell at the same rate/at a faster rate/at a slower rate**
The... **barely changed**...
The... **increased markedly to**...
The... **fluctuated between ... and** ...
The... **peaked during.../in** 2000
The **(level of/speed of/amount of) change in**... was **barely noticeable/minimal/modest/quite significant/marked/startling/unprecedented**
Those with...

Language for maps

When asked to write about maps you may need to compare places at two different times, or discuss locations or layouts.

Compass directions

It is useful to be able to discuss location using the compass points:

To the north/south/east/west is situated ...
To the north of the (road) there is ....
The store **is located north of** the motorway.
North of the forest is the hotel.
The picnic area lies **to the north of** the shopping centre.
The beach is located **north east/north west/south east/south west of** the caravan park.
If you drive **in a northerly direction** you will reach the castle.
Directly north of the castle is a river.

Options for exiting buildings

It is possible that you might be asked to describe the best way to exit from a building. These sentence starts could be helpful:

• Anyone who was located/working in _____ would **be advised to/should probably choose** exit... because...
• Exit ___ **is probably the best option for those** working in offices ... or ...
• If a person is working in _____ **they would be better off choosing**/making for the exit at... because...
• It would be better to make for exit _____ if located in office ___ in the event of a sudden evacuation.

IELTS Vocabulary Writing Task 1

Locations of places relative to other places

Directly opposite the bank is a hairdresser.
Diagonally opposite the café is a restaurant.
Right next to the car park is a school.
Facing the school is the police station.
Above the bank are some apartments.
Underneath the cinema is a large car park.
Some distance away is the motorway.
In the same zone/area there is a hospital.

Then and Now – comparing maps for two different times

The shop **has been replaced by** a car park.
A road **has been constructed** where the garden used to be.
The hospital **has been enlarged/further developed** to include a…
The hotel **has been modified/reduced** in size.
The old town hall **has been demolished/renovated/redesigned/relocated**.
The car park has **doubled/tripled in size**.
The park is now **half/a quarter of** its original size.
There are now **high-rise apartments/low-rise town houses/rows of town houses** in the town centre.
The **access road/road leading to the castle has been widened/made narrower/made straighter**.
More facilities **have been added**.

Language for Process Diagrams

Have a look at these sentence starts/items of vocabulary when responding to a process diagram.

The diagram illustrates/shows…
The first step in the process of… is/**involves (+ing)** the…
The process of (+ing) … **begins with**…
The next step/stage in the process **involves (+ing)** the/a…
In the stage after that, _____ _____the… is (+ passive)
Along with…/Together with… it is (+passive)
During that stage (** *if something happens within a time period*)
Next, …
After that, …
The penultimate stage/step involves (+ing)…
The final step involves/is…/**consists of…**(+ing)
To summarise…/These, then, are the steps/stages in ___(+ing) a _____

Note: (+ing) means a word ending in –ing, as in: send**ing**/sign**ing**/sell**ing**/mak**ing**
(+passive) mean passive form of the verb, as in: is **delivered**/is **sent**/is **transferred**/is **signed**/is **sold**

Language for Bar Charts

The bar chart is another typical frame for the presentation of statistical information. Expressions from above may be useful but these could also help.

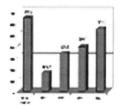

- The **data** in the chart **indic**ate that...
- **In percentage terms**, (household access to computers or internet) in 2008 was/ stood at ...%.
- The **corresponding figure** for (Spain) was...
- **Rates** of access
- **The pattern changed** in...
- ...**fell**, then **recovered**...
- The percentage of (households on annual incomes below 50,000 a year with access to computers) in 1998 **was/totalled/comprised** 34%
- Access to (computers) **among those with** (incomes below $20,000 a year) **reached a level of** ... in 2010.
- In 1998 **there were** 34% of households **with**...
- 34% of households on annual incomes below 50,000 had access to computers in 1998. **This percentage dropped marginally/rose slightly** in 1999.
- **Turning to** access to internet... **it can be seen that...**
- **Compared with those** (on higher incomes), **a much smaller/larger percentage of** the (lower income group) had access to the internet.

- **In comparison with** the (lower income group), **those on** (incomes over $50,000) **had proportionately more** than twice as much access to computers **and three times as much** access to the internet.

- **Overall**, the table **shows** that those (on higher incomes) had much greater access to both (computers and internet) **across the** three years.

I'm sure you haven't read all these sections at the same time. You have?
Hey, don't over-do it, OK?

It's probably better to use this section as a resource when you are practising writing Task 1 answers. Gradually you will find that your answers will start to read more like the samples in the earlier sections of this book. But, remember, every writer is a unique writer, so try to find and value your own particular style even if you use some of these items of vocabulary or formulaic patterns.

Good luck! Keep trying!

IELTS VOCABULARY — WRITING TASK 2

Writing Task 2 places different kinds of demand on your language skills, and involves, of course, an ability to justify your point of view by developing ideas and examples based on your own knowledge of social issues.

Varied and appropriate use of vocabulary is vital to the development, clarity and precision of your ideas, especially as your Task 2 score carries more weight than Task 1.

Let's have a little look at some options for enriching your use of vocabulary.
Are you ready?

Expressions for the Introduction paragraph

Of course, the topic of the essay will determine some of the vocabulary used in the early sentences; however, it is useful to have a range of options when stating what the essay is going to do or what view it will try to put forward.

Essay Type 1 — Indicate and Support Your Level of Agreement

(Essay topic)… is **a significant/major/an ongoing issue/growing problem/issue/a challenging dilemma in the modern world/in a globalised world/nowadays/currently/these days.**

Tackling/Addressing/Solving/Making headway with this issue is **challenging/complex** especially **given limited resources/the pressure of modern life/the speed of social change.**

Some believe/are of the opinion that…; others suggest that…/point to the fact that…/are convinced that…

This essay **will express/articulate** its **full agreement** with this view **and will offer/indicate/suggest/put forward/outline** reasons for this position/**argue/justify** this **position/stance/standpoint**.

This essay **will agree/accord in part** with …, and **will …**

This essay **will express/assert its complete disagreement** with … and …

Essay Type 2 — Present a two-sided Discussion

This essay **will discuss/explore/examine** both points of view and **then offer/present** a personal **view/viewpoint/perspective/**on this **dilemma/issue/situation**.

Both **standpoints/perspectives** will be **analysed/scrutinised** and then a **personal slant/take** on the issue will be **put forward/advanced**.

Essay Type 3 — Discuss Advantages & Disadvantages

There are **numerous/a range of/various/a plethora of/a myriad**... **pros and cons/benefits and pitfalls/positive and negative aspects** ...**with regard to/in terms of/with respect to/ regarding**... *(Essay topic)*

One **clear/definite/obvious/unequivocal/indisputable/undisputed/advantage of**...

Essay Type 4 — Explain & offer Solutions or Consequences

This essay **will explain/outline/offer/identify/nominate/highlight some key reasons why** *(Essay topic)* is ... and **will suggest/will propose** what can be done.../(someone/some organisation) should do.../**a range of measures/steps** that can be taken to improve the situation/**some options/possibilities** for **improving/changing** the situation.

...will **identify/propose/briefly highlight**... one or two/just a few... **likely/potential/probable/possible**... **consequences/knock-on effects/outcomes of**...

Finishing off your essay

Sometimes the final sentence can be used to make a final comment or to offer an interesting thought or prediction. This is a final chance to brighten up the vocabulary.

It remains to be seen whether or not.../if...
What the **future holds is a mystery,** but it may well be that...
Looking into my own crystal ball, I would predict that...
It will be **fascinating to see/intriguing to see** if...
In the short term... will probably... ; **in the long term**, the situation seems far less predictable...

Choosing topic vocabulary for the body paragraphs

One of the challenges of Task 2 is that you have no idea what the topic is going to be about. It could be on almost anything. We have tried to put together some vocabulary resources on typical topic areas.

One of the reasons why some IELTS candidates have difficulty in achieving a higher vocabulary score is that they know some individual words but can't always use them naturally, because they don't know the collocations (the other words that usually 'go with' the word they may know) that help to make the vocabulary appropriate and fluent.

You will notice that although we occasionally use single words, most of the time we offer expressions which involve collocation, or even sentences. This is both to give you some possible ideas for topic content and to help you build 'natural-sounding' vocabulary strings. We have also put many verb forms together in their infinitive form under 'T' for ease of access. Hope this works for you.

Topic vocabulary for the body paragraphs (all essay types)

A Animals :: Pets

A aggressive dogs

B being bitten by a dog

C (the) cost of keeping a pet

E exercising a dog sufficiently
exotic pets

G guard dogs
guide dogs

L losing interest in your pet

N (a) nation of dog lovers
(the) need to commit time to looking after a pet
neglecting a pet

O obedience training

P pet food
pets as companions
preferring pets to people

T taking a dog for a walk
to abandon a pet
to give a pet away
to treat a pet like a child
to underestimate the impact of pet ownership

U unusual pets

V veterinary fees

Animals :: Animal protection

A anti-ageing products

B bears

C cosmetics

E endangered species

I (the) illegal export of animals
(the) illegal trade in…

L (the) loss of natural habitat

M maintaining numbers

N national parks

P park rangers to protect animals from poachers

R rhinoceros horn

S selling rare species on the black market

T to prioritise the wellbeing of endangered species
to trade illegally in exotic species

U (the) use of animal parts in traditional medicine

W (the) World Wildlife Fund

Animals :: Zoos

A animals showing signs of boredom

B being attacked by an animal
breeding program

C cooperation between zoos

D *(the)* difficulty of reproducing

E each animal's natural habitat
(an) escaped animal

G giving large animals enough space to roam freely

K keeping children entertained

M maintaining public interest

R restricted enclosures

S safety issues in zoos
school visits
souvenirs

U *(the)* upkeep of a zoo is expensive

Z *(a)* zookeeper
zoos' educational programs

B Books and Reading

A autobiographies

B biographies
(a) bookshop

C *(the)* classical works of fiction
cooking books

D detective stories

E *(an)* e-book
encouraging children to read

F fiction

I it's a book about...

L literary treasures
(a/the) local library

N non fiction
novels

P *(a)* page-turner *(means – a book that really makes you want to keep reading)*
plays
poetry

R reading a book on a tablet
reading a book takes too long
reading an actual book
reading for pleasure
(the) reading habit
reading has lost some popularity
reading on the train/flight/bus
reading to children at bedtime
romantic fiction

S stimulating a child's imagination
store thousands of books easily
(a) successful genre

T to be glued to a book *(idiom)*
to borrow books
to buy books on the internet
to find reading boring
to not be able to put a book down
to read between the lines *(idiom)*
to read in bed
to read only very occasionally
to read voraciously
to read widely
travel books

C Climate change :: Signs

 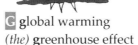

C cyclones

D drought
dwindling water supplies

E El Niño events
extreme weather events

F floods

G global warming
(the) greenhouse effect

H hotter summers

I it is scientifically clear that human activity exacerbates the situation

L La Niña patterns

M *(the)* melting polar ice caps
milder winters

R record temperatures
(a) reduction in agriculturally productive land
rising sea levels
rising sea temperatures

S shorter winters

Climate change :: Causes

a air pollution

c climate skeptics

e excessive carbon footprint in the developed nations

g greed

i *(the)* inability of politicians to act early to modify economic activity
increasing population
industrialisation
insufficient evidence

l *(a)* lack of education about the fragility of the planet
(a) lack of international agreement on action

n natural variation in weather patterns

o over-farming of livestock

r reliance on oil-based economy
(the) rich world over-consumes resources

Climate change :: Solutions

a applying a carbon tax

c carbon-offset schemes

e educating children about sustainability

f forging new and binding international agreements

g growing low carbon crops

i individual action to consume less
international action to alter lifestyles and reduce harmful economic activity

n nuclear energy

p policing the implementation of global agreements

s *(a/the)* shift from animal to plant farming
solar energy
(a) switch to green energy

w wave energy
wind farms

Communication :: Internet

a applications

c chat rooms
creating an online identity
(a) cyber bully

d download speed

f finding information

h *(a)* helpful website

i illegal downloading
inappropriate use of the internet

i *(an)* informative website
internet addiction
(the) internet as a means of increasing democracy
internet crime
internet dating
(an) internet provider

m monitoring children's use of the internet

n news online

o online bullying
online learning
online movies

p *(a)* personal website

s *(a)* suspicious website

t *(the)* time spent on the internet is increasing

u *(the)* use of the internet for social interaction

w *(a)* web camera
(the) wider use of e-commerce

Communication :: Mobile phones

A *(an)* **a**nnoying ring tone

C *(a)* **c**ell phone
(a) **c**ell phone plan

I *(the)* **i**llegal use of mobile phones while driving
(the) **i**nappropriate use of mobile phones in public places

M **m**onthly costs

S **s**witching off your mobile

T **t**o have your mobile phone stolen
to lose your mobile phone

T **t**o replace your mobile
to use your mobile phone constantly
to use your mobile phone for emergencies only
too young to have a mobile phone

Communication :: Computers

B **b**attery life

C **c**omputer literacy
computer-based learning
(a) **c**omputer nerd

E *(the)* **e**asy availability of computers

F *(a/the)* **f**ailure to develop interpersonal skills because of over-using the computer

G **g**igabytes
(a) **g**eek

H **h**acking into confidential information/government sites
(the) **h**ard drive

I **i**ntellectual property
internet addiction

L *(a)* **l**aptop computer
low-price computers

M **m**egabytes
memory
(a) **m**ouse
my computer crashed

N *(a)* **n**etbook

P **p**oor posture/back pain/tired eyes
processing speed

R **r**eliability

S *(the)* **s**hort life of a computer
(a) **s**oftware update
spending all your free time in front of a computer screen
(the) **s**teadily reducing price of computers

T **t**echnophobic
(a) **t**ouchpad
to be a social networker
to email constantly
to search the internet
to twitter

U *(an)* **u**pgrade

(the) **u**se of computers in elementary school

Crime and Policing :: Crime

B **b**reaking and entering

D **d**rug trafficking

E **e**arly release

F *(a)* **f**irst offence
found guilty (or not guilty) by the jury

H *(an)* **h**abitual offender
held in custody

M **m**oney laundering

O **o**n trial for...

P *(a)* **p**arking offence

R **r**eleased on parole

S **s**erving a prison sentence for...
(a) **s**peeding offence

T **t**ax evasion
tax fraud
to be drunk and disorderly

T **t**o be under arrest
to blackmail *(someone)*
to carry an offensive weapon
to carry out a physical assault
to commit robbery with violence

to commit a crime
to murder *(someone)*
to undertake/carry out a robbery

U **u**nder-age drinking

IELTS Vocabulary Writing Task 2

Crime and Policing :: Policing

C *(the)* chief of police

D death in custody
drug raid

E *(an)* escaped offender

F *(a)* full investigation

H *(a)* high speed chase
hunt for a criminal

I inspector of police

M military police

P plain–clothes police
(a) police car
police cells
(a) police constable
police corruption
(a) police dog
(a) police sergeant

S special weapons assault team
(the) superintendent of police

T to hold back a crowd
to accept a bribe
to arrest
to ask for legal representation
to be heavy-handed
to be under suspicion
to break up a disturbance
to breathalyse
to charge someone with an offence
to contact an informant
to cooperate with the police
to elicit a confession
to find a witness
to give a warning

T to give chase
to handcuff
to have bail refused
to identify a suspect
to interview a suspect
to lie to the police
to make a false arrest
to patrol the streets
to question a suspect
to release on bail
to release without charge
to search someone
to spot someone on close circuit television
to take into custody
to use a police baton
to use excessive force
to withhold evidence from…

U uniformed police

E Education :: School years

B being absent
broadly-based curriculum

C class sizes
corporal punishment

D dealing with behavioural problems

E empathetic teaching
exam nerves
exam-oriented curriculum

F face-to-face teaching
fear of failure

L learning social skills
limited attention span
(the) level of discipline in schools

I *(the)* importance of creativity
inclusive classrooms *(means - including disabled or slow learners in the mainstream classroom)*

M making school subjects interesting and relevant
mixed schools

O online learning

P poor performance
preparing students for the workplace

R reading age
rising absenteeism

S single sex schools
(the) social status of teachers is declining in…

T teaching life skills
teaching skills
test-driven
treating pupils more as adults

V violence in schools

Education :: College or university

A aspects of university life
assignment-driven courses
(the) availability of lecturers for support

B *(the)* benefits and drawbacks of online course components
building independence
buying a university place

C *(the)* cost of studying in another city or country
(the) costs of a degree

D *(the)* decline in Arts subjects
(the) decline in social opportunities for networking

E education for life or education for work
elite universities
entry based on merit

F flexible study arrangements

H having to combine study with part-time work

I increased fees

L language support
(the) long-term debt caused by tuition fees'

M making friends

N *(a/the)* need for degrees that can be completed quickly

P practical degrees linked to occupations
(the) proportion of international students

R reduced government funding

S specialising too early

T taking more responsibility for your studies

U universities are lowering/raising their standards
universities are now more like businesses
university entrance exams
university league tables

Entertainment :: TV / radio

A adverts

C cartoons
channel-hopping
children's programs
(a) comedy show
(a) cooking program
(a) couch potato
current affairs programs

D documentaries on social issues
(a) drama series
dumbed-down program content

E endless adverts

G *(a)* game show host

I interrupted by the adverts

L late-night movies
local radio

M *(a)* movie made for tv

N *(a)* news announcer
(a) news broadcast

P pay channels
pay tv
(a) police series
poor reception
pop music stations
program content
programs on…

R *(a)* radio announcer
(a) radio shock jock
(a) radio station
(a) reality tv show
(a) repeat

S *(a)* serial
(a) series of documentaries
serious programs
(a) soap opera
superficial content

T talk shows
(a) talk show guest
(a) talk show host
(the) remote
to watch too much tv
(a) tv announcement
(a) tv celebrity
(a) tv channel
(a) tv meal
a tv show

U unsuitable for children
unsupervised viewing

W *(a)* weekly tv program
(a) wide-screen tv

IELTS Vocabulary Writing Task 2

Entertainment :: Film / movies

A *(an)* **a**ction movie
(an) **a**dventure movie
(an) **a**nimation
at the end of the movie…..

C *(a)* **c**ameo performance
(a) **c**omedy film
(a) **c**urrent release

F *(a)* **f**ilm director
(a) **f**ilm festival

H *(a)* **h**orror movie

I **I** couldn't take my eyes off the screen
it was filmed in…
it's being shown at the…
it's on at 9pm

M **m**ovie stars

O *(an)* **o**ld movie
(an) **O**scar-winning performance
(an) **o**ver-rated star

R *(a)* **r**omantic comedy

S *(a)* **s**cience fiction film
she gives a powerful performance as…
special effects
(a) **s**pellbinding performance
(a) **s**upporting role
(a) **s**uspense film

T **t**he action takes place in…
The best part of the movie is when…
The film drags…
The film draws you in immediately
The film is about…
The main characters are played by…
The movie lasts about 100 minutes
This movie stars Brad Pitt
to show a movie at…
to star in…

U *(an)* **u**nder-rated actor

Environment and sustainability

B **b**leached coral

D **d**evelop sustainable farming methods

E **e**ncourage education about the environment
endangered species
environmentally-friendly
environmentally-insensitive building development
erosion

F **f**ood production methods
future wars based on access to reliable supplies of food and water rather than territory

H **h**unting whales

I **i**llegal
impact on the environment
increased salinity
increasing levels of toxicity
international agreement on environmental protection

O **o**il pollution
oil spills
over-fishing

P **p**olluted waters

R **r**enewable energy

S **s**ea warming
species are losing their habitats
stopping whale hunting

T **t**o care enough about the environment
to damage the environment
to degrade the environment as a result of intensive farming
to feed a growing world population
to move to renewable energy sources
to plan for a sustainable future
to pollute the environment
to protect and maintain water quality
to protect the environment for future generations
to reduce levels of waste
to reduce our carbon footprint
to tread lightly on the earth

H Happiness

C *(the)* constant creation of unnecessary consumer needs

H happiness depends on having basic needs met
happiness is a goal that many people aspire to
happiness is a state of mind
happiness is a temporary state
(the) happiness of giving

K keeping active rather than dwelling on things
keeping life simple

L leading a life that gives space for the important people in your life
(a/the) link between unhappiness and depression

N *(a/the)* need for a government ministry for the promotion of happiness

P permanent happiness
(a) positive outlook on life

P prevents happiness
(the) pursuit of happiness

S *(the)* secret of happiness
surveys suggest that people in affluent countries are often less happy than people who are living simple lives in developing countries

T thinking of others more than yourself
to find happiness unattainable
to have a happy nature/personality
to yearn for happiness
training yourself to think positive thoughts

Health :: Health problems

A allergies

B bacterial infections from hospitals
being overweight

C *(a)* cancer sufferer
chronic lifestyle diseases
constant costly improvements in medical technology

D depression
(the) diseases of aging
diabetes
drug dependency

E eradicating infectious diseases
expensive drug treatment

F faulty drug tests

G *(a)* global pandemic

H heart disease
higher life expectancy
higher proportion of elderly people

I inadequate sun protection
Inadequately-tested drug treatment
infectious diseases
influenza strains
insufficient government expenditure

L lack of exercise
low motivation

M malaria

N not eating healthily

O overwork

P poor diet
poor self image
poor work-life balance
poorly paid nurses
profit-driven, global pharmaceutical companies

R repetitive strain injury
resistant viruses
resurgence of tuberculosis

S sexually transmitted diseases
(a/the) shortage of doctors
skin sensitivity
sleeping disorders
spiralling costs
stress
(a) stressful job
symptoms of depression

T too many fatty foods
tuberculosis

U uncontrollable health costs

IELTS Vocabulary Writing Task 2

Health :: Health care

A *(an)* annual medical check

B being aware of risk factors
blood tests

C *(a)* check up
compulsory vaccination
(a) cosmetic procedure
(a) cosmetic surgery

D dental care
dental treatment

E early detection
ensuring a healthy diet
(an/the) extraction

F *(a)* filling

G giving up smoking
greater knowledge of the genetic basis of many diseases

H health education
health insurance
holistic approaches
hospital treatment
hospital waiting lists

M maintaining healthy gums
more information available about health issues and disease prevention

O *(an)* organ transplant
outpatient treatment

P prevention is better than cure
preventive care
promoting a healthy lifestyle

R reducing the length of hospital stay
regular monitoring of early symptoms

S signs or symptoms
(a/the) shortage of organ donors
(a) surgical operation

Health :: Sleep problems

B *(the)* build up of sleep deprivation
burning the candle at both ends *(saying)*

C *(a)* chronic lack of sleep
constant napping

D disturbed sleep

E *(the)* effects of stress on sleep

G going to bed too late
(a) good night's sleep

H health risks of inadequate sleep

I *(the)* importance of melatonin to sleep
(an) increased risk of stroke or heart attack
insomnia
irregular working hours

R rapid eye movement sleep

S shift work
sleep apnoea
sleep deprivation
sleep medication
sleeplessness

T to avoid caffeine in the evening
to be a poor sleeper
to get to sleep
to go to bed worrying
to have difficulty falling asleep
to keep waking up
to read before going to sleep
to see a sleep therapist
to sleep fitfully
to sleep late/sleep in
to sleep on and off
to sleep soundly
to wake up feeling tired

U *(the)* use of meditation
(the) undoubted importance of sleep to wellbeing

Holidays and travel

B *(a)* **b**umpy landing

C *(a)* **c**rowded flight

F *(the)* **f**light attendants were very helpful/rude
(the) **f**ood in economy/business class was awful/surprisingly good/tasteless

I *(the)* **i**n-flight entertainment broke down

O **o**ne of the local customs involves …ing

S *(a)* **s**mooth take off/landing
sniffer dogs

T **t**o bargain with…
to be attacked by…
to be bitten by a mosquito
to be charged for…
to be constantly harangued by local traders/beggars
to be late for your flight
to be overcharged

T **t**o be ripped off *(informal)*
to be stopped at customs
to be stung by a jelly fish
to book a holiday to…
to book tickets
to buy souvenirs
to change money
to check-in at the airport
to collect your baggage from the carousel
to complain to the hotel receptionist/manager about…
to experience some turbulence
to find the departure hall
to get sunburnt
to go on a bus tour to..
to go on an excursion to…
to go through the x-ray machine
to have a delay
to have a trouble-free flight
to have an up-to-date passport
to have something confiscated by customs
to have your baggage searched
to have your flight cancelled

T **t**o lose your bags
to need a visa
to never want to go to… again
to pass through customs
to pay through the nose for…*(idiom)*
to put on sunscreen
to read through brochures
to relax by the hotel pool
to stay in a budget hotel/backpacker hostel/luxury hotel/room only/bed and breakfast/an ensuite room/with a beautiful view of…/over the bay/of the river
to sunbathe
to swim in the sea
to take a taxi to/from the airport/hotel
to take in the night life
to take some wonderful photos of…
to try out the local food
to wait for hours at the airport
to want to return to…
to watch the in-flight movies
(a) travel agency/agent

IELTS Vocabulary Writing Task 2

L Languages

A *(an)* **a**rchaic expression

C **c**ode switching

D *(the)* **d**ominance of English
dynamic nature of language

E *(an)* **e**ducated language user
error correction

F **f**irst language acquisition
(a) **f**ormal language

G *(a/the)* **g**lobal language
(the) **g**rammar

I *(an)* **i**diolect
(an) **i**nappropriate expression
incorrect grammar
it is our local dialect

L **l**anguage as a functional tool of communication
language as a marker of identity
language as a means of creating imaginative cultural masterpieces
language is becoming more informal

L **l**anguage is changing
(a) **l**anguage is dynamic
(the) **l**anguage is now only spoken by...
(the) **l**anguage learnt in colonial times
(a) **l**anguage that is dying out
learning language in context
loan words

M **m**aintaining your first language

O *(the)* **o**fficial language

P *(the)* **p**ronunciation of...

R *(the)* **r**ange of meaning
(a) **r**egional accent
resistance to Anglicised expressions

S *(a)* **s**ociety where the language is spoken
speaking with a terrible accent
subtle meanings of language

T **t**o be completely fluent in...
to encourage people to speak
to find it easy to learn
to forget a language
to go to language classes
to immerse yourself in the culture
to improve rapidly
to know some slang expressions
to know the basics of a language
to learn a completely different language from your own
to learn a new language
to learn vocabulary
to lose a language
to make slow progress
to not be able to understand language spoken at normal speed
to practise every day
to speak like a native speaker
to speak several languages
translation methods

U *(a)* **u**niversal language

W *(the)* **w**ritten form of the language

Leisure activities

A 'All work and no play...'

C **c**amping
carrying out voluntary work
community work in...

D **d**o-it-yourself activities like renovating a kitchen or painting the house

F **f**ree time

G **g**ardening

H **h**ealthy, outdoor activities
hiking

I *(the)* **i**mportance of having a hobby after retirement
the **i**mportance of leisure to a balanced lifestyle

L **l**eisure time
leisure-time activities

M **m**ountaineering

R **r**ock climbing

S **s**ky diving

T **t**heme parks
to be a couch potato *(idiom)*
to be interested in personal growth activities like meditation
to do nothing
to do something creative
to eat out at good restaurants
to enjoy the opera
to go for a picnic

T **t**o go jogging regularly
to go to the theatre
to go to concerts
to go to the beach
to go to the fitness centre
to grow your own food
to have a hobby
to learn new things
to live a life of leisure
to need more leisure time
to relax in front of the television
to try something new
to use leisure time wisely
to volunteer to...
to walk in the park
too much leisure in retirement
trekking

W **w**alking

N Nutrition :: Diet

anorexia

(a) **b**alanced diet
balanced nutrition

caffeine intake

dietary supplements

excessive sugar intake

(a) **h**igh-protein diet

I couldn't maintain my diet
insufficient dietary fibre

(a) **l**ow, carbohydrate diet

(a) **M**editerranean diet
mild obesity
my diet didn't work

(an) **o**bsession with losing weight

(a) **s**pecial, low-fat diet
stress-fuelled overeating

to change your diet
to eat a healthy diet
to eat less processed food
to eat more fresh fruit and vegetables
to gain weight
to go on a diet
to lose weight
to maintain liquid intake
to need more protein
to overeat
to restrict your intake of…
to watch your diet

(a) **v**egetarian diet

Nutrition :: Food / drink

adjusting your food intake
alcoholic drinks
allowing food to digest properly
anxiety about eating

bland tasting food
bottled water

carbonated drinks
cheese
chemically-treated food

dairy products
decaffeinated coffee

eating good food
eating on the run
eating slowly
energy drinks
expensive food

fast food
food additives
food advertising
food markets
food packaging
food shortages
foods that are damaging to your health
foods that are good for you
fresh fruit juice
fruit

genetically modified food
government policy towards labelling
growing control of the supermarket chains
growing your own food

health benefits of moderate wine-drinking
(a) herb garden
home-cooked food

imported food
inadequate food labelling
instant meals
international foods

locally-grown food

milk

olive oil
organically-grown foods
overcooked

(the) **p**opularity of food programs on tv
processed food
pulses

raw food
rice
rising grocery bills

salad
shopping for food daily
(the) slow food movement
snack foods
spicy food
staple crops
supermarket brands
sushi

targeting children
tasteless
tasty food
to stop snacking between meals

undercooked

vegetable garden
vegetables

(the) **w**eekly trip to the supermarket

yoghurt

IELTS Vocabulary Writing Task 2

P Parents and children

A (an) abused child
(an) average child

B badly-behaved children
bringing up children in today's world is very challenging

C (a) child born on the wrong side of the tracks
(a) child from a wealthy family
(a) child who is out of control
children these days have less respect for their elders
children who have everything

D (a) demanding child
depending on parents for everything
disciplinarians
disobedient children

F feeling close to your parents

G (the) generation gap
(a) gifted child

H helping out at home

I in my grandparents' time
inter-generational conflict

L lack of respect for parents
leaving home too early

M my parents are always there for me
my parents are very traditional

N (a) nagging child
(a) needy child
(a) neglected child

O open-minded
over-protective parents

P parental expectations
parental guidance
parenting skills
parents need to teach children more self discipline
parents who split up when the children are young
permissive parents
(a) poor family
progressive parents

R refusing to take responsibility for their own life
respecting your parents

S (a) single-parent family
(a) spoilt child
(a) stubborn child

T to be more influenced by your mother than your father
to be responsible for the upbringing of your children
to drift apart from your parents
to follow your parents' advice
to have parents who are very liberal
to have your grandparents living with you
to hold traditional values
to let your grandparents go into an aged care facility or home
to miss your parents
to need your own space
to not talk openly to your parents
to obey your parents
to tell your parents everything

Population

A (an) aging population

D (a) dwindling population

E economic migration
emigration

G (a) growing population

I illegal entry
immigration
insufficient infrastructure to support the level of population growth

L (a) lower birth rate

M migration

N net migration

O overcrowding
overpopulation

P permanent residency
population growth
population issues

R refugees
(a) reluctance to have a large family
(the) rising costs of child-rearing

S state encouragement to have children
(a) sustainable population

T to adapt
to apply for citizenship
to assimilate into a new society
to be granted citizenship
to be issued with a visa
to seek a better life
to be worried about the kind of future that your children will inherit

Public transport

A assaults on trains or buses
automated ticket systems
C (the) cost of travelling by bus or train needs to be attractive, especially to those who are less well-off
crowded buses/trains/trams
F fare discounts between peak hours
(the) future possibility of electric buses
I investment in public transport is essential for future needs

I (an) important part of urban infrastructure
M (a/the) metro system enables mass public transit in large cities
multi-trip tickets
N (a/the) need for regular services, especially outside rush hours
(a/the) need to limit the use of private cars in cities
P public transport is less environmentally damaging than private cars are

S safety on public transport
schemes to make public transport more attractive
T to reduce congestion by taking public transport
to run intermittently/ occasionally/irregularly
to run on time
to take a bus/train/tram to work
U user-friendly timetables
W well-lit bus stops

R Relationships

A (an) abusive relationship
B (a) baby sitter
(a) blended family
boyfriend-girlfriend
(a) broken family
(a) brother
C (a) caesarean section
E (the) eldest child
emotional abuse
(an) estranged husband
expensive child care
(an) extended family
F (a/the) first child
I identical twins
induced labour
H (a) house husband
L life goes on
M (a/the) middle child
N natural birth
(a) nuclear family
P parenting skills
(a) partner
pregnancy
S shared parenting
siblings
(a/the) sister
step children
T to be a feminist
to be a good listener

T to be against institutional care
to be bedridden
to be betrayed by
to be blind to someone's faults
to be close to your parents
to be co-dependent
to be critical of…
to be grateful for…
to be infatuated with
to be jealous
to be let down by (someone)
to be over-possessive
to be refused access to your children
to be taken in by (someone)
to be the prime carer
to be too macho
to be totally dependent on (someone)
to discuss your feelings
to drift apart
to fall in love
to fall out of love
to fall out with (someone)
to feel a duty towards…
to feel helpless
to feel responsible for…
to find someone else
to find the right one
to find your soul mate
to get married
to get over (someone)
to give the other person enough space
to have a de facto relationship
to have different interests

T to hold in your feelings
to keep in regular contact with
to learn from your mistakes
to live for (someone)
to look after your aging parents
to lose contact with (someone)
to lose mobility
to lose someone
to miss someone
to move on with your life
to need constant care
to never get over the loss of…
to never see someone again
to no longer see eye to eye on
to offer love and support
to pay maintenance
to practice some 'give and take'
to raise your child as a single parent
to respect each other
to separate from
to settle down
to share the household tasks
to share the same interests
to spend quality time with your children
to still be independent
to treat a woman with respect
to trust your partner
(a) toxic relationship
twins
W (a) wife

IELTS Vocabulary Writing Task 2

S Sport

A *(an)* **a**mateur player

B *(a)* **b**rand name racquet
brand name sports clothing

C *(a)* **c**hampion
(the) commercialisation of sport

E *(an)* **e**lite athlete
extreme sports

F **f**itness
football hooliganism

G *(a)* **g**lobal audience
global coverage

I **i**ncome from product endorsement

M *(a)* **m**atch report
(a) medal winner

O *(the)* **O**lympics

P **p**aid too much
(a) professional sportsman

R **r**unning shoes

S **s**pectators
sport has become too much of a business
sport is too commercialized
(a) sports commentator
(a) sports magazine
(a) sports personality
(a) sports report
supporters

T **t**ennis is beginning to take off *(idiom)* in...
to be a dedicated sportsman
to be a fan of...
to be a loyal fan
to be interested in sport
to be a sportsman
to be very good at sports
to dedicate themselves to their sport
to go to every match
to join a sports club
to lose
to make sacrifices in order to get to the top of your sport
to not be sporty
to play for fun only
to play sport for exercise
to play sport regularly
to practise constantly in order to improve
to represent your country
to retire from sport
to take up a sport
to watch live sport
to watch sport on television
to win easily
(a) top athlete
(a) top competitor
(a) top player
top sports stars are overpaid
top sports stars should be good role models for...

W *(a/the)* **w**orld record

Y **y**oung people are less willing to train hard

T Technology

A **a**dvanced technology
automated manufacturing processes

B **b**ioengineering

C *(a)* **c**ollege of technology

D **d**esign costs
developing new manufacturing techniques

E *(an)* **e**lectric car
electronics
(the) environmental impact of technology

F **f**uturistic technology

G **g**ene technology
genetically modified food

H **h**i-tech. industries

I **i**ntelligent robots
intermediate technology

K **k**eyhole surgery

L *(a/the)* **l**ack of technology
laser technology

M **m**edical technology
microchip technology
miniaturisation

N **n**anotechnology
nuclear technology

O **o**utdated
outmoded technology

P **p**atenting
production costs

R **r**esearch and development
robotics

S **s**atellite technology
(a/the) shortage of modern technology
solar technology
space technology
'state of the art' technology

T **t**echnological innovation
technological progress
thermal energy
3D (three dimensional) printers

W **w**ave motion technology

The future

A *(an)* **a**pocalyptic vision of environmental destruction

B **b**attles over resources
(a) **b**leak future

C **c**loning
(the) **c**olonisation of outer space

E **e**lectronic surveillance
endless corruption

F *(a)* **f**uture characterised by unimaginable inventions
(the) **f**uture holds many surprises
(a) **f**uture in which peace reigns supreme

F *(the)* **f**uture looks bleak
(a) **f**uture marked by electronic control
(a) **f**uture of bitter struggles between the 'haves' and the 'have-nots'

G **g**enetic engineering

I *(the)* **i**nability of the human race to manage the planet sensitively

M **m**edical progress

N *(the)* **n**eed to secure a safe world for future generations

O *(the)* **o**ption to live for ever could be achieved
organ replacement will become commonplace

R *(a)* **r**osy future

T **t**o anticipate the future
to be optimistic about the future
to predict the future
to see into the future

U *(an)* **u**ncertain future

W *(a)* **w**ar-torn future
we need a sustainable future
world government

W Work :: Workplace

A **a**nnual bonuses
annual leave

B **b**oring work

C **c**hallenging work

E **e**xciting work

F **f**ringe benefits

I **I** didn't get the job

M *(a)* **m**anufacturing company
(a) **m**ultinational company

P *(a)* **p**art-time position

R **r**ather routine

S *(a)* **s**alary package
(a) **s**oftware company
(a) **s**tarting salary
stimulating

T **t**o apply for a better job
to apply for a job

T **t**o be a casual worker
to be fired
to be flexible
to be offered an interview
to be offered the job
to be posted overseas
to be promoted
to be put on short-time
to be successful
to be underpaid for the responsibility you have
to develop your career and become a…
to fill in an application form
to find work
to find your boss difficult… *(to get on with)*
to get on well with work colleagues
to go for an interview
to hand in your notice
to have a good boss
to have enough to live on in retirement

T **t**o hope to become a…
to lose your job
to make a great deal of money
to multi-task
to quit
to respect your boss
to retrain as a…
to start your own business
to struggle in retirement
to struggle on your earnings
to travel overseas as part of your job
to work for a local business which makes…
to work for an international company
to work full-time
to work in a democratic company
to work in a hierarchical company
to work past retirement age

W **w**orking conditions

Work :: Work-life balance

C caring for elderly parents

S stress often prevents the effective completion of tasks

I to be burnt out
to be under too much pressure
to build up a pension
to change to part-time work
to do something more with your life
to feel too much pressure

I to feel unappreciated as a worker
to find work stressful
to grow as a person
to have insufficient time for your family
to have more time to do the things you enjoy
to have more time to spend with friends
to learn new skills
to lose motivation

I to lose too much sleep because of work
to make more of your life
to need a better quality of life
to need a complete change
to need more holidays
to need more quality time with your family
to plan for retirement
to retire early
to work long hours
to work too hard

Y You can do it!

Congratulations on looking through just some of this vocabulary – you have done really well! We are now at the end of our resource sections.

I can't sit with you when you take the IELTS test but, one way or another, I'll be there cheering you on! Good luck!

IELTS SPEAKING

SPEAKING LESSON

First Questions Answered

Q. **What does the IELTS interview consist of, and how long does it last?**

A. The interview has these main elements:

- You are interviewed by one, trained IELTS assessor.
- The interview is in three parts, lasting a total of 11-14 minutes.
- The assessor asks all the questions.
- The assessor awards your score.

Q. **What is in each of the three parts?**

A. The parts are divided up as follows:

- In **Part 1** the assessor asks you questions on three everyday topics for a total of four to five minutes. There are usually four questions for each topic.

- In **Part 2** you give a short talk on a topic which is given to you beforehand. The topic is on a topic card, such as the one below:

> Talk about someone you know, or know about, who has had an interesting life.
>
> You should say:
> > who the person is
> > where the person comes from
> > what is interesting about that person's life
>
> and explain why that person's life seems interesting to you.

You have one minute to plan your talk and have to talk for one to two minutes.

- In **Part 3** you are asked questions of a more general nature, but broadly related to the topic of your talk. The assessor may respond to your answers to draw out more detail.

Q. How can I be sure I perform well in each part?

A. Practise before the test and follow a systematic routine, like this one:

What you should do:	How?	Why?
Part 1 — answer each question sufficiently.	By understanding each question and responding clearly, fluently and naturally for about 15 seconds or so while varying grammar and vocabulary.	• To keep the rhythm of the test's timing (max. 12 questions in four to five minutes). To give a positive initial impression of level.
Part 2 — plan your talk systematically during the one minute preparation time.	By writing a quick outline of your answer to each of four parts on the topic card.	• To minimize chances of a repetitive, confused talk. To ensure that you talk for long enough, with confidence.
Part 3 — develop your answer to each question in a more formal and extended way using your own knowledge and experience.	By adding detailed explanations or examples using formal phrases like, 'By this I mean…' or 'Let me try to explain it in another way' or 'I'll give you an example from my own society'. Aim to extend each response for about 30 or 40 seconds.	• To sound more mature and more considered. You can become the 'expert' when talking about your own society as an example.

Q. What do I have to do to respond <u>well</u> to the assessor?

A. Your task is to:
- ➢ Speak as clearly and as fluently as you can while answering the questions coherently, with good grammar, flexible and appropriate vocabulary and clear pronunciation and intonation.
- ➢ Relate to the assessor as naturally, confidently and with as much interest as you can.
- ➢ Keep to the timing and rhythm of the test's parts to make the assessor's job easier.
- ➢ Represent yourself authentically, meaning don't memorise answers or sound mechanical. Give real information from your life in a genuine way.

IELTS Speaking Lesson

Q. Do my answers have to be truthful and based on my own life experiences?

A. This is a question for your own conscience! The assessor is not assessing truth value, but most people feel more comfortable when they are representing themselves honestly. If you get a question or topic but it is outside your experience try to talk about something that really happened to a friend or to a relative. For example, imagine a Part 2 topic asking you to describe something you made at school, you can say,

'I'm afraid I never made anything at school but I remember that a friend of mine made a wonderful basket, so I'd like to talk about that'.

The assessor will not penalize you, because you are adapting as well as you can to the situation and it is still connected to your own life. It is your language that is being assessed, not your life.

Q. OK, but should I try to say something nice to the assessor? Is it OK to chat?

A. If the assessor is a more formal type of person, then they might see compliments as your attempt to get a higher score, rather than as sincere. If you chat too much and try to involve the assessor, this may seem over-friendly for a first meeting. The best option is to find a 'middle way'.

Be friendly and pleasant but take the test situation seriously as well. Adapt to the different phases of the test:
- In Part 1 the topics are general so you can use a less formal style.
- In Part 3 you are discussing issues and developing your opinions, so be a little more formal then.

Assessors differ in terms of their personalities, ages, expectations, but they all have a serious job to do and are trying to do it in the fairest way they can. Help them. This will have the most positive impact on them.

Q. Are there 'wrong things' I might say, that will affect my score?

A. The assessor is evaluating your use of language, not your opinions.
If you say something, in Part 3, for example, that the assessor strongly disagrees with, they may try to encourage you to explain in more detail why you have that opinion. But it is probably a good strategy not to express views that are too strong or too controversial in case the assessor is affected unconsciously in a negative way.

Q. How should I dress for the interview?

A. The test takes place in many countries so there are different cultural considerations. In general terms it is better to dress smartly and tidily but not too formally (this may be seen as trying to influence your score). Clothes are, of course, not assessed directly but may have an effect unconsciously on the assessor's impression of how serious you are about the test and how much respect you have for them and for the situation. At the same time you need to feel comfortable in your clothes so that you feel confident and at ease.

Q. When does the assessor give me my score?

A. The assessor is thinking about your individual scores for each of four criteria during the test. These **four criteria** are:

Assessment criteria	Some features affecting your score
Fluency and Coherence	How much do you hesitate? How appropriate and developed are your answers? How do you link ideas?
Lexical Resource	How flexible are you in your choice of words? What range of vocabulary do you have access to?
Grammatical Range and Accuracy	How accurate are you grammatically? What range of sentence types can you use?
Pronunciation	How easy are you to understand? How well can you put feeling into your voice through intonation? How well can you use chunking* and pauses?

See Secret #5 in the 'Secrets of how to impress your assessor…' section, Page 273.

At the end of the interview the assessor gives you a score from 0-9 on each of these four dimensions and then your overall score is calculated by IELTS.

IELTS Speaking Lesson

Q. What is the best way to get from an IELTS 6 to a 7 score for Speaking?

A. This is a frequently asked question as many candidates need the higher score. We consider these to be important ways to lift your score from 6 to 7:

> - Make your spoken English as natural as you can (as much like a native speaker as you can) and add variety (life) to your intonation.
> - Add as much variety and flexibility as possible to your grammar and vocabulary.
> - Show fluency and confidence.
> - Relate well to, and cooperate well with, the assessor.
> - Avoid repetition and reduce simple errors (e.g. wrong tense, wrong subject/verb agreements, lack of plural forms).
> - Answer questions relevantly in Part 1, give a relevant, well-organised talk in Part 2, and extend your answers intelligently in Part 3.

To find step by step guidance take a careful look at our advice in 'Secrets of how to impress your assessor…' later in this chapter. Then, try out the Fitness Activities on page 280.

GOLD STAR ADVICE No. 1:
An interview gives you an opportunity to help to establish a comfortable social relationship. Try to see yourself as the assessor's 'partner' in the interview situation, not the victim of a test interrogation.

What if I...? Some Problem Situations

Q. What if I don't understand a question in Part 1?

A. Use a polite, formal or even idiomatic request to ask for the question to be repeated, for example:
'I didn't quite catch that. Could you repeat it please?'
'I'm sorry but would you mind repeating that please?'

If you heard the question but didn't understand it at all, just say:
'I'm sorry, would you mind moving on to the next question please?'

 Note: The assessor can only repeat questions in Part 1, not explain them.

Q. What if my assessor seems distracted and not interested in the conversation, or stops me before I have a chance to finish. What can I do in this situation?

A. Candidates occasionally report such problems and it is clearly a problem. Your best strategy is to be as lively as you can and to use your voice to maintain interest. Good intonation keeps the attention of the listener usually. If the assessor cuts you off, it probably means that they are worried about the time (i.e. you are taking up too much time for each answer in Part 1) Try to practise giving answers of about 15-20 seconds on average for most of the questions in Part 1.

Q. What if I don't want to talk about the Part 2 topic or don't know much about it?

A. It's probably better to try to talk about the topic you are given, or something close to that topic, than to ask for a different topic, because this causes less disruption to the test timing.

Q. What if I don't understand a question in Part 3?

A. In Part 3 you can use excellent English to ask for clarification if you don't understand the question. For example, you can say:

'Could you phrase that question in a different way, I didn't quite follow it?'
'Do you mean _____ or _____?'
'If I understood you correctly, you are asking _____. Is that right?'

Q. What if my mind goes blank because I'm nervous?

A. If your mind goes blank, buy time with some 'filler' expressions, for example:

'I'm sorry but the word has gone out of my mind completely', or
'I'm afraid I've totally forgotten what I wanted to say'

then try your answer again or start your answer in another way, saying,

'Let me see if I can explain it/answer the question in a different way'

Use an active, positive strategy, don't just freeze or panic!

Q. What if I don't make notes for the Part 2 talk? Or, in the opposite situation, how do I know when to stop making notes?

A. You don't have to make notes but you do need to offer a coherent talk which seems organized, so the cue card and your notes are supposed to help. The assessor will tell you when to stop making notes.

Q. What if I can't talk for two minutes in Part 2?

A. You only have to talk for a minimum of one minute. If you stop before the two minutes is up, the assessor will check by asking something like, *'Could you say anything else about that?'* If you have spoken for at least a minute it is OK to answer *'That's all'*. Or, you can continue, like this:

Example

Assessor:	Could you say anything else about that?
You:	*Mm, what else can I say?...Well...* (and continue)

Q. What if I take a moment to think while answering and there is a bit of silence, will it ruin my score?

A. If you are only thinking before answering, no it won't. If you hesitate too often in the middle of sentences because of struggling for words or accuracy, then this might affect your score negatively.

Q. What if I freeze when speaking to this stranger (the assessor), how can I fight that?

A. Different cultures have different attitudes to strangers and the IELTS interview is a sensitive situation for any candidate. You need to keep telling yourself that the assessor is just a person who is interested in you (This is probably true anyway!) and so your job is to seem interesting rather than shy. You are a representative of your country, so talk with pride, don't hide in fear. Try to find native speakers of English to practise with before the exam.

Q. What if I talk for too long, especially in Parts 1 or 2?

A. The assessor will usually signal with a hand if they want you to stop at the end of each section. Just say something like, *'Oh, sorry'* and wait.

IELTS Speaking Lesson

Secrets of how to impress your assessor in the IELTS Interview

Your assessor is a busy person with perhaps 15 candidates to interview.
Maybe you are the last candidate of the day so the assessor might be a little tired. Within the limitations of your English, you need to create a positive relationship with the assessor through the quality of your spoken language and social contact.

 GOLD STAR ADVICE No 2: *Connecting always counts.*
As well as everything you say and how well you say it, the quality of the connection you make with the assessor comes to represent 'YOU' in the mind of the assessor. Be interesting;
make good contact.

Q. How can I create a good impression in the mind of the IELTS assessor?

A. There are certain things that always create a good impression.

Follow these detailed suggestions and your Interview will be appreciated by your assessor:

1. Take care when building your answers

Explanation
The assessor has to judge whether or not you have answered the question coherently. This means whether your ideas are linked together in an 'easy to follow' way.

Why is this important?
Linking ideas clearly creates a good impression of you as a good communicator because you try to help the listener as much as you can.

Example

 I like pets. Pets are friends. Many people have pets. People are less lonely.

 *I like pets **because** pets are friends. People have pets **so that** they are less lonely.*

2. Extend your responses – say it, explain it, support it.

Explanation
If you use a structured and organized approach when starting a response, especially in Part 3, this will help you to extend your response and make it more coherent. It will also give you more opportunities to display a wider range of sentence types and vocabulary.

Example

Assessor:		Do you think weddings are a good idea these days?
You:	Say it	*Well not really, in fact I suppose I'm a bit anti-weddings.*
	Explain it	*By saying this I suppose I mean that at many weddings today there seems, to my mind at least, to be too much emphasis on display and perhaps not enough attention given to deep meaning.*
	Support it	*For example, I've seen many of my friends' marriages fail and this has made me a little pessimistic about expensive, 'showy' wedding ceremonies that seem mainly about displays of wealth. It's the deep commitment of two people that is the core of a marriage.*

3. Try to use your own personal experience when appropriate

Explanation
Your own experiences are often easier for you to talk about.

Why is this important?
Your own life and culture can be used to generate examples and this helps to extend an answer, especially in Part 3.

Example

I think friends are easier to talk to than relatives.

Friends are much easier to talk to than relatives. In my country, generally speaking, people talk more openly to their friends than to their relatives because our culture is... I'll give you an example from my own situation...

4. Try not to drift off topic

Explanation
It's important to make your answers respond to the questions relevantly and coherently.

Why is this important?
'Relevance' here means that your reply fits the usual expectations of an answer to that question and responds to the central intention of the question. If your answer is relevant it tells the assessor you understood the question appropriately and listened to it fully.

Example

Assessor:		What do you imagine will happen to marriage in the future?
You (Response 1):		*I'm not sure if I'll get married in the future. I want to get a good job and build my career so that I don't have to worry too much about money. Maybe I'll think about getting married after that.*
You (Response 2):		*I think marriage will become less popular, at least in this society, because many young people are becoming more self-centred. They seem to think less about families and more about their own needs. Perhaps in the future this will make them less willing to make a major commitment like marriage, less willing to take responsibility.*

Response 1 is not really relevant to the question, which is asking about marriage in general, not the candidate's marriage. Response 2 is more relevant.

5. Improve your pronunciation

Explanation

The better your pronunciation is, the easier you are to understand. If your pronunciation is weak, it may not be easy to perfect it immediately, but you can make some helpful adjustments.

Example

Part 1 topic about cooking:

Assessor: How often do you cook your own meals?

First of all, the assessor won't want to hear an unbroken answer in a flat, monotone voice, as in:

You: *'Idon'tcookveryoftenperhapstwiceaweekbecauseIsometimesworklate andthenIjustbuyfastfoodonthewayhome'*

So, here are some important ways of improving your pronunciation:

Try skilful 'chunking'

'Chunking' involves speaking in blocks of words and then taking a tiny pause. It helps to build a slightly slower rhythm consisting of clear blocks of meaning. This helps the listener. But, you mustn't make the pauses too long or too mechanical, or fluency is lost and it sounds unnatural and even hesitant. So the original response might be improved like this:

You: *I don't cook very often [mini-pause] perhaps twice a week [mini-pause] because I sometimes work late [mini-pause] and then I just buy fast food [mini-pause] on the way home.*

Apply good stress and rhythm

You also need to remember to stress the main information-carrying parts of your responses. So, as well as chunking and 'quick-pausing', you would stress the following elements (in bold type) more heavily than others, to communicate key information clearly, while maintaining appropriate rhythm by saying the parts between in an even-timed way:

You: *I **don't COO**k very **of**ten [mini-pause] perhaps **TWI**ce a **WEE**k [mini-pause] because I sometimes **WORK la**te [mini-pause] and then I just buy **FAS**t **FOO**d [mini-pause] on the **way HO**me.*

IELTS Speaking Lesson

You also need to be careful to pinpoint correct stress inside words (e.g. souven**IR**, not sou**VE**nir; **MAN**ager not man**AG**er; **IN**ternet, not in**TER**net).

Remember there are classes of words that are normally stressed (nouns, verbs, adverbs, adjectives) but also those that **aren't** normally stressed (prepositions, articles, linking expressions, pronouns) unless a particular contrast is being made (e.g. **I** love her, but **YOU** don't).

Practice <u>intonation</u> to inject life into your voice

Finally, to introduce a little more intonation ('voice music') into your responses you could add a comment which shows your attitude or feeling, by using strong stress PLUS a higher tone and slower pronunciation, so that your response finally becomes::

You: *I don't **COO**k very **of**ten [mini-pause] perhaps **TWI**ce a **WEE**k [mini-pause] because I sometimes **WORK la**te [mini-pause] and then I just buy **FAS**t **FOO**d [mini-pause] on the **way HO**me. [pause] I bet it's [higher tone] **R E A L** l y   **B A** d   for me!*

6. Use variety of vocabulary

Explanation
If you keep repeating the same simple words, the assessor realizes that you don't have much flexibility and are unable to vary your vocabulary, or express precise meaning.

Why is this important?
Variety makes you sound more interesting and more flexible as an English speaker.

Example

My dog is nice. He's a very nice pet. He likes nice walks. It's nice to walk with him every day. Every day I go with him for a walk.

My dog has a very friendly nature and is a very loving pet. He really enjoys his walk every day, and I get a great deal of pleasure from these daily outings as well.

7. Use up-to-date idioms or colloquial vocabulary <u>occasionally</u>

Explanation
Hearing occasional, everyday idioms, phrasal verbs or colloquial expression makes the assessor feel that you are similar to them in your cultural style. This is persuasive.
On the other hand, **outdated idioms sound strange**, so choose and use carefully.

Example 1

 Too basic

Q: Tell me about your favourite food.
A: *I like curry.*
Q: Why?
A: *Because it's spicy... and it's very hot... I enjoy going to different Indian restaurants...*

 More varied & interesting

Q: Tell me about your favourite food.
A: *I'm really **crazy about** curries.*
Q: Why?
A: *Well, they're so spicy...sometimes they're so hot they can almost **take your head off**... but I really enjoy **trying out** different Indian restaurants...*

Example 2

 Q: Do you like studying in Australia?
A: *I feel a bit like a **fish out of water**, so it's **not really my cup of tea**.*

 Q: Are you lonely sometimes?
A: *Well I try to **keep a stiff upper lip**.*

These idioms are less often used these days and can sound a little old-fashioned and unnatural, especially when used by a younger, non-native speaker, who is not very fluent.

8. Reduce simple grammar mistakes

Explanation
Constantly making simple grammar mistakes doesn't always affect communication or understanding but creates a negative impression. It tends to suggest that you haven't worked hard to conquer those mistakes from your early years of learning English.

Why is this important?
To get a higher score you need to sound as much like a native speaker as possible. Native speakers rarely make basic grammatical errors.

Example

 With grammar mistakes

Q: Which other language would you like to learn?
A: *I like learn French*
Q: Why?
A: *It is interested language. My father speak French. He learn it when he's a child I like to talk him in French.*

 Without grammar mistakes

Q: Which other language would you like to learn?
A: *I'd really like to learn French*
Q: Why?
A: *It is such an interesting language. Actually, my father speaks French. He learnt it when he was a child. I'd really like to be able to talk with him in French.*

9. Respond to any comments made by your assessor

Explanation
Sometimes your assessor will comment on your answer (as opposed to asking you the next question). Here is an example of how to respond in a natural way:

Example

Assessor: It sounds as though you don't really trust the idea of marriage.

You: ***Does it? Maybe you're right.*** *I think it's definitely true that marriage seems more risky these days, as in this type of society people are more selfish, more independent and less respectful of tradition and so they may not feel so deeply connected to any promises they make.*

10. Cooperate with the assessor's time restrictions

Explanation
The assessor has to cover the three parts of the interview according to a strict time schedule so you need to help the assessor with this, not cause stress.

Why is this important?
If you talk for too long when answering, for example, Part 1 topic questions, the assessor has difficulty asking all the 12 questions. Conversely, if your answers are too short, the assessor doesn't use the minimum time for Part 1 (four minutes).

Example

After the Part 2 talk, the assessor asks a quick question. Give a shortish answer so that the assessor has enough time for Part 3. Try to give longer answers in Part 3.

Talk topic: 'Your best friend'. The assessor is asking a quick rounding-off question:

Assessor: Do you see your best friend very often?

You (Response 1): *Yes I do, very often.*

You (Response 2): *Yes, of course. I see him every day when I'm in my country. I phone him up as soon as I get back and we meet, in a café maybe, and talk about all the things that we want to do together, you know, like going to the cinema or having a meal at our favourite restaurants, like the one in the city centre where we always went when we were at school together. The food there is great and pretty cheap still.*

You (Response 3): *Yes, of course. When I go back home we meet up and plan what to do together. We see each other most days, and send text messages to each other all the time.*

Response 1 is too short, Response 2 is too long, and Response 3 is about the right length.

IELTS Speaking Lesson

11. Treat the assessor as your equal, not as your boss

Explanation
The interview is a social experience between two strangers, where one (the assessor) has the questions and controls time, but doesn't control your answers or your personality.

Why is this important?
Although confidence is not being assessed directly, in western cultural terms it makes you seem weak and limited if your answers show a lack of positive energy and low self-confidence – this suggests you are allowing yourself to be dominated by the situation.

Example

Assessor: Are you good at cooking?

You (Response 1): *No, I'm not good at cooking, I'm very bad at cooking.*

You (Response 2): *Well, I'm not the best cook in the world, but I can cook simple things, and I enjoy eating what I cook, even if others don't.*

Response 1 sounds negative, too self critical, whereas Response 2 sounds more positive, but realistic; not over-confident.

12. Try to make appropriate eye contact

Explanation
In western cultures eye contact is an accepted part of a conversation even with someone who has authority over you.

Why is this important?
In the IELTS interview you are not just using English you are creating a brief social relationship with your assessor. The assessor needs to feel comfortable too. If you make appropriate eye contact, it gives the impression that you are interested and so the interview feels more comfortable for the assessor as they can more easily make contact with you. Actually it is hard for the assessor to make regular eye contact as they have to read the words on the page in front of them accurately. Try not to be put off by this.

Example

You could make gentle, positive eye contact when:
- listening to questions or instructions
- when giving your answers

13. Don't ask about your performance at the end of the interview

Explanation
When the assessor announces that the interview has ended, don't ask any questions about your performance—this may annoy the assessor, who is not permitted to comment on your performance. Just say something polite and leave.

Example

Assessor:		That's the end of the interview.
You (Response 1):		*Great. How did I do? Was I OK? I was pretty nervous - hope that didn't show.*
You (Response 2):		*OK. Thank you. It was really nice talking to you. Is it all right to leave now?*

SPEAKING FITNESS ACTIVITIES

The fitness activities in this section will help you to tell some of the differences between a stronger response and a weaker response, and to improve your own responses when you try the IELTS Practice Interview.

PART 1 » Answering questions on three everyday topics

Fitness Activities 1–16 for Part 1 of the IELTS Speaking Test

 Activities 1–5 will help you to build stronger responses to questions on Topic 1:

> **Topic 1**   Let's talk about your home

1. **Question: 'Do you live in an apartment or a house?'**

    Which of these possible responses seems the most appropriate, and why?

    a) 'A house.'

    b) 'I live in a house in West Beach; I've lived there for about 2 years now.'

    c) 'I live in a house. The house is big.'

2. **Question: 'Is it a good place to live? (Why?/Why not?)'**

    Which response is not really answering what the question is asking?

    a) 'Yes, it's the suburb that is near the city centre, with all the best shops.'

    b) 'Not really, as it's located in a very noisy part of town and the landlord never does anything about our complaints.'

    c) 'Yes it's a really good place because the rent is reasonable and it's near to the train station.'

3   **Question: 'Is the area where you live pleasant? (Why?/Why not?)'**

   Which response is a good one? What seems wrong with each of the other two?

   a) 'It's pleasant, yes. It's pleasant because it has very pleasant parks nearby. These parks are nice and big, with nice flowers, and nice trees.'

   b) 'Yes, it's great. There are plenty of parks, with tennis courts, and many varied, native plants, flowers and trees. Also the houses are all well-built and up-to-date.'

   c) 'Yes it has…er…it has pleasant surroundings…er…and very attractive parks, with sports…erm…facilities…and…very little…erm poll…pollu…pollution.'

4   **Question: 'What facilities are there near your home?'**

   Which seems the best way to ask for this question to be repeated?

   a) 'I'm sorry I didn't catch that. Could you repeat it please?'

   b) 'I don't understand. Can you say it again?'

   c) 'What are 'facilities', please? I need to hear the question again.'

5   **Which response to the Topic 1 question in activity 4 seems the clearest?**

   a) 'There are facilities, yes, there are a park, I go sometimes, a sports ground for I think for soccer. Kids go there, from street where I live.'

   b) 'There are lots – a park, for example, which I go to sometimes, and a sports ground, for soccer, I think. Some of the kids from my street go there.'

   c) 'Near my home are lots facilities, like there is a park for me to go there and a soccer sports ground for street kids from where I live in.'

IELTS Speaking Fitness Activities

Activities 6–9 will help you to build stronger responses to questions on Topic 2:

| Topic 2 | Let's move on to talk about friends |

6   **Question: 'Do you have many friends or just one or two?'**

   Complete this response using the expressions in the box below.

   'I have _____ of friends... some from right back when I was at school, others from various jobs I've had, and there are the friends I play _____ with. I've always been a _____ sort of person so I find it easy to _____ on with people when I _____ them. But, I _____ I'd say I only have one or two _____ friends – friends I completely trust, I _____.'

   | suppose   mean   true   meet   sport   friendly   get   loads |

7   **Question: 'How often do you see your friends?'**

   Which response has some high level vocabulary and idioms in it?

   a) 'I don't have much chance to catch up with my old friends at the moment, as I'm studying here in Australia and they're not, but I often bump into my new friends at college here, and we hang out together.'

   b) 'Most of my old friends are back at home, and I'm here in Australia. I have lots of new friends from college and we like to meet up and do things...all sorts of things together. It's good.'

   c) 'Wow...Let me see...I don't see my school friends much...as they're at home and I'm not...if you know what I mean...so I don't see them often...but my new Aussie, college friends...well, of course, I see them all the time...too much maybe!'

8 ***Question: 'Are you good at making new friends? (Why?/Why not?)'***

Which response is the most grammatically accurate?

a) 'As I say, I'm pretty good at make friend because I'm easygoing and I like meet new people when I'm going out to parties or thing like that.'

b) 'As I'm saying, I like people so it's easier making friends. I'm good at chatting, you say 'small talk' I think. People seem like me maybe because I laugh much.'

c) 'As I said just before, I'm a bit shy but I make friends quite easily, maybe because I'm a good listener, and I like asking questions and showing interest in people.'

9 ***Question: 'Which are more important – friends or family (Why?)'***

Which response seems the most interesting and varied answer?

a) 'I think family is more important, because everyone has a family. Friends sometimes don't last but your family is with you for ever. You always have a family – parents, brothers, sisters and if you're lucky, your grandparents, of course. It's normal to have a lot of family around you.'

b) 'Family definitely. They are with you and care for you from the beginning of your life, they shape the person you become, they always support you and love you unconditionally. They will always be there if you get into difficulties. Friends don't always feel the same level of responsibility.'

c) 'Both are important, but family is more important. I really love my mother, and she loves me. It's natural I suppose but it's important to me, and to her. My friends like me and I like them but it's not the same really. It's a different feeling, less important really, at least for me.'

Activities 10–13 will help build stronger responses to questions on Topic 3:

| Topic 3 | Let's talk now about cars and driving |

10 *Question: 'Can you drive? (Why?/Why not?)'*

Which response uses the most advanced and varied linking expressions?

a) 'I can't drive at the moment; however, I'd like to learn because it will be useful, even though I don't need to drive as part of my job, as I work in an office.'

b) 'I can drive, yes. I learnt last year and I have a small car, but I don't drive very often. Petrol is much too expensive for me and I'm only a student.'

c) 'I've been driving for ten years. In my country it is not easy to learn to drive because lessons are so expensive so it cost me about $800 to get my licence.'

11 *Question: 'Is traffic increasing on roads in your country?'*

Which response seems the most relevant?

a) 'There are many cars on our roads, especially taxis. The roads never seem to be quiet, and it's always so noisy and there is a lot of pollution. It's not really safe to drive these days.'

b) 'The roads are increasing but we need more because the population is increasing very rapidly too. Everyone wants a car and luckily we make our own cars now and they are quite cheap.'

c) 'It's increasing rapidly, yes. This is mainly because more people can now afford to buy cars, and so the increasing levels of traffic are very noticeable – more traffic jams, and more accidents.'

12 ***Question: 'How can car accidents be stopped?'***

Which response seems too direct and perhaps even a little impolite?

a) 'It's probably unlikely that car accidents can be stopped completely. Life is often too hectic, so people have more difficulty concentrating and the roads are busier. All these factors put ever greater pressure on drivers, I think.'

b) 'They can't. It's not possible. Think about it. Can you drive and answer your mobile phone and remember what you need to buy from the shops, and talk to the children in the back seat. Nor me. That's why there are accidents.'

c) 'It's not possible, really. If you think about it, many drivers have a lot of stress when they drive – stress from other people in the car, mobile phones, time pressure. Put all these together and it's not surprising that accidents happen.'

13 ***Question: 'How do you feel when you are in a car that is going very fast?'***

In which response is hesitation managed most successfully?

a) 'I feel…erm I feel scare…scared because I don't always…I don't trust the driving…sorry
the driver. If I know the driver…and I know the driver drives…erm, safer, I mean safely, then I could…can relax a little bit'

b) 'I feel…scare…sorry I meant to say, I feel scared, because I don't always…how can I put it, I don't always trust the driving, I mean driver. If I know the driver…erm or more important, if I know the driver drives…safer, or rather, safely, then I could…or can relax a little bit'

c) 'I feel…I feel scare…scared because I don't always…I don't trust the driving…the driver. If I know the driver…and I know the driver drives…safer, sorry, safely, then I could…I'm sorry, can relax a little bit.'

IELTS Speaking Fitness Activities

 Activities 14–16 will help you to develop your pronunciation skills

14   **Building Awareness of 'Chunking'**
Good speakers group the words they speak into 'chunks', which are units of meaning separated by little pauses. This helps the listener to absorb information more easily. The pauses are only very short otherwise fluency is lost and instead the listener may think you are hesitating.

Example

Compare A with B:
A   IcomefromTehranit'sareallybusycitywithmanymarketsandmosques
B   I come from Tehran • It's a really busy city • with many markets and mosques

Now try to 'chunk' the following responses from Part 1 in a similar way

1) I'msorryIdidn'tcatchthatCouldyourepeatitplease?

2) Yesit'sgreatTherearepletyofparkswithtenniscourtsandmanynative plantsflowersandtrees.

3) AsIsaidjustbeforeI'mabitshybutImakefriendsquiteeasilymaybebecauseI'ma goodlistenerandIlikeaskingquestionsandshowinginterestinpeople.

Finally, practise saying each sentence in 'chunks', using only very short pauses.

15   **Building Awareness of Stress and Rhythm**
English is a stress-timed language, which means that it follows a pattern a bit like a drumbeat, so some words or sounds are spoken more loudly (stressed) and others are spoken more quickly and softly in a fairly regular time. This establishes rhythm.

Example

Let's imagine you want to say this sentence:

'I went for a meal last night but the waiter forgot my order'.

To apply stress and create rhythm you would need to say it a little like this:

I wENt for a MEal last nIGHt • but the WAIter forGOT my ORder

What is happening in this version of the sentence? Let's analyse it:

➢ Only part of each stressed word receives the strongest sound **(MAIN STRESS)**
➢ Some words also have some stress but it is less strong (eg last, but, my)
➢ The end of a stressed word may become weakly pronounced in order not to disturb the rhythm (eg the 't' sound in 'went' and 'night' may hardly be heard)
➢ All the unstressed parts (highlighted, e.g t for a, al last n) are spoken at a faster speed, and each occupies about the same time length, to maintain a spoken rhythm.
➢ The listener 'catches' the information because it is the information-carrying words that are stressed (**went, meal, night, waiter, forgot, order**)

Analyse these spoken responses from Part 1, using the style in the Example

a) It's normal to have a lot of family around you.

_____

b) …so the increasing levels of traffic are very noticeable.

_____

c) It's probably unlikely that car accidents can be stopped completely.

_____

d) …I'm a good listener, and I like asking questions and showing interest in people.

_____

Now, practise saying each sentence and try to build the 'drumbeat' of stress, and the rhythm this generates.

16 **Building Awareness of Intonation**
Intonation is like the 'song' of a language – it helps you to express your feelings and your personality. But some languages invite more variety of 'song' than others. When you speak English, it really helps to develop a good range of tones (from high to low) because:
   ➢ it adds interest to your voice and to the meanings and feelings you are expressing
   ➢ it makes the listener feel more focused and more connected to you as a person

A good time to use intonation in IELTS is when you are expressing something you have strong feelings about.

Example

Assessor: Do you like driving?

Speaker A: I LOVE it • it's my TOtal PASSion • I feel complETEly alIVe when I DRIve.

Speaker B: L O VE   T O tal P A S Sion   E T E ly alIVE
                I   it • it's my   • I feel compl   when I DRIve.

Speaker B lifts the tone on some of the stressed words and also says them a little more slowly at the same time to show how much feeling is involved.

Look at these Part 1 responses. Try to identify parts where a speaker might try to communicate feelings using a higher tone, and a slower delivery.

a) I really love my family, especially my grandmother; she's such a beautiful person.

_____

b) I make friends really easily; in fact I get super excited when I meet new people.

_____

c) I'm a terrible driver. I get totally nervous in heavy traffic, and when I get out of the car I feel like a total wreck! I'm so annoyed with myself about it!

_____

Practice saying these responses in a way which communicates the feelings.

 Now listen to Part 1 of Practice Interview 1 (Questions)

Listen to the questions on the recording (or see Page 373) and practice answering as if you were in a real IELTS interview. (Total audio time for all three parts of the interview is 11 min.)

If possible, record your answers for later analysis. For example, you could analyse how long your responses were, how varied, fluent, grammatical, and interesting.
This is part of learning about, and managing your spoken performance.

STOP the recording when you get to Part 2 of the Interview.

PART 2 » Giving a short talk on a topic

In Part 2 the assessor gives you a topic card. On the card, there is guidance on what aspects of the topic to talk about.

You have one minute to prepare and during that minute you can make notes on a piece of paper. Then you talk for one to two minutes.

Fitness Activities 1–7 for Part 2 of the IELTS Speaking Test

Activities 1–7 will help you train yourself to prepare effectively for the talk and deliver a relevant and coherent speech.

Topic Card: An interesting life

> Talk about someone you know, or know about, who has had an interesting life.
>
> You should say:
>
> who the person is
> where the person comes from
> what is interesting about that person's life
>
> and say why that person's life seems interesting to you

1. To practice in getting ideas, choose either a), b) or c) below and list four interesting things about the life of the person you choose:

Person / Interesting things	1	2	3	4
a) Someone you know well				
b) A famous person				
c) Yourself				

IELTS Speaking Fitness Activities

2. Imagine a candidate who received the topic card on a person with an interesting life, and has chosen to talk about their brother.

Match the notes (a-k), about the candidate's brother, with the 4 parts of the topic card.

Notes

a) my brother, Pierre
b) born deaf
c) brilliant scholar
d) 5 years' older than me
e) now lives New Zealand
f) took risks, unlike me
g) born Paris
h) now an artist
i) sailed solo to NZ
j) met his wife in NZ
k) never allowed disability to spoil his life

Topic Card   Notes (a-k)

1) Who the person is   _____
2) Where the person comes from   _____
3) What is interesting about that person's life   _____
4) and say why that person's life seems interesting to you _____

3. Which beginning to the talk (a, b, or c) seems the most appropriate to you, and why?

a) My brother is interesting. His name is Pierre. He is five years' older than me so I'm the younger one. He comes from Paris originally but now he is in New Zealand

b) All right. Well, I suppose all lives are fascinating in some ways, but I'd like to talk briefly about my brother, Pierre. His life has been really extraordinary, at least in my opinion. Let me explain.

c) Pierre is my brother. He's my older brother in fact – five years older. He has had an interesting life, for sure, very interesting. Mine has been not so interesting. He was born in Paris, in fact we both were born there.

4 **Sometimes candidates have trouble talking for two minutes, for different reasons.**

   Which two of these candidates are having trouble and for what reasons?

   a) My brother Pierre, is from Paris. He is interesting because he is deaf. He has done many things – he was good at school, he was an artist, he sailed to New Zealand on his own and got married there. Why is he interesting? Because he never let disability spoil his life, he took risks, not like me.

   b) We born…were born…in France…in Paris. His name, my brother's name…is Pierre…and he is five years' more…five years' old…five years' older…of…I mean, than I…me. So…she is…his…he is my grand…big brother…and my…I am a…baby…the baby for…of the family.

   c) My brother, Pierre, in fact he's my older brother, as there's five years' difference in our ages, was born in Paris, actually very close to the centre of Paris, where our parents had a very popular local bakery . Although he was born deaf, Pierre was brilliant at school, especially at mathematics and Art…

5 **The last part of the topic card usually asks you to explain why you think something, so it is an opportunity to offer your opinions instead of just information.**

   Which one of these last parts does this the best?

   a) Why my brother is interesting? He is interesting because he has done all those things – sailing, art, moving to a new country. He has done more things than me. I didn't travel much and don't take many risks, like he does. I tend to stay at home.

   b) My brother has always seemed especially interesting to me because he was born deaf and this created distance between us. As a younger brother I wanted to look up to him, but it was not easy as his disability made him seem so different. But he inspired me because he never let his deafness stop him from taking risks, or from seeking adventure.

   c) His life is interesting. It is not easy to be a deaf boy and he has still managed to do lots of things, often things that are risky. Sailing to New Zealand was risky but he did it, and he did it alone. It took him nine months, but he finally got there to New Zealand. We met him there…the whole family met him.

IELTS Speaking Fitness Activities

6   If you stop talking after only a minute or so, the assessor may invite you to say more. This is a good opportunity to enrich your use of language. If you end just before the two minutes, you can signal the end of your talk.

Which of these ways of ending your talk seems the most appropriate and polite?

a) I finish now.
b) That's it, no more to say. I said it all.
c) I think that's all I have to say on this topic, for now, anyway.

7   The assessor may ask you a 'rounding off' question after you have finished your talk. You should answer it briefly but try to answer in an interesting way.

Which of these answers seems the most appropriate?

Assessor: Do you see your brother very often?

a) No, not really. I live in Paris still and he's in New Zealand. It's a long journey to go from France to there, or even the other way…it takes a long time, too long for me.

b) No, not often. He doesn't make contact very often…he's busy. I think he's too busy to make regular contact. I'm quite usually busy too most of the time, I must say.

c) Not as often as I'd like. He came over to Paris last year for our parents' 30th wedding anniversary but flights are a bit too expensive for us to get together regularly.

Now listen to Part 2 of Practice Interview 1 (Questions Only)

Listen to the recording and practice answering as if you were in a real IELTS interview.

1. After the introduction to Part 2, **pause** the recording for **one minute** to make notes. Here is the topic card:

   > Talk about a time when you were a child and got into trouble.
   >
   >   You should say:
   >
   >   how old you were
   >   what you did that got you into trouble
   >   what happened afterwards
   >
   > and say why you still remember this occasion

2. After the one minute, **start** the recording again. After you hear, 'Could you start talking now, please', **pause** the recording again and start talking.

3. Start the recording again after **two minutes** and listen to the rounding off question.

4. Answer the question.

STOP the recording when you get to Part 3 of the Interview.

PART 3 » Answering questions related to the topic of your talk

In Part 3 the assessor asks you some questions broadly related to the topic of your talk. This is your opportunity to take your use of spoken English to a higher level. The assessor usually starts with a simpler topic.

Fitness Activities 1–5 for Part 3 of the IELTS Speaking Test

 Activities 1–5 will help you to build stronger responses to questions in Part 3:

1   Which response (a, b, or c) to the first question, extends the topic most but at the same time answers the question relevantly?

   Assessor: Let's talk about exciting activities. Can you tell me about some exciting leisure activities in your culture?

   a) There are many exciting activities in my country. You can do sports, of course, like soccer, and basketball, or you can do more exciting activities like mountain climbing or skiing. It all depends on your interest and your money, of course. Some of these sports cost a lot of money so not everyone can do them. I wasn't able to do such things as a child.

   b) It's true that these days people are more interested in exciting activities, even dangerous ones, In my country skydiving has become popular, and also hunting for wild boar. Hunting is dangerous because it is unpredictable, partly because the boars are aggressive and can run very fast. This mix of danger and excitement seems increasingly attractive, at least to some people.

   c) I think it all depends on what you think is exciting. I'm not a very brave person so many things are exciting for me. Some of my friends, however, love excitement and like to do more interesting things. If I go for a picnic in the mountains, this is really exciting for me, not the food of course, but the steep places and the views.

2   Occasionally the assessor may respond to your answer with a rounding off question.

   Which response (a, b, or c) seems the most relaxed and natural?

   Assessor: Why don't you like dangerous activities?

   a) I don't know. I don't like them. They seem rather stupid to me. I never liked to do dangerous activities when I was younger, and I'm the same now. I like an easy life not a difficult life. In a nutshell, I like to stay in the land of living.

   b) Why do you think I don't like dangerous activities? I like some. I like skiing for example. That's dangerous sometimes. Some people get killed from skiing accidents, but I never think of that. I like this sport too much.

   c) Well, maybe I'm just a bit of a coward, though I don't think so. I like to think I'm just sensible, that's all. Everyone has to decide what they can or can't do, and so I just try to be careful. I don't think I'm alone, I'm sure many people are like that.

3   The next question might ask you to imagine the situation in the future.

   Which of these responses (a, b or c) has the greatest variety of grammar?

   Assessor: Do you think in the future people will choose to lead more dangerous lives?

   a) Yes, I do for sure. I think people will try to do very unusual things like space trips or they will go on endurance walks in dangerous places with no guide or maybe they will even sleep in haunted houses or shoot rapids on a log.

   b) Yes, more and more dangerous, you're right. It is part of life. People always want to go beyond their limits and other people are happy to take their money and to organise some new dangerous activity, like shark hunting.

   c) It seems likely that this trend will continue, yes. This is probably because people psychologically seek danger even though they know it's risky. However high the risk, there are always people who are willing to have a go.

4 The assessor may now move to a slightly more complex topic. This is your chance to discuss ideas in a more complex way using a good variety of language.

Which of these responses (a, b, or c) has the richest use of vocabulary?
Circle any word that you think is a higher level vocabulary item.

Assessor: Let's talk now about the best ways to build your life. Can you explain why nowadays more young people wait until they are older before they get married?

a) I suppose there may be a whole host of reasons, but generally speaking, I think the pressure of building a career is stronger now. In fact, sometimes young graduates struggle to find permanent jobs and if they have a succession of temporary positions they probably don't feel financially secure enough to face the responsibility of marriage. Also, most marriages depend on both partners having the potential to earn good salaries, so for many women a career is built first, and marriage and family is put off until later.

b) I think there are many reasons but many people need a career today and it is very difficult to find a good job, even if you have been to university. Some people have one temporary job after another and don't think they have enough money to get married. Today husband and wife often both have jobs, and actually both need jobs. Many women try to have a good job before they think about getting married and having children. They will probably work again too even when their children are young.

c) You have to have a good job these days, it's very important, because it's hard to find a really good job - I mean a job that is not part-time or just for a few months. So without a real job and a good salary many men and many women don't have the confidence to get married, and to have children, especially as children are expensive too! This is a problem for many women, I think, who know they must probably work and have children, so they try to get a good job first and they marry later, have children and then try to work part-time.

5 The assessor only needs to use 4 minutes minimum for Part 3 so may not use the full 5 minutes if already confident to judge your level. So, develop all your answers to Part 3 questions with as much range and variety as possible.

In this final question, the assessor asks for comparisons.

Which response (a, b, or c) uses the most effective linking expressions between sentences (e.g. 'However', 'For example') to build coherence in the response?
Read these responses and mark the linking expressions.

Assessor: Do you think your life has been more interesting than your parents' lives?

a) I don't think it is easy to answer this question. I have certainly travelled more than my parents but it's not easy to say my experiences have been more interesting. My parents had a simple life when they were young but it was rich in its own way. They had more regular contact with members of their extended family – erm cousins, aunts, uncles, and grandparents. I have to say I don't even know some of my cousins as they live in other countries, and are dotted all over the world. Perhaps my life has been less interesting in terms of contact with wider family. Their family life was richer, for sure.

b) To be honest, I can't really say. Even though I think I've had more opportunities to travel than may parents did, it's not very easy to compare different experiences in terms of level of interest. While my parents' early life was simple, it did have its own richness. Compared to my upbringing, for instance, theirs involved more regular contact with family members. For example, they spent more time with cousins, aunts, uncles, and grandparents, whereas I haven't met some of my cousins, simply because they live in other countries. So, from that point of view, my life has probably been less interesting than theirs.

c) This is an interesting question. I don't think interest can be compared…it's very personal. OK I know I have travelled more than my parents did. It was interesting for me but different from their early life. My parents' early life tended to be simple but to them I'm sure it was really interesting. I know they had a lot more contact with family members like cousins, aunts and uncles and grandparents than I've had. In fact I don't know many of my cousins and have never even met them. They live all over the world in different countries. So my parents' family life was definitely more interesting than mine, I believe.

 Now listen to Part 3 of Practice Interview 1 (Questions Only)

Listen to the recording and practice answering as if you were in a real IELTS interview. If possible, record your answers and listen to them. It's good practice to re-record your own responses, each time trying to improve some aspect of your language – pronunciation, grammar, vocabulary, fluency and coherence.

IELTS Speaking Sample Interview

 RATED SAMPLE IELTS INTERVIEW (Audio time: 12 min)

Did you answer all the questions for the practice interview in the previous section? Well done! For comparison, you might now like to listen to Pragnesh practising a full, IELTS interview. Here's what to do:

1. Start the sample interview recording and follow the transcript below.
Pause the recording any time you want to compare what Pragnesh says with the suggested 'better responses' alongside the transcript.
2. After you have listened to the interview, read the detailed analysis of his performance, noting the discussion of the four IELTS assessment criteria.
3. For practice, try answering each of the assessor's questions yourself!
4. Later, try some of the many test practice questions/topics (Pages 314-330) and try out one or two of the many idioms (Pages 307-313).
5. It's an excellent idea to record your own responses and to analyse your own spoken English while trying to move it closer to IELTS styles.

Pragnesh Speaking Interview Transcript, Part 1

Speaker	Original Version	A better response would be...
Assessor:	Hello my name is Sally Robinson. Could you tell me your full name, please?	
Pragnesh:	*Er hello Sally, my name is Pragnesh...Pragnesh Takka but you can call me Pragnesh, if you like, yeah*	*Er hello Sally, my name is Pragnesh...Pragnesh Takka but you can call me Pragnesh, if you like*
Assessor:	Can I see your identification?	
Pragnesh:	*Yeah, sure... here is my passport, and I guess that should serve the purpose*	*Yes, of course... here is my passport, I imagine that should serve the purpose*
Assessor:	Thank you. Now in Part 1 of the interview I'm going to ask you some questions about yourself.. Let's talk about where you live, Pragnesh. What kind of apartment or house are you living in at the moment?	
Pragnesh:	*Er..I live in er...a three-bedroomed house...at the moment, er... which is single storey...yeah*	*Er..I live in a three-bedroomed house...at the moment, <u>it has just a single storey</u>*
Assessor:	And what do you like about your house?	
Pragnesh:	*Er well our house is located in one of the close roads so that's er I guess that is the most er beautiful thing I like about that...we don't have much of ...an... a traffic er going through the street... so that is good... er...we have got er a lovely neighbourhood as well...er...in close look we have only eight houses there...very good neighbours.. yeah it's nice place to live in*	*Er well our house is located in a <u>cul de sac</u> <u>which I suppose is the most attractive thing</u> <u>about it</u>...we don't have much traffic <u>going past</u> <u>the street... which is good</u>...we <u>live in a lovely</u> <u>neighbourhood</u> as well...with only eight houses there... and very good neighbours... yeah <u>it's a</u> <u>really</u> nice place to live in*
Assessor:	How far is your house from public transport and shops?	

IELTS Speaking Sample Interview

Speaker	Original Version	A better response would be…
Pragnesh:	Well..er..we are just one street away from the public transport..er we can use it..er..as and when needed...er we are a little bit far from the shopping area er but I guess like er it's OK we most of us... most of the time we rely on..er private transport. I have got my own car so er shopping and things are not too bad to go through...so that's quite OK with me at the moment	Well..we are just one street <u>away from public transport</u>..so <u>we can easily use it</u> as and when needed...we are a little bit far from the <u>shopping centre</u> er but <u>it's generally OK because most of the time we rely on</u> private transport as I have my own car so shopping and <u>things like that</u> are not <u>hard to do</u>...so <u>overall everything is really good at the moment</u>
Assessor:	If you could change er one thing in your house, what would it be?	
Pragnesh:	Er...well...er I'm quite happy at the moment so it's a difficult question for me to answer...er... but I guess...er I might go more er near the shopping area that will help me when ...er... I don't have my own car so I can go easily there ...go walking there...er... I guess that will help me	Er..well..as I said, I'm quite happy at the moment so it's a difficult question for me to answer..but <u>perhaps it might be more convenient.er to be located a little nearer</u> to the shopping area as that <u>would help</u> me <u>whenever I didn't have my car and could easily walk there. I think that would be helpful</u>
Assessor:	Thank you. Let's go to talk about eating now. What foods do you eat that are really healthy?	
Pragnesh:	Er...well...er I'm a vegetarian person so er...er main part of er like er quite lot we rely on salads and fruit and er that I guess is..quite a healthier part of my diet...mm	Er..well.I'm <u>a vegetarian</u> so the main part of ...so we rely quite a lot on salads and fruit and that <u>I suppose is the healthiest aspect</u> of my diet..mm
Assessor:	Do you eat sweet things very often?	
Pragnesh:	Oh yes I love my sweets	Oh yes I love <u>sweet things</u>
Assessor:	Why?	
Pragnesh:	er like culturally a part of India where I belong...like...er...er sweet is a core er...component of our food anyway, so er most most of time we have sweet at least once or twice a day... so...er I have grown in that culture and I love my sweets	er well culturally, <u>in the part</u> of India where I belong <u>sweet things</u> are a core component of our food anyway, so most of the time we <u>eat sweet things</u> at least once or twice a day... and <u>as I grew up</u> in that culture, I love <u>sweet things</u>
Assessor:	Are you eating healthier food now than you were when you were a child?	
Pragnesh:	Er..unfortunately not...er...as a kid...er well I was er grown in an environment where my parents...er ...used to er encourage more healthier foods now than what I'm having now I don't have any limitations on that ...and I guess I'm not the right person to choose my foods.	Er...unfortunately not as a child...er well I <u>grew up</u> in an environment where my parents...used to encourage <u>me to eat healthy foods but now they are not around so no one is putting any restrictions on my diet</u> ...and <u>I'm probably not the best person</u> to choose my diet.
Assessor:	I'd like you to talk about your evenings now, Pragnesh. (**Yeah**) How do you usually spend your evenings?	

IELTS Speaking Sample Interview

Speaker	Original Version	A better response would be…
Pragnesh:	Er…most of time when I er return from…from work…er I spend my evenings er with family er…I'd prefer to go out for walking…er but unfortunately it's not possible all the time…er but whenever time permit I would prefer to go out for the walking with family and… er that's what I like…er we have got lovely er…garden near our pl…our house so that's where I want to go.	…most of the time <u>after I get back</u>..from work…er I spend my evenings with family. <u>Actually, I'd prefer to go out for walks</u>, but unfortunately it's not always possible…but whenever time <u>permits</u> I <u>enjoy going out for walks</u> with my family and …<u>there's</u> a lovely garden near our house so that's where <u>we like</u> to go.
Assessor:	Are you ever tired in the evening?	
Pragnesh:	Ah…yes…a few days It depends how busy you are at work and that's the reason I said earlier cause it's not possible all the time but when I'm not tired I would go for walking and things, yeah	Ah…yes…<u>on some days</u>. It depends how busy <u>I am</u> at work and <u>as I said earlier even though</u> it's not possible all the time, when I'm not tired <u>I really enjoy walking, and things like that</u>
Assessor:	Do you sometimes eat late in the evening?	
Pragnesh:	Er I would say quite often…er I'm a late-night person so I like to fini…tidy off my…all… most of the things doing late night…and even as…er…eating…like…er… culturally we have our er dinner er most of time…quite late as well, yeah	Er I would say quite often…er I'm a late-night person so I like to finish off … <u>any work I need to complete, late at night</u>…and <u>in my culture we tend to</u> have our dinner <u>quite late most of the time,</u> anyway
Assessor:	Mm..Thank you.	

Pragnesh Speaking Interview Transcript, Part 2

Speaker	Original Version	A better response would be…
Assessor:	Now I'm going to give you a topic and I'd like you to talk about it for one to two minutes. Before you talk there will be one minute to think about what you are going to say, and to make notes. Is that OK?	
Pragnesh:	Er yeah sure	<u>Er Yes, that's fine</u>
Assessor:	So here's a pencil and a paper for making notes and here's your topic. Er could you talk about an occasion when someone gave you money	
Pragnesh:	OK **(preparation time begins)**	
Assessor:	All right. Remember, you have two minutes for your talk, so don't worry if I stop you. I'll let you know when the two minutes is up. So could you start talking now, please?	

IELTS Speaking Sample Interview

Speaker	Original Version	A better response would be…
Pragnesh:	Yeah, sure. Er…well…er… I er remember the occasion when I er received some money from my dad on er my birthday when I was in Year 10 er I remember it very well 'cause that was the time when I wanted the money very badly er I was grew up in an area like in a time when er video games are quite new and I was…er like we were one of the middle class families so I didn't use to get a lot of pocket money and I didn't manage to get one of those video games from my saving from my pocket money er…	<u>Yes certainly. Well</u>, I remember the occasion when I received some money from my dad on my birthday, when I was in Year 10. I remember it very well because that was the time when I wanted the money very badly. <u>I'll explain why. I grew up during the time when video games were quite new.</u> We were one of the middle class families so I didn't use to get a lot of pocket money and <u>I couldn't manage</u> to <u>save up enough to</u> buy one of those video games.
	One of my very close friend got a video game as a gift on his birthday and I was.. I used to be very jealous with that and I desperately wanted to buy one of those video games …erm…er …and unfortunately I was short of money so I couldn't er afford that…er but luckily my birthday came up and I er received a handsome money from my dad.	<u>However</u>, one of my very close <u>friends was given</u> a video game as a gift on his birthday and I was.. er I used to be very jealous <u>of him</u>, and desperately wanted to buy one of those video games <u>for myself</u>. Unfortunately I was short of money so I couldn't afford it…but luckily my birthday <u>came along</u> and I received a handsome <u>sum of money</u> from my dad.
	That was the time when I liked it a lot and I straightaway bought my video game from that and yeah so er well those days like er…before that birthday most of the time I used to get gifts on my birthday and er I was not having a choice to what to buy from that so I was forced to use what I was given as a gift but when I received money I got the choice to er decide where I can spend my money and luckily I had enough money so that I managed to give a er party for my friends from the money spared after buying the video game…yeah	At that time I <u>liked getting money a lot</u> and straightaway <u>I bought</u> my video game. <u>Perhaps I should say that</u> before that birthday most of the time I used to get gifts on my birthday and so <u>I had no choice</u> of what to buy and was forced to <u>make use of the gifts I was given</u>, but, when I received money <u>on that occasion, for the first time I could choose</u> where to spend my money…<u>in fact</u>, luckily I had <u>more than enough</u> money <u>so I even managed</u> to <u>throw a party</u> for my friends from the money <u>left over</u> after buying the video game.
Assessor:	Thank you. Do people often give you money?	
Pragnesh:	Er…not now er but as a kid I used to get er money quite often er traditionally like when there was some ok like festival comes in er we used to go to our parents and grandparents and we used to get either money or gift as a like their best wishes.	Er…not now, but as a kid I used to be <u>given</u> money quite often…traditionally when there was <u>some sort of festival</u> we used to go to our parents and grandparents and we used to receive either money or gifts from them <u>with their best wishes.</u>
Assessor:	Thank you. I'll take the paper and pencil back now (**Yeah**)	

Pragnesh Speaking Interview Transcript, Part 3

Speaker	Original Version	A better response would be...
Assessor:	So you've been talking about some money that someone gave you and I'd like to discuss with you a few more questions related to this topic (*Sure*) So, first of all let's consider money as a gift...erm When do people often give money to others in your culture?	
Pragnesh:	*Er on like quite of... quite often during the festival season when we go to elderly people oh erm our parents and grandparents they offer money or gift as a best wishes. Er...and then er on birthdays or when you achieve something in your studies or erm your exams...yeah*	*Er well, quite often <u>money is given</u> during the festival season when we go to <u>visit the older generations</u>, like parents and grandparents, and they offer money or gifts...and then also on birthdays, <u>as I told you earlier</u> or when you achieve something in your studies, or <u>pass your exams</u>*
Assessor:	Do you think giving a present is better than giving money, though?	
Pragnesh:	*er..it depends. Er the answer is yes and no er as a kid er mostly they don't have a rough a gross idea about what they should be spending money on so quite often there is a risk involved that er kids can be spoiled by giving them money er but er and at the same time er if they receive a gift as a present then they don't have the choice as well...so er it's a difficult one to answer on.*	*er. <u>I think</u> it depends. <u>Probably</u> the answer is <u>both yes and no</u>. <u>Most kids</u> don't have <u>a clear idea</u> about what they should be spending money on so quite often there is a risk involved that kids can be spoiled if <u>they are given money</u>, but at the same time if they receive a gift as a present then they don't have any choice so it's a difficult one to answer <u>definitively.</u>*
Assessor:	Well do you think parents give money to children more often now than in the past?	
Pragnesh:	*er... with my best knowledge er 'yes' is the answer 'cause these days kids are more particular about what they want and quite often they get annoyed when they don't get the gift what they want so erm at the same time parents are they are quite busy with work and everything so they try to avoid spending time on getting the right gift rather they would give money to the kids I don't know whether that's a right or wrong thing.*	*er.. <u>To the best of my knowledge</u>, I think 'yes' is the answer because these days kids are more particular about what they want and quite often they get annoyed when they don't get the gift they want. At the same time parents <u>these days are quite busy at work</u> and everything, so they try to avoid <u>wasting</u> time trying to get the <u>perfect</u> gift and would <u>rather</u> give money to their kids. <u>I can't decide</u> whether that's a right or a wrong thing, though.*
Assessor:	Thank you, Pragnesh. Let's talk now about money and personal values. Er..why do you think so many people these days want to be rich?	

IELTS Speaking Sample Interview

Speaker	Original Version	A better response would be…
Pragnesh:	er well these days the gap is er increasing quite a lot between rich and poor people and er with globalisation or more often or more so with the audio visual medias people know what rich people can do and that's why they want to achieve all those things that they don't have in their life er…so…er now even the poor and middle class people can see the lifestyle of celebrities and more rich people and they want to get all those things for they don't have in their life so they er spend er…money's very important for them.	er Well these days _it's true_ the gap _between rich and poor people is increasing noticeably._ But, _with globalisation and with the spread of audiovisual media_ people now know _how rich people live_ and that's why they want to _acquire_ all those things that they don't yet have in their own _lives_. _Nowadays_ even the poor and middle class people can see the lifestyles of celebrities and _other_ rich people and so they want to _surround themselves with_ all the _material goods_ they don't have in their lives and this is why money _has become increasingly important_ to them.
Assessor:	What about you, could you live a simple life in the future and live without money?	
Pragnesh:	I would love to, but the honest answer is no I would rather have er more money and decide where I can spend them.	I would love to, but the honest answer is no. I would rather have more money and then decide _what to spend it on._
Assessor:	Finally, let's talk a little about money in the world. Erm what is your explanation for why the wealth gap between rich and poor people is becoming wider in many societies?	
Pragnesh:	Er well er a difficult question for me to answer I've never given er thought to that er but. er I guess like er er with current economical policies er where er they are trying to er get more equalisation in the society but the risk involved in this that in developed countries like Australia and Canada say they give lots of social er money like er social service money to the poor people and quite often they encourage people not to do work cause if er people can get easy money without working what is currently happening in quite a few developed countries that's one of the major risk involved in that lately quite a few stories are coming up where people declare themself disabled just because they can get easy money so er with the policies government is doing right thing by er getting the poor er trying to improve the quality of life in poor people but at the same time there is a risk involved where er there is a group of people who want to take advantage of that.	Er well that's a difficult question for me to answer _as I've never really given it much thought,_ but _I think that_ the current economic policies, _which are_ trying to _build more equality_ in society, _also involve some risks._ _For instance,_ in developed countries like Australia and Canada _many less well-off people receive_ social _security or social services_ and quite often _this encourages_ them not to work, _for the simple reason_ that if people can get easy money without working, and this is something that is currently happening in quite a few developed countries, then that's one of the _major risks_ involved. _There have been quite a few_ stories lately of people _declaring_ themselves to be disabled just to _make themselves eligible_ to receive easy government money, so, _although by adopting these policies_ governments are doing the right thing by trying to improve the quality of life _of_ poor people, at the same time there is a risk involved _whenever there are groups of people_ who want to take advantage of that.
Assessor:	Thank you Pragnesh That is the end of the interview.	
Pragnesh:	Thank you.	

Analysis of Pragnesh's Sample IELTS Interview

This evaluation is not an official IELTS score; it is a formal evaluation and an impression score prepared by a highly experienced teacher, based on the publicly available IELTS assessment guidelines.

The teacher has tried to analyse the student's strong and weak parts and this will give you a better understanding of how to perform better in the IELTS Speaking Test.

Fluency and Coherence

Pragnesh is typical of many speakers of English from the Indian subcontinent – he is very fluent, and has no difficulty at all in understanding all the questions put to him. His answers all make sense and are appropriate responses, though his answers are not always enriched in terms of content, and his ideas not always well linked.

His way of speaking, however, displays one or two features meriting separate consideration.

- Firstly, he has a constant verbal tic (a sort of repetitive speaking habit) in the form of **the sound 'er' which he uses all the time** (and he **repetitively overuses the word 'yeah' also**, though to a lesser extent). This represents a form of hesitation, but because he speaks so quickly and easily, it seems difficult to classify it as part of a major mental struggle to communicate in English. Nevertheless it is a negative aspect.

- The **speed of his speech**, while showing fluency on the one hand, is also a slight problem, in the sense that he sometimes **swallows words** before they have been uttered clearly or fully. This puts an occasional, slight level of strain on the listener and occasionally weakens the overall coherence of his responses.

- Finally, Pragnesh tends to **repeat the same information** in slightly paraphrased form, rather than trying to develop and enrich the ideas he presents. This reduces the overall quality of coherence in his ideas and possibly also reduces the quality of the connection with the assessor, and the assessor's level of interest in the ideas being expressed.

It is these factors that would need to be weighed up when assigning him a score in this area.

Lexical Resource

Pragnesh has an effective functional vocabulary, meaning that he has no difficulty talking on any subject or in any situation. However, his **range of vocabulary is sometimes limited and repetitive**, and he **tends not to enrich his speech with less common (more advanced) vocabulary** choices which might add more colour, texture, interest and precision. This is related also to his **limited ability to develop ideas.** Occasionally, however, he comes out with something impressive (examples: 'core component' ; ' whenever time permit'; 'short of money'; 'declare themselves disabled'; 'easy money'; 'major risks involved'; 'take advantage of that'; quality of life').

In terms of the final score for this criterion, the only occasional use of less common (more advanced) expressions may not be quite enough to outweigh the overall effect of his generally limited range and repetitive use of vocabulary.

Grammatical Range and Accuracy

Again, Pragnesh is fairly typical of many Indian speakers of English in the sense that he has developed a variety of spoken English that in some ways is not quite standard to, say a British or Australian native speaker of English, since **he makes little grammatical errors constantly (for instance tense errors, word form errors)**, but they are errors which don't impede successful communication or comprehension. At the same time, and, again like many speakers of English from India, he uses English grammar in a somewhat limited way, which means he **doesn't display a very wide range of grammatical options or range of constructions**, which in turn tends to make **his grammatical formulations a little repetitive**. It is these factors that would be limiting his ability to be assigned a really high score.

Pronunciation

This is often a troublesome area of language for Indian speakers of English, as once again they have long experience of speaking English but are exposed to varieties of spoken English that may not be standard and often difficult for native speakers of English in the US, Australia or Britain, for example, to follow. Pragnesh's great strength in terms of pronunciation is his use of intonation. He maintains the listener's interest by frequent changes of tone, and this makes him sound engaging, interesting, and natural. Sometimes Indian speakers are much more monotone with unusual stress patterns that cause the listener to lose the sense of what is being said. Pragnesh is also easy to understand most of the time, except when he swallows the occasional word by speaking too fast. His stress patterns and 'chunking' of phrases are generally effective and aid the listener's comprehension. On balance, then, he is effective in terms of pronunciation, but **might be penalised for the negative impacts of speed of speech** on ease of understanding.

SUMMARY

In terms of IELTS, it is likely that Pragnesh would score quite well for Fluency and Coherence and quite well for Pronunciation and possibly Vocabulary, but might struggle to be rewarded as highly for Grammar. He is a good example of a candidate hovering overall around the **Band 7 level**. There are many IELTS candidates in a similar situation.

IELTS Speaking Sample Interview

How could he gain a higher score?

There are one or two simple things that Pragnesh could do and are within his existing ability.

1. **He could slow down a little** – by relaxing (especially if nervousness makes him speak so fast), and by practicing more under IELTS-like conditions to get more used to the 'rhythm' of the test.

    He needs to be more aware of **achieving balance between speed of speech and content.** Based on this interview it seems clear that in order not to fall silent or to seem limited during the interview, he prefers to use repetition of individual expressions and repetition of ideas. This may not be the best balance. Sometimes non-native speakers of English from India fall into the trap of 'over-talking' (often at high speed).

    He **needs to understand the usefulness and power of short pauses between ideas and 'chunks' of speech.** These pauses act to highlight the ideas being communicated and also give the listener time to follow and evaluate them. In fact, **'over-talking' can sometimes lead to 'under-meaning'** (not actually having many different ideas to offer and using a limited language repertoire). This combination of **fast, non-stop (no pause) speech and low content is very tiring to listen to** and may even reduce the perceived value of the language displayed.

2. He should try consciously to insert more, **higher level or idiomatic expressions** into his answers (especially in Part 3) to give the vocabulary score a chance of being lifted. He probably has more vocabulary at his disposal, but has got into a 'functional' speaking habit (i.e. regarding communication of his ideas in simple language as being enough). In an IELTS test he probably needs to focus on **DISPLAYING** appropriate language, not just answering all questions as if they are everyday conversations. His strategy for this language test encounter should be looking at every question as an opportunity to demonstrate (appropriately, of course) the higher level expressions he knows. Again, more practice can achieve this. At the same time Pragnesh needs to learn how to develop ideas in order to generate greater variety of expression. He could record himself giving answers and then analyse the recording to assess the level of repetition and try to come up with new ideas with which to develop his points and then re-record those sections in order to feel the difference in quality and range of content.

3. He might try to move to a **slightly more formal style** in the latter parts of the test, where the questions can be more abstract, discussion questions. He would also benefit from more practice at **extending and developing slightly more complex ideas** in Part 3 of the interview so that expression of ideas gives rise more naturally to maturity and richness of language.

    Going over typical Speaking topics and thinking about ideas to talk about during exam preparation is a good idea. It may help with developing views and opinions on a wide range of subjects.

4. He should try to make fewer grammatical mistakes. It would probably not be as easy for Pragnesh to change his grammatical patterns very quickly as many of them are by now probably 'fossilized' ('stuck') and represent the variety of English he has probably been using for a long time in a different cultural context. But, nevertheless, he could get more control over his sentence patterns with practice.

TOP SCORE VOCABULARY FOR THE SPEAKING TEST

Using occasional, idiomatic or phrasal expressions in your IELTS interview can enrich vocabulary. However, they need to be used **naturally and only occasionally**.

'Sounding natural' is really important when trying to achieve a higher score. It means being fluent and using language in a way that makes the listener feel they are talking to someone who could belong to the same language community.

Below is a list of expressions, each with a meaning and an example of possible use in the Speaking test. Asterisk (*) shows **the most flexible, and perhaps frequently used expressions.**

Expression	Meaning	How to use in a Speaking test
* a drop in the ocean	a very small amount compared to the amount needed	*Assessor*: Do you give money to charity? *You*: No I don't, mainly because I feel that my $50 donation would only be **a drop in the ocean.**
a lost soul	without direction or purpose	*Assessor*: Do you feel you belong in Australia now? *You*: In some ways, yes, but deep down I'm still a bit of **a lost soul**.
a real can of worms	uncovering a range of complex problems	*Assessor*: Have you ever had to solve a tricky problem at work? *You*: Yes, I once found out that someone at work had a criminal record and it was **a real can of worms** when I tried to sack him.
a straight talker	someone who talks directly and openly	*Assessor*: What can you tell me about your best friend? *You*: My best friend, Paul, is a really **straight talker**; he never just tries to say what I would like to hear.
all at sea	very confused	*Assessor*: Do you adapt well in new situations? *You*: Yes, eventually, but I tend to be **all at sea** at first, until things settle down.
* at the end of the day	finally/in the end	*Assessor*: Overall then, which is more important to you - love or respect? *You*: **At the end of the day**, it all depends on your priorities at different times.
drop dead gorgeous	very attractive	*Assessor*: Do you know a person who is very attractive? *You*: Yes, a friend of mine. She's a beauty; I mean she is **drop dead gorgeous**.
full of beans	has a lot of energy	*Assessor*: Is it true that children have more energy than adults? *You*: Oh yes, my son, for example, is always **full of beans**.

life in the fast lane	to seek many colourful experiences in order to chase success or self-improvement	*Assessor:* *You:*	Do you enjoy taking risks? Well, you only life once, don't you, and I've always liked **life in the fast lane**.
life in the slow lane	life without any excitement or danger	*Assessor:* *You:*	How do you feel about extreme sports? Well, some people go for them, but they're not for me - I prefer **life in the slow lane**.
nothing to write home about	mediocre/not as good as expected	*Assessor:* *You:*	Have you seen any new movies lately? Yes, I saw the new Spielberg movie, but it was **nothing to write home about**.
* over the top	excessive	*Assessor:* *You:*	Do you think a CEO can ruin a company? To blame one person for the collapse of the whole company seems to be a bit **over the top**.
quality time	time spent with someone without distractions	*Assessor:* *You:*	If you could change something about your life, what would it be? I would work less and instead spend more **quality time** with my children.
* the bottom line	the final outcome	*Assessor:* *You:*	Children these days often argue that learning in a classroom should be replaced with online studies, do you agree? The methods may vary, but the **bottom line is** they still need to go to school.
* the tip of the iceberg	the visible part of something but the main part is hidden	*Assessor:* *You:*	Is there any corruption in your country? Yes, one of our government ministers was arrested recently for stealing public money and I'm pretty sure it's only **the tip of the iceberg**.
tough love	helping someone to change their behavior by treating them in a very severe way	*Assessor:* *You:*	Do you believe in strong discipline? Well my dad was really strict, but I think his brand of **tough love** helped me to become more responsible.

Expression (verbal)	Meaning	How to use in a Speaking test
* I fancy a (*something*)	I would like a (*something*)	*Assessor*: Do you have a favourite café or restaurant? *You*: Definitely, there is a little cafe that I always go to when I **fancy a** coffee, and also the cupcakes they serve are heavenly.
* to be a disaster	to end very badly	*Assessor*: Are you good at building relationships? *You*: No, I'm afraid I'm not. My last relationship **was a (complete) disaster.**
* to be a joke	to be ridiculous, or ineffective	*Assessor*: Do you think the government should do more to protect the environment? *You*: With all due respect to the government of my country, their current attempts to protect the environment **are a joke**.
to be a waste of space	to be useless	*Assessor*: If you had a problem, would you ask your neighbour for help? *You*: My neighbour **is a waste of space**; I wouldn't even bother.
to be an outsider	to be a stranger, new to something	*Assessor*: Have you got many friends in the place where you live? *You*: I'm still a **bit of an outsider** in my town, even 10 years after moving there.
* to be put out	to be offended/annoyed	*Assessor*: How did you feel when you didn't get that job? *You*: I **was** a bit **put out** when they sent me the rejection letter.
* to be up against it	to experience difficulties created by a situation or a group of people	*Assessor*: Have you ever been in a difficult situation? *You*: Yes, when I had to apply for my visa and saw all the paperwork involved, I realized that I **was** really **up against it**.
to be up on (*something*)	have good, up-to-date knowledge of (*something*)	*Assessor*: What are your interests? *You*: I like sports, especially football. I'm really **up on** the Premier League in the UK; I know all the teams.
to bite the bullet	to take an unpleasant action or decision	*Assessor*: Have you ever had to make an unpleasant decision? *You*: Yes, I once had to quit a well-paid job. It wasn't a good career move but I just had to **bite the bullet**.
to come together	to happen in a satisfactory way, without problems	*Assessor*: How did you feel when you found a new job? *You*: Like my life was finally starting to **come together**.
to do (*something*) up	to make improvements	*Assessor*: What would you like to change about your house? *You*: Everything! The whole place needs **doing up.**
to drink like a fish	to drink large amounts of alcohol regularly	*Assessor*: Do you think that drinking alcohol can be dangerous? *You*: Well, I suppose if you **drink like a fish**, you have to expect health problems.

IELTS Speaking Top Score Vocabulary

to drive like a madman	to drive like an idiot	*Assessor*: *You*:	How do you feel about bad driving habits? I wouldn't get in a car with a bad driver, such as my neighbour - he **drives like a madman.**
* to drop in on (*someone*)	to spontaneously visit (*someone*) without arranging the visit in advance	*Assessor*: *You*:	Do you ever visit your family without calling first? Well, yes, I enjoy **dropping in on** my mother at the weekend sometimes, to give her a nice surprise.
to drop off	to fall asleep	*Assessor*: *You*:	Do you enjoy your course? Well, I'm usually so tired after my part-time job that I often **drop off** in the middle of the lectures. I don't snore, though!
to eat like a horse	to eat large amounts of food	*Assessor*: *You*:	Do you teach your child about a healthy diet? Well, I'm always telling him that if he keeps on **eating like a horse**, and then just watching TV, he may end up overweight.
to feel a bit of a fool	to feel silly	*Assessor*: *You*:	How did you feel about making that kind of mistake? **I felt a bit of a fool**, I suppose.
* to find a way	to manage to complete a difficult task	*Assessor*: *You*:	Is it important to be adaptable in life? I believe so, and one of my friends is a good example. He always tends **to find a way** to get what he wants.
* to fit in	to be socially adaptable	*Assessor*: *You*:	Do you usually adapt well in new social situations? No, not always. I remember that I never seemed **to fit in** at school, for example.
* to get on (*someone's*) **nerves**	to annoy (*someone*)	*Assessor*: *You*:	Do you always enjoy work? To tell you the truth, my boss **gets on my nerves** sometimes.
* to get on top of	to be in control of	*Assessor*: *You*:	Are you a good student? I'm afraid not - but I'd like to be. I need to **get on top of** all my subject material.
* to get on well with (*someone*)	to understand someone well when you interact	*Assessor*: *You*:	Do you have good relationships with people at work? My team is rather small, it's just my colleague Peter and I, and luckily **I get on very well with him**.
* to get (*someone*) down	to annoy (*someone*) or make (*someone*) feel downcast	*Assessor*: *You*:	How do you feel when you make mistakes in English? It usually **gets me down** because I seem to make so many.
* to get together	to meeting someone	*Assessor*: *You*:	Do you prefer to spend time with family or friends? Well, I enjoy **getting together** with friends – less stressful, to be honest.
to give (*someone*) a talking to	to reprimand	*Assessor*: *You*:	Have you ever had a problem with your supervisor at work? Yes, as a matter of fact, not too long ago my boss **gave me a talking to** about being late for work.

* to go for it	to try it	Assessor:	Are you a focused person?
		You:	I would say so. If I believe something is worth the effort, I really **go for it**.
* to go on and on about	to talk at excessively about	Assessor:	Do you think education is important?
		You:	Personally I don't, but my parents are always **going on and on about** the importance of education.
* to go out of my way	to make an effort	Assessor:	Do you think fairness is important?
		You:	Personally, I do. **I go out of my way** to be fair with everyone.
to go out on a limb	to say or do something very differently from most people	Assessor:	Do others feel the same way as you do about this?
		You:	Probably not, I tend to **go out on a limb** about most things.
to have a stroke of luck	to have a lucky happening	Assessor:	Have you ever been late submitting an assignment to your teacher?
		You:	Unfortunately yes, there was a time when I wasn't able to finish my homework in time but I **had a stroke of luck** because my teacher was suddenly ill with flu for a week.
to jump up and down	to be agitated or annoyed	Assessor:	What did your parents think when you left your current job?
		You:	Oh my dad **jumped up and down** for a while until I explained that I had been headhunted by a better company.
to land a …	to achieve something, perhaps with a bit of luck	Assessor:	Have you changed jobs recently?
		You:	No, personally I haven't, but my sister has just **landed a** great job as a lawyer.
to live it up	to enjoy life while spending a lot of money	Assessor:	How do you feel about saving money?
		You:	I just like to **live it up**, so with such an extravagant lifestyle I never save much.
to make a meal out of (*something*)	to take longer than necessary doing something	Assessor:	What do you find the most difficult thing about supervising others?
		You:	I suppose it sometimes seems difficult to get people to do pretty simple things. For example, last week I asked my secretary to write a short memo and she **made a real meal out of it**.
to make (*someone*) see red	to make (*someone*) very angry	Assessor:	Are there any forms of behaviour that you find irritating?
		You:	Well, yes, when people fail to take responsibility for their mistakes it **makes me see red**.
* to make up (*someone's*) **mind**	to come to a decision which is unlikely to change	Assessor:	Are you good at making decisions?
		You:	You bet I am! Once I've **made up my mind** to do something, nothing stands in my way.
* to make up with	to resolve differences	Assessor:	Are you a forgiving person?
		You:	I can be, especially with my girlfriend, every time she wants to **make up with** me after an argument.

IELTS Speaking Top Score Vocabulary

* **to overdo it**	to do too much	*Assessor*: *You*:	How do you feel about dieting? Dieting can be helpful, but people shouldn't **overdo it**.
to play their hearts out	to make a real effort	*Assessor*: *You*:	Have you ever been to a music festival in your country? Yes, and actually I really enjoyed the street musicians the most because they were **playing their hearts out**.
to put it bluntly	to express an opinion in a harsh form	*Assessor*: *You*:	Do you think professionalism is important? I think it is very important. I have no respect for people who, **to put it bluntly**, are no good at what they do.
to put it diplomatically	to express an opinion in a gentle form	*Assessor*: *You*:	Do you perform well at work? **Putting it diplomatically**, I have much room for improvement.
to put (*someone's*) **life on the line**	to do everything possible	*Assessor*: *You*:	Did you try hard enough to get that contract? I pretty much **put my life on the line** to get that deal to succeed.
* **to put** (*something*) **off**	to postpone something	*Assessor*: *You*:	Have you ever had to change your vacation plans? Yes, unfortunately. On one occasion due to pressure at work I had to **put off** my vacation for a few weeks.
* **to run out of time**	the time allocated has ended	*Assessor*:	We've **run out of time**, so that is the end of the Speaking test.
to run (*someone*) **down**	to criticize (*someone*)	*Assessor*: *You*:	What sort of relationship do you have with your neighbour? My neighbour is a strange person. I don't want to **run him down** but there are certain things about him I don't approve of.
to say it like it is	to speak honestly	*Assessor*: *You*	What do people at work think of you? I think some people respect me because I tend to **say it like it is**; I never try to hide the truth.
* **to see the good side of**	to understand the advantage of	*Assessor*: *You*:	How do you feel about working in the healthcare industry? I can certainly **see the good side of** trying to help people in need.
to set eyes on (*something/someone*)	to see for the first time	*Assessor*: *You*:	How would you describe your recent holiday destination? Quite frankly, as soon as I **set eyes on** Antigua I knew it was the place for me.
* **to take a good look at**	to give careful attention to	*Assessor*: *You*:	Are you worried about your weight? Well, I think I certainly need to **take a good look at** my diet.
* **to take it easy**	to relax	*Assessor*: *You*:	Do you often feel stressed at work? No I don't. I try to **take it easy** as much as I can.

to take it on the chin	to accept consequences stoically	Assessor:	How well do you handle unpleasant surprises?
		You:	Well, I don't fall apart. When my manager told me I was fired, it was a real shock, but I **took it on the chin**.
* to take it out on (someone)	to vent anger on (someone)	Assessor:	What do you think is the secret to having a good relationship in a family?
		You:	Patience. Whenever I am frustrated, I try not **to take it out on** my partner.
* to take (someone) up on (something)	to accept	Assessor:	If your boss were to offer you a better paid position but with additional responsibilities, how would you react?
		You:	I'd still probably **take him up on** that.
* to talk behind (someone's) back	to criticize a person, but only in a conversation with others.	Assessor:	Do you enjoy your job?
		You:	The job is fine, but some of my co-workers are not, especially those who **talk behind your back**.
* to talk (someone) into doing something	to convince (someone) to do something	Assessor:	How would you solve a dispute between yourself and a neighbour?
		You:	I would try to **talk the neighbor into** coming over to my house for a cup of tea. Getting to know each other better would help.
to try to talk straight	to speak frankly and directly	Assessor:	Do you think being honest is important?
		You:	Yes I do. I try **to talk straight** and I expect everyone else to speak openly and directly.
to work oneself to death	to be overworked	Assessor:	Do you think people work longer hours nowadays?
		You:	Yes, definitely. Take my sister for example - she almost **works herself to death**.

IELTS SPEAKING TEST PART 1 – QUESTIONS FOR PRACTICE

In this section you will find a collection of questions of the kind you may be asked in Part 1 of your IELTS Speaking test. It is a good idea to go over as many as you can and answer them, or at least think of something to say. Wherever appropriate, extend your responses for around 10-20 seconds.

The first questions you may be asked

Are you a student or do you work?
⇒ What job do you do?
⇒ What are the most interesting parts of your job? (Why?/Why not?)
⇒ How long are you hoping to stay in this job?
⇒ What's you dream job?

Where do you work?
⇒ Is your job sometimes boring? (Why?/Why not?)
⇒ Do you like your boss (your company)?
⇒ Would you recommend this job to others? (Why?/Why not?)
⇒ Is this kind of job popular in your country?

What course are you studying?
⇒ Which subject in your course do you enjoy most? (Why?)
⇒ What would you like to change on your course?
⇒ What will you do after you finish your course?

How long have you been on your course?
⇒ Which parts of your course have been the most difficult for you? (Why?/Why not?)
⇒ Have you made new friends on your course (Why not?)
⇒ Would you recommend this course to others? (Why?/Why not?)

Other Part 1 topics

Let's talk about television now.
⇒ How often do you watch television?
⇒ What kind of programs do you enjoy watching?
⇒ Is television too powerful, do you think? (Why?/Why not?)
⇒ In what ways is watching television bad for you?

Let's move on to talk about going on holiday/vacation now. Is that OK?
⇒ Where do people usually go for holidays/vacations in your country?
⇒ Where did you last go for a holiday/vacation?
⇒ Would you like longer holidays/vacations? (Why?/Why not?)
⇒ Is going on holiday/vacation sometimes stressful? (In what ways?)

I'd like to talk about getting up in the morning now.
⇒ What time do you usually get up in the morning?
⇒ Do you use an alarm clock? (When?/Why not?)
⇒ Do you like getting up early or not? (Why?/Why not?)
⇒ What do you usually eat for breakfast? (Why?)

Now let's discuss the weather.
⇒ What's the weather like in your country at this time of year?
⇒ Do you like rainy days? (Why?/Why not?)
⇒ Do you ever sunbathe on sunny days? (Why?/Why not?)
⇒ Is the weather changing in your country? (How?)

Let's discuss storms now
⇒ Do you often have storms in your country?
⇒ Are you ever frightened of storms?
⇒ When was the last time you experienced a storm? (Where?)
⇒ Are storms dangerous?

I'd like to talk about supermarkets
⇒ Are there many supermarkets where you live? (Why not?)
⇒ What do you like about supermarkets?
⇒ Are supermarkets too powerful, do you think? (Why?)
⇒ Are traditional markets more interesting than supermarkets? (Why?/Why not?)

Let's talk about roads and traffic now.
⇒ Are roads busy where you live in your country? (Why?/Why not?)
⇒ Is it ever dangerous to cross roads where you live? (Why?/Why not?)
⇒ Are most drivers good drivers in your country? (Why?/Why not?)
⇒ How can traffic on the roads be reduced?

Let's talk about learning to drive
⇒ Have you ever learnt to drive? (Why?/Why not?)
⇒ Is learning to drive expensive in your country? (Why?/Why not?)
⇒ What is the lowest age a person should be able to drive? (Why?)
⇒ Is the driving test difficult in your country? (Why?/Why not?)

Let's talk about eating in restaurants now
⇒ How often do you eat out in a restaurant?
⇒ What is your favourite kind of restaurant? (Why?)
⇒ What kinds of restaurant are popular in your country?
⇒ Do you think restaurant food is too expensive? (Why?/Why not?)

I'd like to move on to talk about clothes now
⇒ Do you have many clothes in your wardrobe? (Why?/Why not?)
⇒ Which clothes in your wardrobe are your favourites? (Why?)
⇒ What do you do with your old clothes?
⇒ Are all new clothes cheap in your country?

Let's talk about sport now
⇒ Which sports are popular in your country?
⇒ Which sports have you tried? (When?)
⇒ Which sports are the most expensive to learn in your country? (Why?)
⇒ How often do you watch sport on television? (Why?/Why not?)

I'd like to discuss friends now
⇒ Do you have many friends or just a few?
⇒ Who is your best friend? (Why?)
⇒ Do you make friends easily? (Why?/Why not?)
⇒ Do you still have any friends from your elementary school? (Why not?)

I'd like to talk about using the phone now.
⇒ Do you enjoy talking on the phone? (Why?/Why not?)
⇒ Are you comfortable using the phone on a train or bus?
⇒ Have you ever lost a phone, or found a phone? (When?)
⇒ Are phones dangerous for children to have? (Why?/Why not?)

Let's move on to talk about eating meat now
⇒ How often do you eat meat? (Why?/Why not?)
⇒ Which kinds of meat are popular in your country?
⇒ Is eating meat good for you?
⇒ Will more people stop eating meat in the future? (Why?/Why not?)

Let's talk about walking now
⇒ How often do you go for a walk? (Why?/Why not?)
⇒ Where do you like to walk?
⇒ Have you ever walked a long distance? (Why?/Why not?)
⇒ Is walking better for your health than running?

Let's talk about cycling
⇒ When did you first try to ride a bicycle? (Why not?)
⇒ How safe is cycling in your country? (Why?/Why not?)
⇒ Is cycling popular in your country? (Why?/Why not?)
⇒ Would you enjoy a cycling holiday? (Why?/Why not?)

Let's talk about music
⇒ Is music from America popular in your country? (Why?/Why not?)
⇒ When do you like listening to music?
⇒ Can you play a musical instrument? (Why not?/Which one?)
⇒ Which musical instrument would you like to learn to play? (Why?)

Let's talk about plane travel
⇒ Are you frightened of flying? (Why?/Why not?)
⇒ Is airline food good, do you think? (Why?/Why not?)
⇒ What can you do on very long flights?
⇒ Is flying bad for your health? (Why not?/In what ways?)

Now let's talk about reading magazines
⇒ What kinds of magazine do you read?
⇒ Where do you most often read magazines?
⇒ Are magazines expensive in your country?
⇒ Which do you prefer - reading magazines or reading books? (Why?)

Let's talk about learning a language
⇒ How many languages have you tried to learn? (Which ones?)
⇒ Do you learn languages for work or for pleasure?
⇒ Is your own language difficult to learn, do you think? (Why?/Why not?)
⇒ Which language would you like to learn? (Why?)

Let's move on to talk about animals
⇒ Do you like animals? (Why?/Why not?)
⇒ Which is the most common wild animal in your country?
⇒ Have you ever seen one? (Where?)
⇒ Are any wild animals in your country dangerous?

Let's talk about noise
⇒ Is it noisy where you live?
⇒ Is noise a bad thing?
⇒ Do you like noise better than silence? (Why?)
⇒ When are **you** noisy?

I'd like to talk about cooking now
⇒ Who is the best cook in your family? (Why?)
⇒ What do you find difficult about cooking?
⇒ What meals can you cook best?
⇒ Why are cooking programs so popular on TV?

Let's talk about neighbours
⇒ Do your neighbours live close to you?
⇒ How often do you speak to your neighbours?
⇒ Do your neighbours ever help you? (How?)
⇒ Are you a good neighbour?

Let's talk about flowers now
⇒ Do you ever give flowers as a present? (When?)
⇒ Are there many flower shops in your country? (Where?)
⇒ Which colours of flower do you like best? (Why?)
⇒ Have you ever received flowers from someone? (Who?/Why not?)

Now, let's talk about colour
⇒ What colours do you often choose for your clothes? (Why?)
⇒ What is the best colour for a car? (Why?)
⇒ Are there some colours which are really popular in your country? (Which ones?)
⇒ Is there a colour that you don't like? (Why?)

IELTS Speaking Test Sample Questions

IELTS SPEAKING TEST PARTS 2 AND 3 – QUESTIONS FOR PRACTICE

In this section you will find a collection of cue cards and questions, similar to those your assessor may ask you in an IELTS test. Try talking on the cue card topics (Part 2 of the interview) and answering the questions following each cue card (Part 3 of the interview), as if you were in a real exam. Remember the time limits (one to two minutes per Part 2 cue card talk and four minutes minimum for answering questions in Part 3).

Note: questions in Part 3 are ranked by approximate difficulty. When practicing, choose at least one question from each group. If you need a higher score in IELTS Speaking, select more B and C questions. Remember to practice building and developing your responses so that they are neither too basic nor too short.

1

Part 2 Cue Card	**Describe a house you really like.** You should say:
	  where it is
	  what it looks like
	  who it belongs to
	and say why you like it so much
	
	Rounding off question: When are you planning to visit this house?

Part 3 Questions — A easy	⇒ Tell me about the types of houses that are typical in your country. ⇒ Why are newer houses better than older houses? ⇒ Will apartments be the main form of accommodation in the future?
Part 3 Questions — B harder	⇒ How easy is it for young people to buy their own house in your country? ⇒ Are the benefits of home ownership greater than those of renting? ⇒ Is owning a home a common dream in your society?
Part 3 Questions — C hardest	⇒ What can governments do to help poor people to find accommodation? ⇒ Is it possible to design and build really cheap houses? ⇒ How could slums best be improved in large cities?

2

Part 2 Cue Card	**Describe a person who you think is special.** You should say:
	  who the person is
	  how you know the person
	  what is special about the person
	and say why the person is so special to you
	
	Rounding off question: Do other people think this person is special?

Part 3 Questions — A easy	⇒ Can you talk about a special person from the history of your country? ⇒ What statues in your home town or city celebrate the lives of special people? ⇒ Who is the most special person alive in the world today?
Part 3 Questions — B harder	⇒ Are most celebrities really special, or just well known? ⇒ Is a person special because of what they do, or because of the kind of person they are? ⇒ Is it easier to be special in today's world of social networking on the Internet than it was in past times?
Part 3 Questions — C hardest	⇒ What special goals does your government have for the future of your country? ⇒ How does your school system help students with special needs (disabled, deaf, for example)? ⇒ Is it better for children with special talents to go to special schools, or not?

IELTS Speaking Test Sample Questions

3

Part 2 Cue Card

Describe the best day of your life. You should say:
- when it was
- who was with you
- what happened on that day
- and say why it was the best day of your life

Rounding off question: Are most days good days for you?

Part 3 Questions		
A easy	⇒	Tell me about the best day in the year to be at home with family in your country.
	⇒	Do you think you've already had your best days or are they still to come?
	⇒	Are the best days of your life similar to those of your parents, do you think?
B harder	⇒	Are too many happy occasions in life becoming over-commercialised?
	⇒	How could every day become the best day of your life?
	⇒	How important is it to accept that life sometimes brings unhappiness?
C hardest	⇒	Should all governments have a Ministry of Happiness?
	⇒	Is it a basic human right to expect one's life to keep getting better?
	⇒	Are the best days of the Earth's life in the past, or in the future?

4

Part 2 Cue Card

Describe a place that you enjoy visiting. You should say:
- where the place is
- how often you go there
- what you do when you are there
- and say why you like it so much

Rounding off question: When will you go there again?

Part 3 Questions		
A easy	⇒	Describe some really popular places in your country.
	⇒	Is it getting more expensive to visit popular places or are they mainly free?
	⇒	What kind of different places do younger and older people like to go to?
B harder	⇒	What makes a place a popular destination for visitors?
	⇒	If a place becomes popular does it usually get spoilt?
	⇒	How important is it for you to learn something new when you visit places?
C hardest	⇒	Is the global tourist industry likely to grow or contract in the current economic climate?
	⇒	How does visiting places overseas contribute to better cross-cultural understanding?
	⇒	Will people enjoy visiting other planets at some point in the future?

IELTS Speaking Test Sample Questions

5

Part 2 Cue Card

Describe a singer, artist or actor you truly admire. You should say:
- who the person is
- what they look like
- what they have achieved professionally
- and say why you admire them so much

Rounding off question: Is this person still popular?

Part 3 Questions

A easy	⇒	Describe someone in your country who everyone seems to like.
	⇒	Is it easier to admire a singer or an artist, do you think?
	⇒	Who most deserves your admiration — a famous person or a friend?
B harder	⇒	How do the mass media build up the reputations of singers and actors?
	⇒	Is admiration a deep feeling or do most people just admire people who are popular?
	⇒	Do you admire the same people as your parents do?
C hardest	⇒	How do schools help young people to understand the qualities that deserve admiration?
	⇒	Who most shapes your personal values – your school or your family?
	⇒	How might admiration change in the future? Will we admire different sorts of people?

6

Part 2 Cue Card

Describe the most unusual person in your family (not yourself!). You should say:
- who the person is
- where they live
- what things they have done in their life
- and say why you think they are unusual

Rounding off question: Do people in your family think <u>you</u> are a little unusual?

Part 3 Questions

A easy	⇒	What kinds of students were considered unusual when you were at school?
	⇒	Are you unusual in any way, or are you totally ordinary?
	⇒	Is it easy or difficult to be a little unusual in your culture?
B harder	⇒	Is being unusual helpful if you want to enter a career involving creativity?
	⇒	If a person is unusual should they always be allowed just to be themselves?
	⇒	How important is it for everyone to be tolerant of unusual people?
C hardest	⇒	Has globalisation created too much conformity through mass consumption of similar products?
	⇒	Is a society that has too much conformity reducing its level of innovation?
	⇒	Will the stronger societies in the future be those which strive for greater conformity or those which encourage individual difference?

7

Part 2 Cue Card

Describe a time when you lost something important. You should say:
- what you lost
- how you lost it
- what happened afterwards
- and say how you felt and why

Rounding off question: Do you often lose things?

Part 3 Questions

A easy
- ⇒ Tell me about something that you found once.
- ⇒ Do people in your country usually keep things that they find?
- ⇒ Are young people more careless with their things than their parents were?

B harder
- ⇒ Why are many parents losing the battle to control their children's behaviour?
- ⇒ To what extent are school students losing respect for their teachers?
- ⇒ What social values are slowly being lost in your society?

C hardest
- ⇒ Has your government lost its vision of a great future for your country?
- ⇒ Is a globalised world causing the loss of national identity?
- ⇒ What should the world never lose?

8

Part 2 Cue Card

Describe an occasion when you had to wait a long time. You should say:
- where you were
- what happened
- how long you had to wait
- and say why you think it was such a long wait

Rounding off question: Do you get angry when you have to wait for a long time?

Part 3 Questions

A easy
- ⇒ Where do you see queues most often in your country?
- ⇒ How acceptable is it to keep people waiting in your culture?
- ⇒ Are older people usually more impatient than younger people?

B harder
- ⇒ What goods or services involve long waiting times? (eg passports, flights, restaurants)
- ⇒ What is the best way to deal with a customer who has been waiting for a long time?
- ⇒ Have many modern businesses been able to reduce waiting times for customers?

C hardest
- ⇒ Is it reasonable for the world's population to wait longer for real action on climate change?
- ⇒ Will it be necessary to wait for ever for world peace or is it coming soon?
- ⇒ How likely is it that the world will end?

IELTS Speaking Test Sample Questions

9

Part 2 Cue Card

Describe a dream holiday you would like to take. You should say:
- where you would go
- who you would go with
- what you would do there
- and say why you think it would be so special

Rounding off question: Would this holiday be expensive, do you think?

Part 3 Questions

A easy	⇒ Talk about some popular holiday destinations in your country.
	⇒ Do people in your country usually take long vacations or short ones?
	⇒ How expensive is it for people to travel abroad from your country?

B harder	⇒ What are the benefits of travelling on a group tour?
	⇒ Are adventure holidays likely to become more popular?
	⇒ How dangerous is it to plan your own travel and travel alone these days?

C hardest	⇒ How beneficial is tourism in your country?
	⇒ How could governments attract more tourists from overseas?
	⇒ Do you believe you will see outer space tourism in your lifetime?

10

Part 2 Cue Card

Describe the friend you have known for the longest time. You should say:
- when you first met
- what you like about your friend
- how often you see your friend
- and say why this person is still your friend

Rounding off question: Where is your friend now?

Part 3 Questions

A easy	⇒ Describe where people usually meet their main friends in your society.
	⇒ Is it important to have both men and women friends?
	⇒ Are friends usually from the same economic background?

B harder	⇒ How has the Internet changed the ways in which people meet their friends?
	⇒ Is making friends on the Internet dangerous?
	⇒ Is social networking on the Internet a good way to maintain friendships?

C hardest	⇒ Are friendships more superficial now than in the past?
	⇒ How possible is it to be a true friend of someone who comes from a different culture?
	⇒ What could governments do to prevent the problem of loneliness among the elderly?

IELTS Speaking Test Sample Questions

Part 2 Cue Card	**Describe something you have kept from your childhood.** You should say: 　　what it is 　　when you first had it 　　where you keep it now and say why you have kept it **Rounding off question**: Would you ever give this _____ to someone?	11

Part 3 Questions	A easy	⇒ Describe the sorts of toys that children have these days in your society. ⇒ How do people usually sell used things in your culture? ⇒ Do your parents still have things from their childhood?
	B harder	⇒ How popular is recycling in your country? ⇒ What things does your local government recycle? ⇒ How could people be encouraged to recycle more often?
	C hardest	⇒ How important is it for every nation to preserve things from its ancient history? ⇒ How could children be helped to be more interested in ancient history? ⇒ Will a nation's history be of less interest to future generations?

Part 2 Cue Card	**Describe an interesting film you saw recently.** You should say: 　　what kind of film it was 　　what the story was about 　　who was in the film and say why you think it was interesting **Rounding off question**: Do you go to the movies very often?	12

Part 3 Questions	A easy	⇒ Describe the kinds of film that are popular in your country. ⇒ Are films from other countries more popular than local films? ⇒ How popular is cinema-going among young people?
	B harder	⇒ Is it a good idea for the study of films to replace the study of literature in schools? ⇒ Is watching the film version of a book better than reading the book itself? ⇒ How important is it to make film versions of a nation's important stories?
	C hardest	⇒ Is national censorship of films necessary, or should people be free to choose what to watch? ⇒ Do governments have a responsibility to provide money for the nation's film industry? ⇒ As more people in wealthy countries have 'home theatres' is the future of the cinema in doubt?

IELTS Speaking Test Sample Questions

Part 2 Cue Card	\multicolumn{2}{l}{**Talk about a favourite toy from your childhood.** You should say: what your favourite toy was who gave it to you when you got that toy and say why it was important to you **Rounding off question:** Where is the toy now?}	13
Part 3 Questions	A easy	⇒ Describe traditional toys that are still popular in your country. ⇒ Do you agree that many children are given too many toys? ⇒ Did your parents have many toys when they were young?	
	B harder	⇒ How important is it for toys to be educational? ⇒ Do you agree that the best toys are the ones you make yourself? ⇒ Which are more helpful to a child's development — toys or games?	
	C hardest	⇒ Do you agree that violent computer games should be banned? ⇒ Will simple toys still exist in the future or will all toys become virtual? ⇒ How important to successful socialisation are the toys a child has?	

Part 2 Cue Card	\multicolumn{2}{l}{**Describe a really nice restaurant you have been to.** You should say: where it is what kind of food they serve what you had to eat there and say why you think it is so nice **Rounding off question:** Do your friends like this restaurant?}	14
Part 3 Questions	A easy	⇒ Describe the kinds of restaurant that are popular in your country. ⇒ Is it getting more expensive to eat in a good quality restaurant? ⇒ How common is it for people to leave tips in restaurants in your country?	
	B harder	⇒ How easy is it to get casual work in restaurants in your country? ⇒ Is being a restaurant waiter an easy job, do you think? ⇒ Are restaurants becoming more aware of the need to serve healthy, organic food?	
	C hardest	⇒ Are international fast food restaurants damaging appreciation of a country's traditional food? ⇒ How useful is it to know about different types of food from other countries? ⇒ Is it likely that local speciality foods will not survive in a globalised future?	

IELTS Speaking Test Sample Questions

Part 2 Cue Card	**Talk about some recent changes in your hometown.** You should say:
	    what the changes are
	    who wanted the changes
	    which people they are affecting
	and say how you feel about the changes
	
	Rounding off question: Is your town changing too fast, do you think?
		15

	A easy	⇒ Describe some of the new buildings in your home town or city. ⇒ To what extent is your town or city preserving its history? ⇒ How serious are the social problems in your town or city?
Part 3 Questions	B harder	⇒ Is change in cities and towns generally positive or not? ⇒ What social principles should govern changes in towns or cities? ⇒ What part should citizens take in choosing changes to their town or city?
	C hardest	⇒ Who benefits most when cities or towns change rapidly? ⇒ How could international organizations have more influence on global changes? ⇒ Is the world changing for the better overall?

Part 2 Cue Card	**Talk about how you spent last weekend.** You should say: where you spent the weekend who you spent the weekend with what you did and say why you liked/disliked spending your weekend in this way **Rounding off question**: Do you go away at weekends sometimes?	16

	A easy	⇒ Describe a typical weekend for most people in your country. ⇒ Is the weekend in your country very different from weekdays? ⇒ How important is it to have some time to rest at the weekend.
Part 3 Questions	B harder	⇒ Why are many people's lives becoming busier? ⇒ Are people in danger of suffering from high levels of stress by trying to do too much? ⇒ How likely is it that stress levels will increase in the future?
	C hardest	⇒ Should governments try to impose legal limits on the number of hours worked each week? ⇒ Is having at least one free day per week an international human right? ⇒ Which is more likely — the disappearance of the weekend, or the disappearance of retirement?

IELTS Speaking Test Sample Questions

17

Part 2 Cue Card

Talk about an older person that you know. You should say:
who the person is
how you know them
what you like about the person
and explain why this person is important to you

Rounding off question: When did you last see _____?

Part 3 Questions

A easy	⇒ Describe how most old people are cared for in your country. ⇒ Are the elderly still respected in your society? ⇒ To what extent are the elderly in danger of becoming the forgotten age group?
B harder	⇒ What is the most appropriate age for retirement in your society? ⇒ Is it better to retire early or work for as long as you can? ⇒ Will most people be able to afford to retire in the future?
C hardest	⇒ What measures could your government take to support the elderly more effectively? ⇒ Do you think governments should provide pensions for all old people? ⇒ Should governments make families legally responsible for total care of their older members?

18

Part 2 Cue Card

Talk about a message you received. You should say:
what was in the message
who sent it
how the message was delivered to you
and what happened after you received the message

Rounding off question: Do you send many text messages?

Part 3 Questions

A easy	⇒ Describe how most people send messages to each other in your society. ⇒ Are most text messages really necessary? ⇒ When are handwritten messages still used?
B harder	⇒ At what age should children start to learn to write? ⇒ Could schools teach handwriting more effectively? ⇒ Is it still important to be able to write by hand neatly?
C hardest	⇒ Is the Internet providing too much written information but too little understanding of our world? ⇒ Do you agree or disagree that an 'open encyclopaedia' like Wikipedia is a good idea? ⇒ What kinds of information will be most important in the future?

19

Part 2 Cue Card	**Talk about your favourite book.** You should say: what its title is what it's about when you read it and say why it is your favourite book **Rounding off question:** Do you read very often?	
Part 3 Questions	A easy	⇒ Talk about the types of bookshops that you have in your country. ⇒ Do you read as many books as your parents? ⇒ How important is reading in your life?
	B harder	⇒ Why are electronic books starting to become more popular? ⇒ Do you agree that electronic books are not as satisfying to read as conventional books? ⇒ Will electronic books totally replace standard books in the future?
	C hardest	⇒ Is it important to stop books from being illegally copied and sold in other countries? ⇒ Do you agree that all books should be available free on the Internet? ⇒ Is writing and publishing your own books (self-publishing) a positive thing to do?

20

Part 2 Cue Card	**Talk about a way you like to relax.** You should say: how you like to relax where you go to relax who goes with you and say why this is how you like to relax **Rounding off question:** Do you get enough time to relax?	
Part 3 Questions	A easy	⇒ What do people usually do to relax in your country? ⇒ Is relaxation considered essential in your culture, or a kind of laziness? ⇒ Are you better at relaxing than your parents are?
	B harder	⇒ Do you agree that companies should encourage their employees to relax? ⇒ How could companies reduce the stress levels of their workers? ⇒ Which is the more effective worker – a relaxed worker or a focused worker?
	C hardest	⇒ Does the medical profession have an effective way of treating anxiety? ⇒ Will the increasing pace of life prevent effective relaxation in the future? ⇒ What could schools do to teach children effective relaxation techniques?

IELTS Speaking Test Sample Questions

Part 2 Cue Card	**Talk about something that you made yourself.** You should say: what it is when you made it how you made it and say why you made this particular item **Rounding off question:** Do you make things very often?	21

Part 3 Questions	A easy	⇒ Talk about things that children in your society often make at school? ⇒ Do families in your society still teach children how to make things? ⇒ Do older people usually know how to make more things than younger people do?
	B harder	⇒ How important is it for schools to encourage creativity? ⇒ Are children born creative or do they learn how to be creative? ⇒ How can parents help their children to develop their creativity?
	C hardest	⇒ Do you agree that many countries are no longer manufacturing as many innovative things? ⇒ How important is it for a country to have a strong manufacturing sector? ⇒ How will manufacturing change in the future, do you think?

Part 2 Cue Card	**Talk about a school you went to as a child.** You should say: what school it was where the school was located what you remember about the school and say what you enjoyed about your school days there **Rounding off question:** Would you send your child to the same school?	22

Part 3 Questions	A easy	⇒ Describe the different types of school most children attend in your society. ⇒ Are children staying at school longer now than in your parents' time? ⇒ How expensive is it to attend a government school?
	B harder	⇒ Do you agree that single sex schools are more effective than mixed sex schools? ⇒ Is home education better for a child than attending a large government school? ⇒ How important is the teacher for successful learning?
	C hardest	⇒ What is a suitable class size for effective learning at elementary school? ⇒ Will teachers be unnecessary in the future if computers can offer more and more, self-learning materials? ⇒ Is the main function of a school to educate, or to train students to conform?

IELTS Speaking Test Sample Questions

Part 2 Cue Card		**Talk about an advertisement you have heard or seen recently.** You should say: what the advertisement was for where you saw or heard it what products or services were in the advertisement and say why you remember the advertisement **Rounding off question:** Do advertisements annoy you?	23
Part 3 Questions	A easy	⇒ Describe the kinds of products that are advertised on TV in your country. ⇒ Do you agree that advertisements in your country are often interesting? ⇒ Is TV advertising more effective than magazine advertising in your culture?	
	B harder	⇒ Should children be used in advertisements to sell things? ⇒ Do you agree that advertising has a powerful influence on children? ⇒ Is it acceptable to try to sell adult clothes or make up to children when they are still very young?	
	C hardest	⇒ How important is it to develop international standards to control unfair advertising? ⇒ To what extent is advertising an invasion of personal privacy? ⇒ How will advertising change in the future, do you think?	

Part 2 Cue Card		**Talk about an enjoyable event that you attended.** You should say: what kind of event it was when and where you attended it what you did at the event and say why you enjoyed the event **Rounding off question:** Do you go to important events very often?	24
Part 3 Questions	A easy	⇒ What are the major events each year in your city or town? ⇒ Do you enjoy attending music or other big events? ⇒ Are there more events now than when your parents were your age?	
	B harder	⇒ Should citizens be free to demonstrate in public any time? ⇒ Do you agree that protesting in the street is an important human right? ⇒ To what extent are people losing interest in street protests?	
	C hardest	⇒ Is it a good idea for governments to try organising more national events each year? ⇒ Do you agree that national events help people to feel they belong to their country? ⇒ In the future will most national events be replaced by international events?	

IELTS Speaking Test Sample Questions

Part 2 Cue Card		**Talk about a garden that you like.** You should say: where it is how often you go there with whom you go and say why you like this garden **Rounding off question:** Did you like gardens when you were a child?	25
Part 3 Questions	A easy	⇒ Describe the nicest parks in your town or city ⇒ Is gardening a popular leisure activity in your culture? ⇒ Do you agree that gardens are important?	
	B harder	⇒ What is the best climate for a healthy garden? ⇒ Will there be enough water for people and for gardens in the future? ⇒ Do you agree or disagree that the best gardens are wild, not planned?	
	C hardest	⇒ Should governments turn city parks into land for new houses? ⇒ How can young people be taught to be interested in gardening? ⇒ Do you agree or disagree that gardens should be organic and free of chemicals?	

Part 2 Cue Card		**Talk about your favourite shop.** You should say: what shop it is what it sells how you came to know about this shop and say why you like this shop **Rounding off question:** What was the last thing you bought from this shop?	26
Part 3 Questions	A easy	⇒ Talk about some shops in your town or city that you don't like. ⇒ How often did you help your mother with the shopping when you were younger? ⇒ Why do many men in families not like shopping?	
	B harder	⇒ Do you agree that shops no longer offer much personal service? ⇒ How important is it for a shop assistant to be friendly? ⇒ Which is better — a supermarket that sells everything or a little corner shop with a lovely owner?	
	C hardest	⇒ How could governments encourage internet shopping, in order to save energy? ⇒ Will internet shopping replace department stores eventually? ⇒ Do you agree that internet shopping could lead to shopping addiction?	

IELTS TEST

IELTS Full Practice Test

FULL IELTS PRACTICE TEST – ACADEMIC MODULE

LISTENING TEST

Test Instructions

 Listen to the recording straight through, **ONCE** only (total audio time: 30 min). Answer the questions while listening to each section. At the end of the test you will have another ten minutes to transfer your answers to the Answer sheet (Page 354).

SECTION 1   **Questions 1-10**

Questions 1-5

Complete the Seafront Backpacker hostel enquiry form.

Write **NO MORE THAN 2 WORDS AND/OR A NUMBER** for each answer.

Seafront Backpacker Hostel
Bay View Heights

Guest Form

Guest's Current Address: *Seaview Hotel*   **EXAMPLE**   *15 Esplanade, Dune Beach*

Family Name of guest **1** _____   First Name **2** _____

Phone No. **3** _____   No of nights required **4** _____

Cost per night: Dormitory **A:** $18 **B:** $15   Weekly Cost (7 nights) **5** $ _____

---

332   IELTS Success Formula :: Academic

Questions 6-10

Choose the correct letter **A, B** or **C**.

6 **Each bathroom at the hostel has…**
   A   no shower but hot water all the time
   B   a shower, and hot water sometimes
   C   a shower and hot water all the time

7 **Which facilities are free?**
   A   Breakfast and car parking
   B   Breakfast and internet
   C   Towels and bike parking

8 **She recommends the road from Dune Beach to Selby because…**
   A   it's near the hotel
   B   it's not busy
   C   it's safer for cycling

9 **The hostel is located:**
   A   in a retirement home on the beach
   B   up a hill on the sea front
   C   along a right turn off Beach Road

10 **Which animal is known to be a problem to the caller?**
   A   fox
   B   dog
   C   cat

SECTION 2 Questions 11-20

Complete the notes below.

Use **ONE WORD AND/OR A NUMBER** for each answer.

Name of machine	Positive (+) features	Negative (–) features	Overall Assessment
Coffee Supreme	can brew 4+ cups of mild/strong coffee water filtration system **11** _____ the taste overflow protection/ drip stop parts easy to **12** _____	no auto grinder **13** _____ watt electrical system	good value for money but **14** _____ performance
Café Delight	combines a **15** _____ coffee maker with an espresso machine steam nozzle + frothing attachment	machine is **16** _____ and large	flexible and **17** _____
Coffeetime Automatic	can make different **18** _____ has electronic disc to calculate water needs automatically auto clean/descale	**19** _____ and too large	bulky but uses current **20** _____ well

SECTION 3   Questions 21-30

Question 21

Choose TWO correct letters from A, B, C or D.

21 Which TWO are purposes of the Student Support Service?
- A   to improve students' independence
- B   to carry out some of the study for the students
- C   to encourage students to make judgments
- D   to help students to build relationships

Questions 22 - 26

Answers the questions below about Wilson's study problems.

Write NO MORE THAN ONE WORD AND/OR A NUMBER for each answer.

What is Wilson's main problem?	22 _____
What part of an assignment is often not clear to him?	23 _____
With which aspect of his essay problems will the special session help?	24 _____
What is one of Wilson's other problems with essay writing?	25 _____
With whom can Wilson talk about the drafts of his essays?	26 _____

Questions 27-30

Complete the Report on Grace's problems.

Write **NO MORE THAN ONE WORD AND/OR A NUMBER** for each answer.

REPORT

Grace has difficulty keeping up with **27** _____ on her Nursing Course.

She says that lecturers speak too quickly and are not always **28** _____.

She thinks that recording lectures **29** _____ time.

Grace is not sleeping well; seems worried about her family.
I suggested that she should talk to a counsellor from a different cultural **30** _____.

I offered to help her to make the appointment.

SECTION 4 Questions 31-40

Choose the correct letter **A**, **B** or **C** according to what the lecturer says:

31 Management research now understands that...
   A organisations need a structure
   B feelings affect relationships significantly
   C workplace relationships can only be effective with rules

32 Emotional intelligence is...
   A an aspect of IQ
   B a range of abilities linked to feelings
   C an important management task

33 Empathy essentially involves...
   A imagining another's feelings
   B understanding certain conditions
   C feeling natural enough

34 Managing other people's feelings is helpful to...
   A self motivation
   B popularity of the organisation
   C leadership skills

35 In a happy workplace, people are...
   A intelligent and technically competent
   B cooperative and respectful
   C aware of the importance of quality

Complete the sentences below.

Write **ONE WORD ONLY** from the lecture for each answer.

A manager with a healthy self image will probably be a **36** _____ influence in workplaces.

Our perceived self is our inner **37** _____ of ourselves.

Our desired self focuses on what is **38** _____ within ourselves.

Our presented selves require us to behave according to what is **39** _____ by others.

The three aspects of the self are not performed individually, but **40** _____.

READING TEST

Test Instructions

You have **ONE HOUR** to answer 40 questions in three sections. You must transfer your answers to the Answer sheet (page 354) during this time. Allow approximately 20 minutes for each section.

READING PASSAGE 1

Read Passage 1 below and answer **questions 1-13**

Why are women becoming unhappier?

A The 21st century American woman enjoys the benefit of more, and better domestic appliances, higher incomes, more control over fertility and relationships, and better education. So it is paradoxical that the improvements in the objective situation of women in the USA and other industrialised countries over the past 40 years have not been accompanied by perceptions of increased happiness. In fact, women seem to perceive themselves to be both less happy than they were in the 70s and less happy now than men.

B Stephenson and Wolfer's review of the sociological data indicates that, historically, women reported higher levels of subjective well-being than men. By the twenty-first century, women reported happiness levels on a par with, or perhaps lower than those reported by men. Compounding this trend among adults, the US Monitoring the Future study, which since 1976 has been surveying approximately 15,000 US twelfth graders each year about their attitudes, has found that young men have raised levels of happiness, while young women have become slightly less happy.

C Sociologists seem to be unsure about the reasons. Data are inconclusive in terms of whether women now work more hours than men as a result of social changes. However, Hochschild and Machung's work hints at the possibility that women still carry the emotional responsibility in the home and that this is now more challenging for them. Increased divorce rates and growing numbers of children born out of wedlock may have added to women's emotional burdens. Yet, research data tend to suggest that levels of happiness are not significantly different between those women with, and those without children. Other sociologists like Kimball and Willis suggest that the hopefulness and idealism that accompanied the growth of the women's movement in the 70's have gradually weakened. Perhaps connected to this, the largest decline in happiness among women was among the group that had attended university, though this reflects the steadily increasing proportion of women who have been attending college across the past 40 years. In fact, irrespective of the age, marital, labour market, or fertility status of the group analysed, data suggest that both the absolute decline in happiness among women in the United States, and the even larger decline relative to men, seems to be widespread. In Europe, trends are similar with perhaps an even greater decline in the happiness of women relative to men. The attempt to find a critical, explanatory variable has so far proven elusive, however.

D With which aspects of their lives are women now less satisfied? A number of survey questions have explored satisfaction across a number of domains: work, financial situation, family, health, and job satisfaction. Women remain similarly satisfied with their work when compared with both the past, and with men. With financial situation perceptions have changed. Women begin the sampling period reporting financial satisfaction that is similar to that for men. However, women's financial satisfaction declines through the 80s and 90s, and, by the end of the sample period, women are substantially less satisfied with their household financial situation than are men. What is more, the magnitude of the decline in women's satisfaction with their financial situation is similar to the decline in women's happiness overall.

E On average, women are less happy with their marriage than men, and women have become less happy with their marriage over time. However, men have also become less happy with their marriage; thus, the gender gap in marital happiness has been largely stable. Marital happiness is more closely linked to general happiness for women, with the correlation between overall happiness and marital happiness being 0.4 for married men and 0.5 for married women. When asked to rate their health on a four-point scale from poor to excellent, women throughout the period report lower health satisfaction than do men. In contrast, men's subjective health assessment has not changed much over this period.

F Returning to the teenagers, it seems that the subjective well-being of girls is falling and the well-being of boys rising. There appears to be increasing ambition among young women beyond the domestic sphere, with greater importance attached to being successful and being able to find steady work, or making a contribution to society. These data arguably suggest that women's life satisfaction may have become more complicated as women have increased the number of domains in which they wish to succeed. Moreover, the data point to rising pressures beyond the much-discussed work-family trade-off.

G One possibility is that broad social shifts such as those brought on by the changing role of women in society fundamentally alter what measures of subjective well-being are actually capturing, leading to falling average satisfaction as it becomes difficult to achieve the same degree of satisfaction in multiple domains.. Perhaps the puzzle is less one of finding out why women see themselves as less happy and more one of unravelling why men's happiness has not declined in line with women's happiness.

Questions 1-5

Reading Passage 1 has 7 paragraphs, A-G.

Which paragraph contains the following information?

Write the correct letter, **A-G**, in boxes 1-5 on your answer sheet.

1   The proposition that women may be less happy because they no longer have the same feminist, political dreams of 40 years ago.

2   The view that for women to be as satisfied with their lives is more complex because of the larger number of fields in which they want to excel.

3   The parallel size of the reduction in women's satisfaction with their financial circumstances and their general happiness.

4   The view that perhaps it may be more important to focus research on the explanation of why men's happiness levels have held up better.

5   The seeming contradiction between the improvement in women's actual living conditions and the decline in how happy they perceive themselves to be.

Questions 6-10

Do the following statements agree with the information given in Reading Passage 1?

In boxes 6-10 on your answer sheet write

    TRUE   if the statement agrees with the information
    FALSE   if the statement contradicts the information
    NOT GIVEN if there is no information on this

6   It makes little difference to perceptions of happiness if a woman is a mother or not.

7   Younger women are feeling a sense of declining happiness.

8   Twelfth-grader young men view themselves as healthier than their young, female counterparts.

9   The link between marital happiness and overall happiness is stronger for men than for women.

10   Men's perceptions of their health have been more stable than women's across the survey period.

Questions 11-13

Complete the summary below.

Choose **ONE WORD ONLY** from the passage for each answer.

Write your answers in boxes 11-13 on your answer sheet.

Women in the USA **11** _____ themselves to be less happy than 40 years ago, despite improvements in their lives. Men's levels of happiness have not **12** _____ to the same extent. The explanation for this is still a **13** _____.

READING PASSAGE 2

Read Passage 2 below and answer Questions 14-26

The changing vocal world of the humpback whale

A   In the dark world of the world's oceans, whales depend on echolocation – the use of sound for navigation. Only 1 per cent of surface light travels to a depth of 100 meters; at 600 meters the sun's illumination equals that of starlight. Lacking an external ear, they detect sound waves via a fat pad between mandible and middle ear. Among the cetaceans, humpback whales are recognized by scientists as one of the most vocally diverse and exciting species. The cetologist, Peter Beamish, tested the navigational skills of humpback whales in the dark. After building a maze in a Newfoundland bay for a humpback rescued from a fishing net, he blindfolded the whale with rubber drain plungers. Before being set free, the humpback managed to find its way through the maze, thereby demonstrating the effectiveness of echolocation.

B   In 1967, the biologist Roger Payne started making and analysing recordings of the sounds of humpbacks off Bermuda. Working from hundreds of hours of tape recordings taken on the breeding ground, Payne contended that the sounds they heard were more than idle chatter. They described the sounds as notes uttered in succession which together formed a recognizable sequence or pattern in time. In other words, they were songs with distinctive themes. All the whales in a breeding group appeared to sing the same songs, over and over again.

C   Scientists have been studying humpback whale songs for nearly fifty years, but there are strange things about them which resist explanation. For instance, only the male whales sing these amazing songs, so it is generally assumed that the song is to attract the attention of females. However, no one has ever seen a female whale approach a singing male. Instead, other males seem to be more interested. When they approach the singer, he stops singing, and the two males go off silently together for a little while, and then they separate.

D   In any year, whales sing identical songs in Hawaii and Mexico, breeding areas that are 4,500 kilometres apart. How is this possible? Perhaps they hear the songs across long distances or learn them during the summer months, when different groups gather in the north to feed. More remarkable than the geographic consistency is the change in calls over time. Slight variations in the songs occur each year. But, as with evolution, these changes can make huge leaps in a short time. Variation in whale songs is evidence that cetaceans have culture, which can change over time and vary across oceans. The Australian biologist, Mike Noad, and colleagues, found evidence of a 'cultural revolution' in the Southern Hemisphere. In 1996 two male humpbacks from the Indian Ocean arrived in the Pacific with a new song. Within two years, all the Pacific males had changed their tune, picking up the migrants' songs. An explanation of this switch is not so straightforward. A preference for novelty is one possibility, though this theory seems to be contradicted by the observation that all whales in a particular area sing the same song in a given year. Although the cause of this dramatic change is still unclear, the knowledge that cetacean cultures endure and change over time, and that culture is not the unique domain of humans is likely to radically transform perception of these mammals.

E   Unfortunately, whales, and an understanding of their calls, are under a new threat. Noise that degrades information exchange comes in many forms, and it may change the use of a communication system and possibly derail communication all together. Dependency on sound makes whales vulnerable to the rising level of noise in the oceans. The number of cargo ships has tripled in the past 75 years, with larger vessels plying the seas each year. These human-generated, chronic sounds are akin to a smog of acoustic noise. Fishermen employing depth finders and acoustical gear in their search for fish add to this noise. The constant underwater din, which can impact whales' ability to hunt and reproduce, is punctuated by intense pulses from seismic air guns, used to plot oil and gas deposits along the ocean shelf. Among the loudest sounds produced by humans, these pulses reach across entire oceans and may be responsible for recent whale strandings.

F   Naval exercises using high-decibel mid-frequency sonar for antisubmarine training can also harm whales. Mass strandings of beaked whales have occurred around the world after military tests. In 2000, 13 beaked whales and two minkes stranded in the Bahamas after the US Navy deployed mid-frequency sonar. Four of the whales had unusual haemorrhages near their ears. In 2002, 14 beaked whales were stranded in the Canary Islands after a test. Ten of them had gas bubbles in their blood vessels, clear evidence of decompression sickness. The whales may have reacted to the ear-splitting noises by heading for the surface too quickly, disoriented by the sonar. Given that symptoms of the bends have never been found in these deep-diving whales, it is also possible that the noises caused the bubbles to form in the bloodstream of vulnerable whales. There is evidence that, in the laboratory, cetaceans attempt to avoid noise and increase breathing rates, a sign of stress. In the acoustic smog of the modern ocean, there may be nowhere for dolphins and whales to go. Noise can also affect communication. Humpback whales change their songs in the presence of active sonar, extending their calls to compensate for the acoustic interference on their breeding grounds. The situation is unlikely to improve in the near future.

Questions 14-17

Reading Passage 2 has 6 paragraphs, A-F.

Choose the correct headings for paragraphs **A-D** from the list below.

Write the correct number, **i-viii**, in boxes 14-17 on your answer sheet.

	List of Headings
i	The darkness of the ocean's waters
ii	Song variation as evidence of whale society
iii	Some mysterious features of whale song
iv	Understanding whale song
v	How humpback whales detect sound
vi	Sounds and distance
vii	Males and females
viii	Recording of whale song
ix	The threat of noise

EXAMPLE	ANSWER
Paragraph E	___ ix ___

14   Paragraph A   _____
15   Paragraph B   _____
16   Paragraph C   _____
17   Paragraph D   _____

Questions 18-21

Choose the correct letter, **A, B, C** or **D**.

18 How did Roger Payne characterise the sounds in his early recordings?
    A   They were signs that whales were chattering when they were feeling lazy.
    B   The sounds were only made when whales were breeding.
    C   The sounds seemed to reflect repeated topics of musical 'conversation'.
    D   The sounds were successful in helping whales to recognise one another.

19 What does the writer say about humpback whale song in terms of male and female reactions?
    A   Songs are definitely mating calls initiated by males.
    B   Males are interested in following females when the song is being used.
    C   When they hear a male singing, other males want to sing.
    D   The songs seem to lead to a strange silent pattern of behaviour among male.

20 What does the writer say about the quality of noise in today's oceans?
    A   Noise from ships is creating a clear grading of sounds under the ocean.
    B   The noise is a confusing blend of sounds which is ceaseless.
    C   Noise in the ocean today is similar to that made by trains on railways.
    D   Sounds of fish add further volume to the ocean noise.

21 Which is the most likely combination of explanations for whale strandings, according to the writer?
    A   Stress and military testing
    B   Sonar pulses and decompression sickness
    C   Ears splitting and avoidance behaviour
    D   Faster breathing rates and haemorrhages

Questions 22-26

Complete the summary of paragraphs D, E and F (questions 22-26 below).

Use **ONE** word from the list (A–O below) for each answer.

Write the correct letter, **A-O**, in the boxes 22-26 on your answer sheet.

Whales sing identical songs across long distances. But, slight changes in the songs occur each year. Such **22** _____ of whale songs is evidence that cetaceans have culture, which can vary across oceans. The knowledge that whale **23** _____ both endure and change indicates that culture is not just **24** _____ to humans. This is likely to transform how these mammals are perceived.

Increasing ocean noise seems to **25** _____ information exchange among whales and may disrupt communication altogether. The constant underwater din affects their hunting and breeding ability, and may be responsible for strandings.

Strandings have also occurred after military tests. The whales may have reacted to noise by **26** _____ too quickly. The situation is not likely to improve soon.

A moderation	B floating	C lessen
D species	E numbers	F effect
G restricted	H available	I modification
J damaged	K societies	L share
M surfacing	N groups	O diving

READING PASSAGE 3

Read Passage 3 below and answer **Questions 27-40**.

Wave energy – a UK perspective

Waves are generated by the wind as it blows across the ocean surface. They travel great distances and so act as an efficient energy transport mechanism across thousands of kilometres. The energy can be captured by various devices, which produce enough movement either of air or water to drive generators that convert the energy into electricity.

A The energy contained in ocean waves can potentially provide an unlimited source of renewable energy. Ocean waves are created by the interaction of wind with the surface of the sea and the UK has wave power levels that are amongst the highest in the world. The initial solar power level of about 100W/m2 is concentrated to an average wave power level of 70kW/metre of crest length. This figure rises to an average of 170kW/metre of crest length during the winter, and to more than 1,000kW/metre during storms. Wave energy converters extract and convert this energy into a useful form. The conversion usually makes use of either mechanical motion or fluid pressure, and there are numerous techniques for achieving it. The mechanical energy is then converted to electrical power using a generator. Wave energy converters can be deployed either on the shoreline or in the deeper waters offshore. East-facing sites in the UK are unsuitable because of the limited energy associated with easterly winds, while bottom friction reduces power levels where the water depth is less than 80 metres. As a result, the inshore resource is usually only one-quarter or less of the deep-water resource.

B The three main types of wave power machines either sit on the shoreline or are free-floating.

Oscillating water column
An oscillating water column is a partially submerged, hollow structure that is installed in the ocean. It is open to the sea below the water line, enclosing a column of air on top of a column of water. Waves cause the water column to rise and fall, which in turn compresses and depresses the air column. This trapped air is allowed to flow to and from the atmosphere via a Wells turbine, which has the ability to rotate in the same direction regardless of the direction of the airflow. The rotation of the turbine generates electricity.

Buoyant moored device

A buoyant moored device floats on or just below the surface of the water and is moored to the sea floor. A wave power machine needs to resist the motion of the waves in order to generate power: part of the machine needs to move while another part remains still. In this type of device, the mooring is static and arranged such that the waves' motion will move only one part of the machine.

Hinged contour device

A hinged contour device is able to operate at greater depths than the buoyant moored device. Here, the resistance to the waves is created by the alternate motion of the waves, which raises and lowers different sections of the machine relative to each other, pushing hydraulic fluid through hydraulic pumps to generate electricity.

The main problem with wave power is that the sea is an unforgiving environment. An economically-viable wave power machine will need to generate power over a wide range of wave sizes, as well as withstand the largest and most severe storms and other potential problems such as algae, barnacles and corrosion.

C   Due to lack of long-term commercial operating experience, actual cost data is virtually non-existent. The estimates always show projected cost per kWh, falling over time due to better designs and increasing unit size. Given the state of technology there is little doubt that many designs can generate electricity but the key question is can they do so cheaply. It would be straightforward to build very strong devices capable of withstanding all the storm conditions expected - the difficulty is constructing at minimum capital cost and having minimum operating cost (for maintenance and repair) so that the overall cost of generation is kept as low as possible and is competitive with alternative forms of generation.

D   There are two wave power devices in the UK. Total installed capacity currently stands at 1.25 megawatts. The first type of device is the LIMPET (Land Installed Marine Powered Energy Transformer), a 500-kilowatt shoreline oscillating water column on the Scottish island of Islay. The second, the 750-kilowatt Pelamis sea snake, is an example of a hinged contour device. It is the first deep-water grid-connected trial and is currently installed at the European Marine Energy Centre in Scotland, where it has been undergoing testing.

E Marine energy could provide around 20 per cent of the UK's electricity needs but only if there is sufficient investment in the appropriate technology. In the short-term the initial set-up costs of marine energy are high as it requires extensive research and development. Yet it is clear that sufficient investment now could lead to a strong UK marine energy sector. The UK is in prime position to accelerate commercial progress in the marine energy sector and secure economic value by selling marine energy devices, developing wave and tidal stream farms and creating new revenues from electricity generation.

F Wind-generated waves on the ocean surface have a total estimated power of 90 million gigawatts worldwide. Due to the direction of the prevailing winds and the size of the Atlantic Ocean, the UK has wave power levels that are among the highest in the world. Wave energy has the potential to provide as much renewable energy as the wind industry.

Questions 27-30

The reading passage has 6 paragraphs A-F.

Which paragraph, A-F, contains the following information?

Write the correct letter, **A-F**, in boxes 27-30 on your answer sheet.

27   Some discussion of the economic potential of wave energy in the UK.

28   General data on rates of power relative to wave height and length.

29   A brief analysis of factors affecting economic viability.

30   Current operational power capacity.

Questions 31-35

Do the following statements agree with the information given in Reading Passage 3?

In boxes 31-35 on your answer sheet write

    YES   if the statement agrees with the claims of the writer
    NO   if the statement contradicts the claims of the writer
    NOT GIVEN if it is impossible to say what the writer thinks about this

31   The sea bed and restricted water depth both have an impact on the energy potential of waves.

32   Generators are more effective with the buoyant-moored device.

33   Wave energy devices need to be able to cope with plants or organisms which might attach themselves to the machinery.

34   Projections usually assume unit costs will increase as innovative, larger machines are developed.

35   One of the devices currently being tested is joined to the main electricity network.

Questions 36-40

To which device does each statement apply?

Choose one device from the box below and write the correct letter, **A-C**, next to questions 36-40.

A	Oscillating water column
B	Buoyant moored device
C	Hinged contour device

36   This device is attached to the sea bed and is usually visible above the water level.

37   This device enables independent movement and varies the height of its different parts.

38   This device is tube-like and some of it is not visible above the level of the sea.

39   This device produces energy largely from alternation of air pressure.

40   This device relies principally on the variation in wave movement to produce fluid pressure which is then converted into energy

WRITING TEST

TASK 1

You should spend about 20 minutes on this task.

The following table shows average daily water use in households in the USA before and after the application of water efficiency measures.

Summarise the information by selecting and reporting the key features, and make any relevant comparisons.

Average daily water consumption USA (in gallons)

Use \ Year	2011	2012 (After water efficiency measures)
Shower	11.6	8.8
Washing machine	15.0	10.0
Dishwasher	1.0	0.7
Toilet	18.5	8.2
Bath	1.2	1.2
Water leaks	9.5	4.0
Household taps	10.9	10.8
Other uses	1.6	1.6
TOTAL	69.3	45.3

Write at least 150 words.

TASK 2

You should spend about 40 minutes on this task.

Write about the following topic:

> Some people believe that spending money and living for today makes more sense than saving for the future.
>
> Do you agree?
>
> Give reasons for your answer and include any relevant ideas from your own knowledge or experience.

Write at least 250 words.

SPEAKING TEST

 Now listen to the recording of <u>Practice Interview 2 (Questions)</u>

Listen to the recording and practice answering as if you were in a real IELTS interview (total audio time: 11 min).

1. Listen to the **Introduction** and **Part 1** and respond to each question.

2. After the **introduction to Part 2, pause** the recording for one minute to make notes on the task for your short talk. (* The task card is below)

3. After the one minute, **start** the recording again. After you hear, 'Could you start talking now, please', **pause** the recording again and start talking for a minimum of one and a maximum of two minutes.

4. **Start** the recording again after two minutes maximum, listen to and answer the rounding off question. Then just **continue** as the interview moves into **Part 3**.

Remember, Part 3 should last for a minimum of four minutes, so just pause the recording if the next question starts before you have finished answering the previous one.

Here is the Task Card for Part 2 of the Interview.

> Talk about your favourite movie star.
>
> You should say:
>
> who your favourite movie star is
> what kinds of movies they have appeared in
> what sort of person you think they are in real life
>
> and say why you like this movie star so much

Practice Listening Test Answer Sheet

#		#	
1		21	
2		22	
3		23	
4		24	
5		25	
6		26	
7		27	
8		28	
9		29	
10		30	
11		31	
12		32	
13		33	
14		34	
15		35	
16		36	
17		37	
18		38	
19		39	
20		40	

Practice Reading Test Answer Sheet

#		#	
1		21	
2		22	
3		23	
4		24	
5		25	
6		26	
7		27	
8		28	
9		29	
10		30	
11		31	
12		32	
13		33	
14		34	
15		35	
16		36	
17		37	
18		38	
19		39	
20		40	

ANSWERS & TRANSCRIPTS

Listening Fitness Activities – Answer Sheet

Fitness Activity 1		Fitness Activity 6	
1.	A	1.	533 East 67th St
2.	A	2.	93014269
3.	V	**Fitness Activity 7**	
4.	V	1.	Thursday(s)
5.	C	2.	5 / five
6.	C	3.	ATSTIX
Fitness Activity 2		**Fitness Activity 8**	
1.	C	1.	B/bookshop
2.	B	2.	morning(s)
3.	A	3.	M/music
Fitness Activity 3		4.	B/beauty
1.	admission	5.	Thursday
2.	select	**Fitness Activity 9**	
3.	middle	1.	adopted
4.	design	2.	habit
5.	distributed	3.	efficiency
Fitness Activity 4		**Fitness Activity 10**	
1.	jams	1.	how long
2.	inefficiency (built-in)	2.	(brief) notes
3.	(the) left	3.	eye contact
4.	(It) improved / an improvement	4.	speaking slowly
Fitness Activity 5		5.	P/project
1.	372	**Total: 40 answers**	
2.	11:30		
3.	bag		
4.	Singapore		

Note:
1. '/' means alternative answer
2. '( )' means optional part of the answer

Reading Fitness Activities – Answer Sheet

Fitness Activity 1		Fitness Activity 8	
1.	vi	1.	I
2.	iii	2.	A
3.	viii	3.	P
4.	vii	**Fitness Activity 9**	
5.	i	1.	FALSE
Fitness Activity 2		2.	TRUE
1.	A	3.	TRUE
2.	C	4.	NOT GIVEN
3.	D	5.	TRUE
Fitness Activity 3		6.	TRUE
1.	electricity	7.	TRUE
2.	moved	8.	FALSE
3.	flood	**Fitness Activity 10**	
4.	science	1.	iv
5.	consumer	2.	vii
Fitness Activity 4		3.	ii
1.	C	4.	viii
2.	B	**Fitness Activity 11**	
3.	D	1.	devastated
4.	A	2.	support
Fitness Activity 5		3.	solution
1.	YES	4.	150,000ML/water
2.	YES	**Fitness Activity 12**	
3.	NOT GIVEN	1.	damage/disintegration
4.	NO	2.	upstream
Fitness Activity 6		3.	weatherboard shed/shed
1.	C	4.	bitter
2.	B	5.	$200 million
3.	E	**Fitness Activity 13**	
4.	E	1.	stability
5.	D	2.	evaporator
Fitness Activity 7		3.	particles
1.	$2.5 billion	4.	pale tan
2.	flooding/flooding in Gympie	5.	vitamin D
3.	higher gates/floodgates/higher floodgates		
4.	water crisis		

Note:
1. The actual IELTS Reading test has only 40 questions numbered 1-40.
2. '/' means alternative answer.

Writing Task 1 Fitness Activities – Answer Sheet

Task Type: Map	
1. b 2. c 3. b 4. a 5. b 6. c	Planning the Introduction
7. indicates / essentially / increased / improved 8. 1) '…changes in….' 　2) '…between 1980' 　3) '…and 2008' 9. task / overview / present / past	Writing the Introduction
10. b, e 11. west (or western) / east (or eastern) / northern (or north) / southern (or south) 12. 1) In 1980 the Center <u>had</u>… 　2) There was <u>an</u> auto shop… 　3) …<u>on</u> both levels 13. d	Writing Body Paragraph 1
14. b 15. by/On/with/by/to/on/with/to 16. numerous / significantly / pedestrian link to / periphery / disappeared / built 17. c	Writing Body Paragraph 2
18. a 19. d, e 20. To sum up (or 'Overall' / 'To summarise'), by 2008 there was more choice at the (Shopping) Centre, and better transport options for visitors.	Writing the Conclusion

Writing Task 1 Fitness Answers

	Task Type: Process Diagram	
1.	a	Writing the Introduction
2.	shows / covers	
3.	1) ...the main <u>steps</u> 2) ...in <u>buying</u> 3) ...<u>viewing</u> and making	
4.	steps / buying / issues	
5.	The first step / Then / Once / As soon as / After / After that / Once	Writing the Body Paragraph
6.	First, housing needs <u>are established</u>. Then affordable areas <u>are looked for</u>. Next, a house <u>is chosen</u> and an offer <u>made</u>. If it is accepted, a 10% deposit <u>is paid</u>.	
7.	<u>Present passive</u>: is rejected / is required / is made / is carried out / is paid / is cleared (*Any two*) <u>Present perfect passive</u>: has been chosen / has been accepted	
8.	1) principal 2) purchase	Conclusion

	Task Type: Graph	
1.	a	Writing the Introduction
2.	indicates / seems / had "Overall it seems that caravan parks had slightly higher occupancy rates and less fluctuation than hotels."	
3.	higher/ less/ than	
4.	increased / fell back / peaking / returned / recovering / steady	Writing Body Para. 1
5.	a	
6.	a, c	Writing Body Para. 2
7.	(1) marginally / (2) noticeably / (3) substantially / (4) massively	
8.	higher / less	Conclusion
9.	a) ...across the period surveyed b) ...across the years studied c) ...across the months compared	

IELTS Success Formula :: Academic

Writing Task 1 Fitness Answers

Task Type: Table		
1.	The <u>table</u> <u>presents</u> data on access to computer and internet for two income levels in Australia in 1998-2000. Access levels <u>were</u> greater for the higher income group, but <u>increased</u> generally for both groups across the three <u>years</u>. Overview sentence: 'Access levels were greater for the higher income group, but increased generally for both groups across the three years.'	Writing the Introduction
2.	a) two income levels b) the higher income group	
3.	'the corresponding percentages across the three years'	Writing Body Paragraph 1
4.	incomes / falling / recovering / marginally /corresponding / double	
5.	Access to computers for those on incomes below $50,000 was 34% in <u>1998</u>, falling marginally to 33% in 1999 before recovering strongly to <u>37%</u> in 2000. For the above-<u>$50,000</u> group the corresponding percentages across the three years were more than double at <u>69, 71 and 77%</u> respectively.	
6.	'Starting from' / 'the figure increased slightly to' / 'then' / 'from' / 'to' /'and then to'	Writing Body Paragraph 2
7.	1) the figures were much higher 2)…the overall increases less dramatic	
8.	1) To sum up 2) Summing up 3) To summarise	Writing the Conclusion
9.	upper / much higher / lower / more rapidly	

Task Type: Chart		
1.	'coffee consumption increased, especially for those in the older age cohorts.'	Writing the Introduction
2.	a	Writing Body Paragraphs
3.	age ranges, (the 75+) category, age cohorts, older groups, younger groups	
4.	i) a ii) c iii) a iv) b	
5.	it is clear that consumption was fairly similar (C) 6% in the 55-64 group and 3% in the 75+ cohort. (F) rates ranged among these five age cohorts from 12% up to 14%. (F) older groups showed some increase but at lower rates (C) The older, middle age ranges predominated, (C) followed by 14% of 35-44 year olds and 13% of 18-24 year olds. (F)	
6.	A sample conclusion: 'To summarise, coffee consumption increased for all age groups but more rapidly for the middle and older age ranges.'	Conclusion

360   IELTS Success Formula :: Academic

Writing Task 2 Fitness Activities – Answer Sheet

	Task Type 1: Indicate and support your level of agreement	
1.	a (but it is often the case that a writer is not 100% in agreement with a statement)	Planning your answer
2.	c	
3.	b (but 4 possible if short of time)	
4.	c	
5.	a (time pressure encourages brevity)	
6.	c	Writing the Introduction
7.	a, d	
8.	a) Shopping is likely to grow in popularity. b) Shopping is not likely to die out. c) Overspending is likely to cause problems. d) It is highly unlikely that shopping will ever bring happiness.	
9.	people (consumers); selfish (self-centred); careless (less disciplined)	
10.	a) Shopping makes consumers selfish. b) Shopping makes consumers dangerous. c) Shopping makes consumers spend unwisely. d) Shopping makes consumers ill-disciplined.	
11.	c	Writing Body Para 1
12.	a) …enable them to pay their bills b) …are available to help…	
13.	c	Writing Body Paragraph 2
14.	Examples: a)…higher education is important b)…travelling has become so popular c)…people work so hard d) Love (*You need to believe this!*)	
15.	show (depict); wish (desire); look (appearance); shoppers (consumers); feeling good (wellbeing); not good enough (inadequate); goods (products); social good (community welfare)	
16.	a, b	
17.	a), b) Your choice! c) more d) more	Writing Body Paragraph 3
18.	d	
19.	c	
20.	b	
21.	a) + b) – c) + d) –	
22.	a	Writing the Conclusion
23.	all too tempting; ever-busier working lives a) all too / far too all too / far too b) ever-growing c) ever-busier d) never-ending	
24.	b, c, e	

Writing Task 2 Fitness Answers

	Task Type 2: Present a two-sided Discussion	
1.	c	Planning your answer
2.	b	
3.	b	
4.	a	
5.	b	
6.	a	Writing the Introduction
7.	a) economic uncertainties b) pure romance is under challenge	
8.	a) problem b) issue c) topic d) problems / issues	
9.	b, d, e	Writing Body Paragraph 1
10.	a) + iii) b) + iv) c) + ii) d) + i)	
11.	Your choice, so answers will vary	
12.	a) often seem b) often seem c) often seem to struggle d) often seems to know	
13.	Your choices, so answers will vary	Writing Body Paragraph 2
14.	a) wedding cake b) marriage ceremony c) marriage partner d) job opportunity	
15.	a (1), c (2), d (3), b (4)	
16.	a, c	Writing Body Paragraph 3
17.	a) commitment / infatuation b) reputation / proximity c) nutrition / taste	
18.	Your choices, so answers will vary	
19.	a, d, f	Writing the Conclusion

	Task Type 3: Discuss Advantages & Disadvantages	
1.	b	Planning your Answer
2.	c	
3.	a) pros and cons b) prolonging work past	Writing the Introduction
4.	c	Writing Body Paragraph 1
5.	1. benefits 2. enables 3. seems 4. provides 5. individuals	
6.	Disadvantages: c (or b also seems possible) Supporting examples: a	Writing Body Paragraph 2
7.	1. On <u>the</u> other hand 2. <u>a</u> full time job 3. <u>the</u> workforce	
8.	a) demanding b) remaining c) undertake d) prevent	
9.	b	Writing the Conclusion

Writing Task 2 Fitness Answers

Task Type 4: Explain & Offer Solutions or Consequences	**Planning your Answer**
1. b 2. c 3. Your choices, so answers will vary	
4. a) reasons for this phenomenon b) the key to making family life better	**Writing the Introduction**
5. a) First of all / In the first place b) Lastly / Finally c) All in all / Taken together d) So / Consequently e) In the same way / Similarly f) Thereby / thus g) Putting it another way / In other words h) The result of this is / As a result i) Such that / so…that j) This can lead to a situation in which / This cam mean that	**Writing Body Paragraph 1**
6. a) Line 1: big change b) Line 3: biggest social task c) Line 4: good value d) Line 5: good time e) Line 5: big role	**Writing Body Paragraph 2**
7. a) harder and longer work b) less family time 8. Your conclusion, so answer will vary	**Writing the Conclusion**

Speaking Fitness Activities – Answer Sheet

Part 1 Q	Answer	Explanation
1	b	a) is too short, and even sounds a little rude c) is still too abrupt and too general
2	c	a) 'place' here means the house, not the suburb b) not sufficiently relevant as it introduces the 'landlord'
3	b	a) too repetitive c) too much hesitation
4	a	b) not polite enough c) asks for an explanation, which assessor can't give
5	b	a) and c) have grammatical problems and lack linking expressions – they are therefore unclear
6		'I have **loads** of friends……some from right back when I was at school, from various jobs I've had, and there are the friends I play **sport** with. I've always been a **friendly** sort of person so I find it easy to **get** on with people when I **meet** them. But, I suppose I'd say I only have one or two **true** friends – friends I completely trust, I **mean**.'
7	a	b) and c) don't have the higher level vocabulary and idioms that a) has (**to catch up with** my old friends, **bump into** my new friends, **hang out** together).
8	c	
9	b	
10	a	b) and c) use only simpler links: 'and / but / because / so' ; a) uses a wider range: 'even though / however / because / as'
11	c	a) talks more about roads; b) talks about roads and cars (not traffic)
12	b	b) is too direct because it has imperatives, which often seem impolite ('Think about it') and also uses the short, direct forms which can sound abrupt and opinionated ('They can't. It's not possible'). a) and c) use less direct language which sounds more polite.
13	b	Unlike b), responses a) and c) don't show the wider range of strategies for managing hesitation and for retaining a sense of fluency.
14 *	1) I'm sorry, • I didn't catch that. • Could you repeat it, • please?
	2) Yes • it's great. • There are plenty of parks, • with tennis courts • and many native plants • flowers • and trees.
	3) As I said just before • I'm a bit shy • but I make friends quite easily • maybe because I'm a good listener • and I like asking questions • and showing interest in people.
15 *	a) It's **NOR**mal to have a **lot** of **FAM**ily a**round** you.
	b) …**so** the inc**REA**sing **lev**els of **TRA**ffic are **very NO**ticeable.
	c) It's **prob**ably un**LIK**ely that **CAR** accidents can be s**TOP**ped com**PLETE**ly.
	d) …I'm a goo**d LIS**tener and I like asking **QUES**tions and **show**ing **IN**terest in **peo**ple.
16 *	a) I **REALLY LOVE** my family, esp**EC**ially my grandmother; she's such a **BEAUT**iful woman.
	b) I make friends **REALLY EAS**ily; in fact I get **SUPER** excited when I meet new people.
	c) I'm a **TERR**ible driver. I get **TO**tally nervous in heavy traffic, and when I get out of the car I feel like a **TO**tal **WRECK!** **SO** I'm annoyed with myself about it!

* **Note:** slight variations are possible.

Speaking Fitness Answers

Part 2 Q	Answer	Explanation
1	Various	Not Applicable
2 1)	a), d)	Not Applicable
2 2)	e), g)	Not Applicable
2 3)	b), c), h), i), j)	Not Applicable
2 4)	k), f)	Not Applicable
3	b)	(a) is too abrupt and has no introductory sentence; (c) is rather repetitive and suggests the speaker lacks 'true' fluency and flexibility; (b) has a short introduction and establishes some expectation in the listener.
4	a), b)	(a) is unable to use linking words to make his talk smoother and more connected; (b) is uncertain of correct grammar and creates too much hesitation through self correction.
5	b)	(a) has poor grammar and wanders away from a focused answer by starting to talk about himself rather than his brother; (c) also drifts away from the question by focusing on what his brother did rather than why his brother's life interests him
6	c)	(a) and (b) are very short and direct statements, which often sound a little impolite; in (c) the use of 'I think', and '..for now, anyway' helps to soften the ending and makes it sound more polite by extending it a little;
7	c)	(a) and (b) are too repetitive (lack richness) and thus less interesting

Part 2 Complete Talk

Interviewer: *Could you start now, please?*

Candidate: *All right. Well, I suppose all lives are fascinating in some ways, but I'd like to talk briefly about my brother, Pierre. His life has been really extraordinary, at least in my opinion. Let me explain. My brother, Pierre, in fact he's my older brother, as there's five years' difference in our ages, was born in Paris, actually very close to the centre of Paris, where our parents had a very popular, local bakery. Although he was born deaf, Pierre was brilliant at school, especially at mathematics and Art. He also loved the outdoor life and always liked water. As a teenager, I think he was about 14, he went on a course and learned how to sail. He took to sailing like a duck to water, I suppose you could say. After finishing school, he sailed solo to New Zealand in a small sailing boat. This seemed amazing... and really adventurous to me, his little brother, especially as I was a bit of a stay-at-home geek, ...at that time, anyway. Now, where was I? Oh yes. In New Zealand, he met a beautiful, Maori girl, actually she's not deaf, and eventually they got married. He went to Art School over there and is now a well-recognised artist. I've seen some of his work...it's pretty good. He paints landscapes mainly, or to be more precise, I should say, seascapes. I suppose my brother has always seemed especially interesting to me because he was born deaf and as children this created distance between us. As a younger brother I wanted to look up to him, but it was not easy as his disability made him seem so different, so self-contained and unique. But he inspired me because he has many talents, and never let his deafness stop him from taking risks, or from seeking adventure. In some ways, he is still a mystery to me, always intriguing, almost a bit mythical. Er...I think that's all I have to say on this topic, ...for now, anyway.*

Interviewer: *Thank you. Do you see your brother very often?*

Candidate: *Not as often as I'd like. He came over to Paris last year for our parents' 30th wedding anniversary but flights are a bit too expensive for us to get together regularly.*

Speaking Fitness Answers

Part 3 Q	Answer	Explanation
1	b	(b) is probably the most effective response as it provides two good examples of exciting activities and then develops one of those activities (boar hunting) in an interesting way. (a) offers plenty of examples but they are not really relevant to the idea of 'exciting'. Also this response loses its focus by starting to talk about money and personal interests. (c) starts well by questioning the meaning of 'excitement' but then just talks about personal things, and loses relevance. NOTE: Responses (a) and (c) might negatively affect final score on 'fluency and coherence' because examiners usually can sense if a candidate is 'filling' time with 'easy to use' language rather than having enough richness, flexibility and control.
2	c	(c) seems the most natural, as the candidate is genuinely reflecting on his/her own reasons and then suggesting that caution is not unusual. The candidate doesn't seem to feel any sense of shame in admitting a sort of lack of courage, which is a personal style of response quite common among adults in western-style cultures. (a) is also an honest response but seems abrupt because it has no 'lead-in' expressions such as 'I like to think that I'm… ' in response (c). The examiner might consider this response a little too direct and unsubtle. (b) This response contradicts the questioner, but contradicting in response to a question is fine. However, again, this response is also a little too direct and fails to give any reasons, in response to the 'why' in the question. So it's not really a very relevant answer either.
3	c	c) is the response which has the greatest variety of sentence connecting expressions (because / even though / however / who are…) Although this response sounds a little more formal than the others as a result, it is displaying flexibility of grammar more effectively than the other responses . (a) and (b) sound natural and have good vocabulary but display less variety of clause connection.
4	a	(a) has the richest use of vocabulary (a whole host of reasons, / generally speaking / the pressure of building a career / struggle to find permanent / a succession of temporary positions / feel financially secure / face the responsibility / depend on both partners / potential to earn / is put off) (b) and (c) are good, relevant answers but are a little more repetitive in terms of vocabulary use - the word 'jobs' for example is over-used.
5	b	(b) is the most competent at linking ideas in a varied way (Even though… / more …. than / in terms of… / While… / Compared to… / For example,.. / whereas… / because… /so from that point of view…). (a) and (c) are good answers but rely a little too much on simple linkers such as 'but' or 'and' or 'so' to link ideas.

IELTS Full Practice Test Answer Sheet (Academic)

Q#	Listening test	Reading test
1	Wong	C
2	Jacqui	F
3	014830579	D
4	7	G
5	$90	A
6	C	TRUE
7	B	TRUE
8	C	NOT GIVEN
9	B	FALSE
10	C	TRUE
11	improves	perceive
12	replace	changed
13	750	puzzle
14	limited	v
15	regular	viii
16	bulky	iii
17	convenient	ii
18	drinks	C
19	pricey / pricy	D
20	technology	B
21	A, D *(both needed)*	A
22	writing	I
23	Title / titles	D
24	planning	G
25	structuring / structure / disorganised / disorganized	C
26	tutor	M
27	lectures / lecturer	E
28	clear	A
29	wastes / waste	C
30	background	D
31	B	YES
32	B	NOT GIVEN
33	A	YES
34	C	NO
35	B	YES
36	positive	B
37	view	C
38	missing	A
39	expected	A
40	interact / together	C

Note:
1. '/' means alternative answer,
2. '( )' means optional part of the answer

Listening Fitness Activities - Transcripts

Listening Fitness Activity 1 (Page 21)

Chris: …We've all just met so perhaps we should start by an introduction with a bit of background from each of us.

Anna: OK. I'm Anna. I finished three years of a Languages degree in <u>Sweden, where I come from</u>. This year I decided to study overseas to get to know a different part of the world. I'm also a big fan of European cinema, especially French and Italian.
Those are the languages I majored in along with English. To me, film is a great way to learn about the rest of the world. <u>I was in the film club at my university</u> so when I saw the notice asking for volunteers, I thought it would be a good way to meet people and get involved in something I really enjoy.

Veronica: Thanks, Anna. My name is Veronica and I come from Italy. I'm <u>doing graduate studies in English Literature</u>. I went to some of the films in the festival last year and enjoyed them. I especially liked the video interviews. That was when I decided to get involved. <u>I used to do film reviews for our student newspaper back home</u>

Chris: Hi I'm Chris from Scotland and I'm in 4th year Journalism. Cinema is my hobby. <u>Last year I joined the organizing committee,</u> just like you have now, and somehow, this year I've ended up in charge. I'm actually able to use my coordinating work on the festival towards a credit for one of my courses. I <u>have to write up a report on the festival with recommendations</u> so that's an extra motivation for me. So I hope this is going to be a good experience for us all.

Listening Fitness Activity 2 (Page 22)

Mark: … Any other trends that you thought were significant?

Evelyn: Well what's really interesting is what the article called 'mobile meals'. In other words more and more Canadians <u>are eating meals away from home, but</u> NOT just eating more junk food.
They are projecting a <u>40% increase</u> in snack food sales over the next three years and the growth is coming from healthy snacks – you know the ones that have less cholesterol and fat, such <u>as muesli bars</u>, health food bars and those types of products. Apparently in the food marketing jargon they are called "nutritious portable foods" which means healthy snacks!
The other major trend is that young people are doing more of the food shopping these days so marketing has to be aimed more at them, as well as more conventionally at the mother.

Listening Fitness Audio Transcript

Listening Fitness Activity 3 (Page 23)

Veronica: ... Where does the funding come from? What kind of budget do we have?

Chris: The festival is subsidised by the student council. We generate money through advertising and through admission charges. We'll go over the budget in detail a little later. But we've got lots of work to do in the meantime.

Anna: I guess we have to start pretty soon.

Chris: Well, I think by the first of March at the latest, we need to select all the films. Then we have to find some advertisers to sponsor the event - that shouldn't be too hard. We'll just start with last year's list. Our deadline for that should be the middle of March. By the end of March we need to design the program. Then we can get posters made up and distributed in April.

Veronica: Like you said, we need some clever promotion - something to generate interest and get people talking. We have 4 months to get ready. It should be enough time.

Listening Fitness Activity 4 (Page 24)

Typewriters in 1873 jammed or got stuck if the keys next to each other were hit in quick succession. To solve this problem, in 1878, the QWERTY keyboard was developed, spacing frequent letters away from each other, and therefore reducing the number of jams. It was not specifically designed to slow down typists, as is generally believed, but the keyboard did create a built-in inefficiency for typists. The most common keys are scattered all over the keyboard rows, many on the left side. Right-handed people have to use their left hand, which is the weaker hand. Typewriter technology improved, doing away with the original rationale for the QWERTY distribution, but the keyboard remained. In spite of its inefficiency, it is the keyboard we all use today.

Listening Fitness Activity 5 (Page 25)

Agent: Ok, who's next, please?

Jenny Lee: I think I am.

Agent: How can I help you?

Jenny Lee: I just came in on flight 372 from Singapore at 11:30 and my luggage hasn't arrived. I've been waiting at the baggage claim for about a half an hour now and everything seems to have come off the plane. The conveyor belt has stopped and all the passengers have gone. So I came here to find out what has happened to my bag.

Agent: Can I see your ticket please?

Jenny Lee: Here it is.

Agent: So you came from Hong Kong today and changed planes in Singapore, right?

Jenny Lee: Yes, the connection in Singapore was a tight one. The plane got in late and I had to rush to get to the next flight.

Agent: That's the problem right there. There wasn't enough time to get your bags onto the connecting flight.

Listening Fitness Activity 6 (Page 26)

Agent:	Now, I need you to fill in these forms. Your name?
Jenny Lee:	Jenny Lee
Agent:	Address?
Jenny Lee:	I guess you want my address here. I'm staying with relatives. Just a minute, <u>I'll have to look it up. It looks like 583, no its 533 East 67th St. in Riverside.</u>
Agent:	Do you have the phone number there?
Jenny Lee:	<u>Yes I do. It's um 93014269.</u>
Agent:	So you came in on Qantas Flight… *(fades)*

Listening Fitness Activity 7 (Page 27)

Thank you for calling ATS Advanced Ticketing System, the call system for all your entertainment needs. Our automated telephone service is designed to answer your questions quickly and easily. The ATS office in the Regency Theatre is <u>open Monday</u> to <u>Thursdays</u> from 10am-5 pm and on Friday and Saturday <u>till 8 pm</u>.
For online bookings and detailed program listings check our website at www.atstix.com.
<u>That's spelled A-T-S-T-I-X.</u> Please listen to the choices available. You may press your choice as soon as you hear it to get more information.

Listening Fitness Activity 8 (Page 28)

Henry:	Look there's the notice that Professor Jones told us he'd be putting up confirming the details of our work experience placements.
Jo:	But I thought that was already arranged.
Henry:	No, he said he'd have to check with the companies that the days we preferred were OK for them – let's see if any have changed. Theresa's not here today, but her name's first – it says <u>the Uni Bookshop</u>, <u>Friday mornings</u>, starting on the 23rd March, so nothing's changed. I'll let her know.
Jo:	What about Manuel? He's not here either. Is he still going to the music store in the High St?
Henry:	If it's <u>Mainly Music</u>, yes he's still down for that, on Friday afternoons, starting on the 9th.
Jo:	Um.. the day's different – it's changed from Tuesday mornings, but that's OK, I'll tell him. He'll really enjoy listening to music all day!
Henry:	Now where's my name…Henry…here it is…I 'm going to <u>The Beauty Shop</u>, and I said I preferred <u>Thursday afternoons</u>…oh good, that seems OK and my start date hasn't changed either. Jo, what day did you opt for? *(fades)*

Listening Fitness Audio Transcript

Listening Fitness Activity 9 (Page 28)

The superiority of the Dvorak keyboard was clearly established. However, it has never been adopted as the keyboard of choice. Why? First or all, bad luck and bad timing on the part of the Dvorak team. First there was the Depression, not a good time for introducing change. But the main factor that worked against the Dvorak system was habit. People were used to the QWERTY keyboard. Computers today could easily switch the arrangement of letters to the Dvorak layout, but it seems that because of habit, the QWERTY layout remains dominant. People felt comfortable with the keyboard they learned on so it was the established patterns of hundreds of millions of typists, manufacturers, typing teachers and typewriter salespeople that have crushed all moves toward keyboard efficiency for over 70 years. It looks like QWERTY keyboard may be with us for a long time yet.

Listening Fitness Activity 10 (Page 29)

Probably the most important part of public speaking is what you do beforehand, by which I mean preparation. This includes practical details such as knowing precisely what your topic is and exactly how long you are expected to talk for. You should also plan the content thoroughly. A good strategy is to write out the content as you intend to say it and then make brief notes, preferably on small cards, which you use to talk from. This way you sound more natural, you incorporate pauses while you look at
your notes and you can then look at your audience while you are speaking. Never read your speech without looking at the audience. Eye contact is a very important part of communicating with an audience; so deliberately move your head and look around at your audience. Pauses are important as most people when they are nervous tend to rush through their speech. Practise speaking slowly, this gives you more time to pronounce your words correctly. It's always easier for your audience to listen to
someone whose speaking is clear and calmly paced so that they can understand the ideas being explained. And the bigger the group the more slowly you should speak. Remember to project your voice, speaking clearly to the person furthest away from you.

Practice Interview 1 (Questions Only) Transcript

Hello, my name is Sally Robinson, could you tell me your full name, please?

OK. And what shall I call you?

Can I see your identification, please?

Thank you. Now in Part 1 of the interview, I'm going to ask you some questions about yourself. Let's talk about where you live:

⇒ Where is your home town or city?

⇒ In what ways is it a nice place in which to live?

⇒ Are any parts of your home town dangerous at night?

⇒ What changes would most improve your home town?

Let's go on to talk about walking now.

⇒ How far do you walk each day?

⇒ Where do you go for a walk if you want to relax?

⇒ What do you enjoy about walking?

⇒ How could everyone be encouraged to walk more?

Let's move on to talk about photos now?

⇒ How often do you take photos?

⇒ What kinds of photo do you most like taking?

⇒ Do you have any really special or favourite photos?

⇒ Why do you think photos may become less important in the future?

Speaking Practice Interview 1 Audio Transcript

Thank you. Now I'm going to give you a topic and I want you to talk about it for one to two minutes. Before you talk there will be one minute to think about what you are going to say, and to make notes. Is that OK? Here's a pencil and paper for making notes and here's your topic. Could you talk about a time when you were a child and got into trouble?

> Talk about a time when you were a child and got into trouble.
>
> You should say:
>
> how old you were
> what you did that got you into trouble
> what happened afterwards
>
> and say why you still remember this occasion so clearly

OK? Remember you have two minutes for your talk, so don't worry if I stop you. I'll let you know when the two minutes is up. Could you start talking now, please?

Thank you.

⇒ Were you a naughty child?

Thank you. I'll take the task card and paper and pencil back now.

You've been talking about a time when you were a child and got into trouble and I'd like to discuss with you a few more questions related to the same topic. So let's consider first of all... children's behaviour.

⇒ Tell me what usually happens to a child in your country when they are naughty.

⇒ That was an interesting answer, erm... to what extent do you think parents today are generally kinder to their children than parents were in the past?

⇒ Thank you. OK Let's move on to discuss the effects of parenting. To what extent do you think it is acceptable to slap children who are naughty?

⇒ So, do you think children who are slapped lose respect for their parents?

⇒ Mm being a parent is complicated isn't it. OK. Finally let's move on to consider punishment in society. Is capital punishment ever justified in your opinion?

⇒ You have obviously realised the complexity of that question, but thinking ahead, do you think punishments in society will get harsher or softer in the future?

I suppose we'll have to wait and see if your view of the future turns out to be right, won't we? Thank you. That is the end of the interview.

IELTS Practice Listening Test Transcript

IELTS Success Formula by Stephen Slater and Simone Braverman. Practice Listening Test.
The copyright to these recordings belongs to the authors.

You will hear a number of recordings and must answer questions on what you hear. You will have some time to read the questions and instructions and to check your work. You will hear each recording once only.

The test is in four sections. At the end of the test you will have ten minutes to transfer your answers to an answer sheet.

Please now turn to Section 1.

SECTION 1

You will hear a telephone conversation between a receptionist at a backpacker hostel, and a tourist. First you have some time to look at questions 1 to 5.

You will see that there is an example which has been done for you. The part of the conversation relating only to the example will be played first now.

(sound of telephone ringing)
Receptionist: Good morning, Seafront Backpacker Hostel, Bayview Heights.
Customer: Oh, hi. I'm a student and I'm looking for some low-priced accommodation on the beach.
Receptionist: Well, our prices are pretty good, and we have plenty of students staying here. But usually we ask you some basic questions for our guest enquiry form first. Is that OK?
Customer: Yes, that's fine.
R: Let's start with your current address. Where are you staying at the moment?
C: I'm staying at the Seaview Hotel, 15, The Esplanade…along the coast, at Dune Beach…
R: Mmm…that's a nice place.
C: Yeah it's great, but it's a bit too expensive for me.

The first part of the address is called 'Seaview Hotel', so this has been written on the form. Now the full test will begin.
Answer the questions as you listen because you will not hear the recording a second time. Listen carefully and answer questions 1 to 5.

(sound of telephone ringing)
Receptionist: Good morning, Seafront Backpacker Hostel, Bayview Heights.
Customer: Oh, hi. I'm a student and I'm looking for some low-priced accommodation on the beach.
Receptionist: Well, our prices are pretty good, and we have plenty of students staying here. But usually we ask you some basic questions for our guest enquiry form first. Is that OK?
Customer: Yes, that's fine.
R: Let's start with your current address. Where are you staying at the moment?
C: I'm staying at the Seaview Hotel, 15, The Esplanade…along the coast, at Dune Beach…
R: Mmm…that's a nice place.
C: Yeah it's great, but it's a bit too expensive for me.
R: Yes, so I've heard. And can I ask you your full name please?
C: It's Jacqui Wong.
R: Can you spell that for me, please?

Full IELTS Practice Test Audio Transcript

C: Ok…. My family name is Wong , that's W-O-N-G
R: uhuh, and your given name?
C: My given name is Jacqui but I spell it in an unusual way, J-A-C-Q-U-I
R: Ok, ….got it….And do you have a mobile phone number?
C: Yes, it's 014…830… 579.
R: Sorry did you say 579 for the last three numbers?
C: That's right.
R: How many nights would you like to stay with us here at the Hostel?
C: Well that depends on the cost. How much is it for one night?
R: In our larger, 12-bed dormitory B, it's only $15 per night,
C: That sounds much better value than the Seaview Hotel. …Look, I know it's short notice… but do you have a vacancy for me for 7 nights, starting from tonight?
R: Well, luckily for you, I think we do. One of our guests had to leave early this morning because her father is sick, ….so I think we can fit you in. By the way, the cost goes down to $90 if you stay for a full week of 7 nights.
C: Really? That's great…and a big relief. My money's running a bit low.

Before you hear the rest of the same conversation you have some time to look at questions 6 to 10.

Now listen and answer questions 6 to 10

C: I'd like to know what facilities you have at your Hostel?
R: Well I suppose our accommodation is a bit simpler than at the Seaview Hotel. We have 2 large dormitories, 3 bathrooms….each with a shower and constant hot water; ….er…we also supply towels, at a small cost; erm… there is free use of the internet, and a TV lounge. There is a small parking charge for cars, but …there's no charge for bikes.
C: Sounds fine.
R: Oh yes…and we offer you a simple breakfast, continental-style, free.
C: That's great…a lot of backpacker hostels don't offer that. By the way, how do I get to your backpacker hostel from here at Dune Beach?
R: Are you in a car?
C: No, I'm on my bicycle.
R: Well, your best bet is to take the road from Dune Beach to Selby. You take a small road off to the right, very near to your hotel on the Esplanade. It's a narrow road, but quiet. I always advise guests on bikes to use it as it's definitely much safer for cycling.
C: OK. Where do I go from Selby?
R: In Selby, just by the Church, you'll see a sign to Bay View Heights. It will probably take you about another thirty minutes.
C: Is your hostel easy to find?
R: Yes it's on the sea front, …. it's located right at the very end of Beach Road… up a hill …next to a Retirement Home. The views of the ocean are really great.
C: Sounds lovely. Is there somewhere safe at your hostel I can keep my bike?
R: Yes…absolutely no problem. You can store it in our hostel garage at night.
C: That's a relief. Oh, I forgot to ask if you have any animals at your hostel?
R: That's an unusual question. Well the manager has a small dog. Other than that, we get the occasional fox in the garden, usually at night. Why do you ask?

C: Well, dogs are not a problem but I'm allergic to cat fur …it makes my skin go red and I come out in a rash…Not sure about foxes.
R: Mmm…sounds painful. But don't worry, no cats or foxes indoors here!

That is the end of section 1. You now have half a minute to check your answers.

Now turn to Section 2.

SECTION 2

You will hear a presenter of a radio program for consumers, discussing different coffee machines. First you have some time to look at questions 11 to 17.

Now listen carefully and answer questions 11 to 17.

Hello there listeners, and welcome to your weekly consumer program, Best Buys. Today we're looking at 3 excellent coffee machines at different prices. We'll look at the pluses and minuses and then give our overall assessment for each machine. So let's get started….

Our first stylish, coffee maker is the simplest one. It's called the **'Coffee Supreme'**. OK…, positive points first. Well,…with this machine, you can brew more than four cups of coffee, either mild or strong. Also, it has a water filtration system with a cartridge and this improves the taste of the coffee. It also has overflow protection and a drip-stop function…. and all parts are easy to replace. But,…on the negative side, it doesn't have an automatic coffee grinder. Also, the Coffee Supreme has only a small 750 watt electrical system. ….So now the verdict. Our overall assessment for this attractive, little machine is that it is good value, but has a rather limited performance.

The next machine is a step up in price but has more options. It's called **Café Delight.** On the plus side, this machine combines a regular coffee maker with an espresso machine. It has a steam nozzle and a frothing attachment for making either cappuccinos or café lattes. Also you can make coffee in two ways – either into a cup or into the 40 ounce glass container which sits on its own warming plate. The downside is that the machine is bulky, because it's about 40 cm wide and 30cm high. But…as a lot of our people seem to like either drip coffee or the stronger Espresso style, on balance, our overall evaluation is that it's both flexible and convenient.

Before you hear the rest of the program you have some time to look at questions 18 to 20.
Now listen and answer questions 18 to 20.

The third coffee machine is the most expensive… but it's really hi-tech. It's called **Coffeetime automatic**. This machine is good because it can make different drinks—…not just coffee, but hot chocolate and tea. It uses an electronic 'disc' which automatically calculates water volume, brewing time and temperature for either coffee, tea, chocolate or milk. You can even make different drinks, one after another. Another plus is that there is an automatic cleaning and descaling system, and an automatic coffee grinder. ….But, on the negative side it's rather pricey and rather large, maybe too large for some small kitchens. In fact if I wanted it in my kitchen I would have to build a bigger kitchen. So our overall assessment is that it's bulky but makes good use of up-to-date technology.
Overall then, I suppose with coffee machines you get what you pay for. But perhaps simplicity is important. So good luck out there when you go shopping and remember…(*fades*)

That is the end of section 2. You now have half a minute to check your answers.

Now turn to Section 3.

Full IELTS Practice Test Audio Transcript

SECTION 3

You will hear a conversation between John Grey, a study support adviser, and two students, Wilson and Grace, who have study problems.
First you have some time to look at questions 21 to 26.

Now listen carefully and answer questions 21 to 26.

J: Thanks for coming along, Grace and Wilson. My name's John Grey and I'm one of the Study Support advisers.... As you are new students and have asked to discuss what we can do to help you with your study problems, I'd like first to outline the purposes and approach to Learning Support here at Broadway University. Then I'll ask each of you to describe the sort of issues you have and then say what we might offer you. Is that OK?
G: Yes.
W: That's fine.
J: OK Let's start then. Well, basically our purpose at Student Support is to help <u>students to become more independent</u>. We do this by showing them effective strategies they can use, not by doing the studying for them. Another purpose is to help students to understand some of the cultural differences between their own culture and the cultural context here in this country. In that sense we are encouraging students to make comparisons but not to make judgements about them. I suppose <u>a final purpose is to help students to build relationships</u> inside our culture by encouraging them to relate openly to us.
But that's enough from me. Perhaps, Wilson, you could talk about the sort of study problems you are having and I'll suggest some options.

W: Well <u>my main problems at the moment seem to be connected with writing</u> rather than lectures or seminars.
J: OK...Could you say a little more about what your problems with writing are exactly?
W: Well, I find <u>I can't understand the assignment titles</u>... they're often unclear to me,....I mean the central ideas... or what is sort of ...underneath the title words. Then usually I can't find enough readings or make a good enough plan.
J: Well.... we have a special session that <u>looks at essay planning</u> in each academic area. You're in Business aren't you, so maybe you could come to the Business essay session.
W: That would be great.
J: Anything else about your writing?
W: I find that the <u>structuring of the essays</u> I write is a real difficulty for me. My <u>essays are always very disorganised.</u>
J: Well, on Tuesdays during each semester we have essay writing sessions and you can make an <u>appointment with a tutor</u> to discuss your essay draft. Would that be helpful?
W: Yes, it sounds good.

Before you hear the rest of the conversation, you have some time to look at questions 27 to 30.

Now listen and answer questions 27 to 30.

J: What about you, Grace?
G: Well my problems are a bit different. I'm having <u>great difficulty following the lectures in my Nursing Course</u>. ...The lecturers seem to come from different countries and they talk really fast and are <u>not always very clear</u>. I can't keep up.
...and I end up with very poor lecture notes.
J: Have you tried recording the lectures?
G: Yes, but I still can't understand them and <u>it just wastes time.</u>

J: Well, you might try talking to your course coordinator to see if some of the lecture notes are in Powerpoint form or whether the lecturers have notes they can give you. Or you might ask one of the local students to let you look at their notes and discuss the lecture with you.
G: I'd be a bit embarrassed to ask the lecturer.
J: Well, one of our Support staff can contact the lecturer for you, if you like, to start with.
G; Oh, OK, thank you.
J: Anything else that's a problem?
G: Well, this isn't really a study problem but I'm finding that I'm not sleeping well.
J: I'm sorry to hear that. Is there something you are worried about?
G: I'm worried about the course, there's too much information to deal with. …Also, I had an email from my parents recently saying that my grandmother is not well and I'm worried about her. I feel I should go back to be with her.
J: It sounds as though you need to talk to someone who can listen in more detail to this situation. We have some really good counsellors from different cultural backgrounds. I know you might not feel comfortable about this but I could help you make a time today, if you like.
G: I'm not sure …it's all rather new.
J: OK…. why don't you think about it…and come back to see me again this afternoon?
G; OK, thanks…I'm so sorry to be a problem to you.
J: You're not a problem at all, Grace, ….we're here to help.

That is the end of section 3. You now have half a minute to check your answers.

Now turn to Section 4.

SECTION 4

You will hear part of a lecture about effective management skills given by a business studies lecturer. First, you have some time to look at questions 31 to 40.

Now listen carefully and answer questions 31 to 40.

Today, in my final talk on effective management skills, I want to discuss with you ideas connected with the place of emotional intelligence in the workplace. In recent years, management researchers have realised that an organisation is not just a place with a structure, with bosses and workers and rules, but is a place where feelings can have a huge impact on the effectiveness of work and workplace relationships.

First of all, then what is emotional intelligence? Well, no doubt you all know about intelligence tests, IQ tests, and the usual measurement of intelligence. Well it has been realised that there are other types of intelligence which can be vital to the tasks of management. Emotional intelligence, or E.I. as it is sometimes called, is one of these. Basically, then, E.I. involves a range of abilities connected to feelings. For example, it involves **self awareness**, or, in other words, the ability to be aware of your own emotions as you experience them. Another dimension of E.I. naturally enough is the ability to recognize other people's feelings, or at least to imagine what other people are feeling under certain conditions. We sometimes call this ability **empathy**. Then there is the ability to **manage your own emotions**, and to manage them in a positive and constructive way, thereby helping to motivate yourself. Finally, E.I. involves the ability to **manage relationships**, which involves the positive management of other people's emotions, and this last ability is part of being an effective leader, as well as being linked to being personally popular, or, as we say in plain English… just knowing how to be 'good with people'.

Full IELTS Practice Test Audio Transcript

It doesn't take much of your or anyone's intelligence to realise how important all these qualities are to a happy and open workplace—a workplace where people communicate openly, trust and respect one another, feel valued and understood, and thus work well together, is more productive, ….and probably… more creative.
But quite a number of otherwise intelligent and technically competent managers are not emotionally intelligent, and this means they need to learn these interpersonal skills in order to become more effective at their jobs.

So what underlies our emotional intelligence? What feeds into emotional intelligence and enables it to be developed? Clearly a key part of being emotionally intelligent is our own view of ourselves, how we see ourselves, or as it is sometimes called, our self-image. With a positive self image, which means, if we like ourselves, we are probably more able to support other people in our relationships with them. So managers with good self images are more likely to be a positive influence inside any organisation,

But self image is neither completely straightforward, nor simple.
Basically there seem to be three central aspects to how we see ourselves.
First, there is our **perceived self,** which basically means what we think we are like, …our internal view of ourselves in our mind's mirror, if you like. If we value ourselves and have high self esteem and self confidence, then other people will feel this in us, and will feel a little of it in their relationship with us.
Then there is how we would like ourselves to be, which is sometimes called our **desired self**, and obviously refers to the gap between what we perceive ourselves to be, and what we think is missing in ourselves, what improvements we would like to make in ourselves, if you like. For example, many shy people would like to be more assertive. But, obviously, if we have *too* much desire to change ourselves, it probably means we may not like ourselves enough the way we are.
Finally there are **the 'selves' we present to others**, our public faces, if you like, or, as sociologists express it, our roles. Roles involve expected forms of presentation of self, a bit like parts in a drama, or a play. For example, if you are a manager, your staff will probably expect you to behave in a certain way because this is what they expect of you. For example, you may be expected to give clear instructions and to make good decisions. Through the effective acting out of their work roles, managers can partly control the impressions other workers have of them, either gaining face, if these workers build a positive view of them, or, losing face if they behave in unusual ways…perhaps at the same time losing their authority.

Of course these three aspects of self image interact. In other words, they operate together at the same time, not in isolation. Research seems to suggest that there is a degree of stability in the main ways we communicate, or in our styles of communication, if you like.

So, overall, then a good manager needs a good self image… and a good manager needs to be able to build and use emotional intelligence. A successful modern organisation cannot ignore these psychological needs if it wants to succeed (*fades…*).

That is the end of Section 4. You now have half a minute to check your answers.

That is the end of the IELTS Success Formula Practice Listening Test. You now have 10 minutes to transfer your answers to the Listening Test Answer Sheet.

IELTS Practice Interview 2 (Questions Only) Transcript

Hello, my name is Ben Fulton. Could you tell me your full name, please?

OK, and what shall I call you?

That's fine, and can I see your identification, please?

Thank you. Now in Part 1 of the interview, I'm going to ask you some questions about yourself. Let's talk about where you grew up.

⇒ Where were you born?

⇒ In what ways has your birthplace changed since then?

⇒ Where would be a good place in your country for children to grow up these days?

⇒ Where in your country would you most like to live in the future, and why?

Let's go on to talk about shoes now.

⇒ When did you last buy some shoes? (What kind were they?)

⇒ Do you buy shoes mainly for comfort or to be fashionable?

⇒ Tell me about your favourite pair of shoes?

⇒ Do you think shoes last as long as they used to?

Let's move on to talk about kitchens.

⇒ What do you enjoy doing most when you are in the kitchen?

⇒ Is the kitchen in your house usually tidy or untidy?

⇒ Do you prefer a kitchen with a gas cooker or with an electric cooker, and why?

⇒ What things are stuck to the front of the fridge in your kitchen?

Thank you. Now, I'm going to give you a topic and I want you to talk about it for 1-2 minutes. Before you talk there will be one minute to think about what you are going to say, and to make notes. Is that OK? Here's a pencil and paper for making notes, and here's your topic. Could you talk about your favourite movie star?

> Talk about your favourite movie star.
>
> You should say:
>
> > who your favourite movie star is
> > what kinds of movies they have appeared in
> > what sort of person you think they are in real life
>
> and say why you like this movie star so much

OK? Remember you have two minutes for your talk, so don't worry if I stop you. I'll let you know when the two minutes is up. Could you start talking now, please?

Thank you.

⇒ Do you go to the movies very often?

Thank you. I'll take the task card and paper and pencil back now.

You've been talking about your favourite movie star and I'd like to discuss with you a few more questions related to the same topic. So let's consider first of all... movies today.

⇒ Can you tell me about some movies that have been really popular recently?

⇒ Mm, some of those sound really good, erm... are movies today better than they were when your parents were young, do you think?

Thank you....an interesting reply. OK Let's move on now to discuss fame and movie stars.

⇒ Is being famous a good thing or a bad thing, do you think?

⇒ I see, so, do you think <u>you</u> could handle being famous?

I suppose many people would feel the same as you do. Finally let's discuss movies and society.

⇒ In what ways do movies help you to understand your society better?

⇒ Ok, that's fine but aren't most movies really made for commercial success rather than to help you to understand society better?

OK, thanks for your ideas, but we'll have to stop now as that is the end of the interview.